Praise For

LIVING FULLY WITH SHYNESS AND SOCIAL ANXIETY

"This highly accessible book is an invaluable resource for people struggling with shyness and social anxiety, as well as those who care about them. The book is loaded with practical information, presented in an engaging and user-friendly style. Recognizing the wide diversity among socially anxious individuals, Hilliard reviews multiple strategies that can be tailored to meet each individual's unique needs." —JAMES D. HERBERT, PhD, Director, Anxiety Treatment and Research Program, Drexel University

"Hilliard's book is a welcome addition to the shyness self-help literature. Ms. Hilliard understands the experience of shyness, its strengths as well as its vulnerabilities. She does a lovely job of normalizing shyness as part of the human condition, while providing concrete strategies to practice new behavior in socially challenging situations. Her warmth is communicated to the reader, who is invited to share the experiences and the victories of those she has treated. The reader will develop strengths, as well as counter inhibitions, in the context of many shy people who are living successful, productive, and satisfying lives." —LYNNE HENDERSON, PhD, Stanford University, Director, Shyness Clinic, Originator, Social Fitness Model

"This is a very thorough and comprehensive book written with clarity and compassion. Erika B. Hilliard, a seasoned clinician, has skillfully brought together insights that are suited for both a professional and lay audience." —LEE PULOS, PhD, ABPP, Clinical Psychologist, author of *The Power of Visualization* and *The Biology of Empowerment*

"Erika B. Hilliard communicates a vast amount of often highly sophisticated information in a deceptively engaging, compassionate, supportive, and easy-to-read format that will be undoubtedly valuable to patients with social anxiety disorder and shyness as well as their therapists." —LISA MILLER, MD, Social Anxiety Disorder Group Therapist, Baylor College of Medicine

ERIKA B. HILLIARD, MSW, RSW
Foreword by PAUL FOXMAN, PhD

LIVING FULLY

WITH

SHYNESS

AND

SOCIAL

ANXIETY

■

A COMPREHENSIVE GUIDE
TO GAINING SOCIAL CONFIDENCE

MARLOWE & COMPANY
NEW YORK

LIVING FULLY WITH SHYNESS AND SOCIAL ANXIETY:
A Comprehensive Guide to Gaining Social Confidence

Published by
Marlowe & Company
An Imprint of Avalon Publishing Group Incorporated
245 West 17th Street • 11th Floor
New York, NY 10011-5300

AVALON
publishing group incorporated

Library of Congress Cataloging-in-Publication Data
Hilliard, Erika Bukkfalvi.
Living fully with shyness and social anxiety : a comprehensive guide to gaining
social confidence / Erika Bukkfalvi Hilliard ; foreword by Paul Foxman.
p. cm.
Includes bibliographical references (p. 303) and index.
ISBN 1-56924-397-2 (pbk.)
1. Bashfulness. 2. Anxiety. I. Title.
BF575.B3H55 2005
155.2'32—dc22
2005001001

9 8 7 6 5 4 3

Designed by *Pauline Neuwirth, Neuwirth & Associates, Inc.*
Printed in the United States of America

To my beloveds—my husband, Don, and three sons, Chris, Jordan, and Jesse; my mother, Alla, brother, Peter, and sister, Lydia; and in loving memory of my father, Emil.

Contents

■ **PART THREE** ■
THE MIND

■ **PART FOUR** ■
THE POWER OF ACTION

Foreword

AS A PSYCHOLOGIST AND director of the Center for
Anxiety Disorders in Vermont, I know that anxiety is the
most common emotional problem in our society, if not the entire
world. Yet only twenty-five percent of people with anxiety seek
professional guidance, and only a fraction receive effective help.
While numerous self-help books are emerging to meet a growing
need for reliable information about managing anxiety, Erika
Hilliard takes a quantum leap forward by focusing specifically on
shyness and social anxiety. These are among the most debilitating
forms of anxiety.

It is likely that you as a reader will be looking for concrete and
specific steps to manage shyness and social anxiety. Fortunately,
Hilliard is an experienced psychotherapist who provides detailed
advice on pertinent topics such as managing physical appearance
(clothing, scent, and body language) to improve social effectiveness. In addition, she offers guidance for improving eye contact,
conversational skills, and interview proficiency. A chapter on how
to develop and maintain friendships addresses a basic need that
is often painfully frustrated in shy, introverted, and emotionally
inhibited people. Hilliard even devotes a chapter to dating, one of
the most anxiety-arousing aspects of social interaction for those
who are shy or socially anxious.

Hilliard knows the territory of shyness and social anxiety from
personal as well as professional experience. This makes her book

warm, authentic, and all the more credible. You can trust someone who has been there, and who has personally done the work to overcome the problem.

In my own books (*Dancing with Fear* and *The Worried Child*) I describe anxiety as the result of three interacting ingredients. The first is biological or genetic, which I refer to as *temperament*. Simply put, some of us are born with a shy, sensitive, or inhibited temperament.

The second ingredient is a set of learned *personality traits*, such as high standards of achievement, perfectionism, desire to please others, sensitivity to criticism, fear of rejection, suggestibility, difficulty relaxing, and frequent worry. Some of these personality traits—such as high standards and a desire to do well—are actually positive and increase our chances of success in life.

The third ingredient is *stress overload*. In virtually all cases of anxiety that I have seen, the symptoms of anxiety appear after a period of high stress. This explains why anxiety symptoms may seem to come and go.

Hilliard's book is compatible with this way of viewing anxiety. For example, she addresses the stress factors in shyness and social anxiety, such as information overload, negative thinking, and time pressure, and she shows how a high-stress lifestyle increases the likelihood of anxiety. Hilliard offers guidance in stress management, including a chapter on using nutrition to calm the body. In addition, Hilliard emphasizes the positive side of shyness and social anxiety—a desire to do well, to please others, and to be successful.

Hilliard also points out that modern technology has changed the way we interact, often reducing opportunities for social interaction and practice of social skills. This rings true. E-mail and cell phones, for example, have taken the place of face-to-face contact between people, even though these technologies allow us to maintain social contact conveniently, inexpensively, and across great distances.

If you find *reassurance* and *structure* to be helpful, Hilliard's book will speak to you with its positive tone and unique organization.

The book offers an optimistic approach with interesting case examples. Organization into sections on mind, body, and action is intuitive, and it is easy to navigate through the chapters to find useful information.

Hilliard's book is also comprehensive. Details that are overlooked by other books on the subject are addressed authoritatively. For example, there is a chapter on "shy bladder syndrome." This is a form of anxiety and tension that interferes with going to public restrooms. You will also find a chapter on public speaking and job interviews.

It has been demonstrated scientifically that cognitive-behavioral therapy is the most effective approach to anxiety. Hilliard recognizes this and provides guidance on using imagery, positive thinking, and new thought habits to be more successful and comfortable. She also spells out the action steps in "desensitization" and "exposure" that are necessary for managing—and overcoming—social anxiety.

I also find group therapy to be an effective form of help for social anxiety. For over twenty years, I have been running weekly groups for shy and anxious clients, and I am repeatedly amazed by the power of this therapeutic approach. A recent group, for example, successfully helped a number of college students return to school after dropping out of their freshman year because of shyness and social anxiety. Hilliard also has many years of experience conducting anxiety groups, and she draws from this work in advising you how to be more comfortable in groups and social situations.

I agree with Hilliard when she suggests that medication is not a good long-term solution for managing social anxiety. For one thing, medication teaches no new skills. Furthermore, many anxious people are uncomfortable with the idea of taking medication and, therefore, they use it inconsistently and with disappointing results. Unpleasant side effects and initial adjustment difficulties can add to the problem. And even when medication is helpful in lowering social anxiety, there is always the question as to what will happen when a person stops taking medication. Will shyness and social anxiety take over?

Let Erika Hilliard guide you through the process of understanding and managing shyness and social anxiety. This invaluable self-help book can serve as your personal therapeutic guide toward greater social comfort and enjoyment of life.

Paul Foxman, PhD
Burlington, Vermont
July 22, 2004

PAUL FOXMAN, PHD, has twenty-five years of experience in private practice specializing in the treatment of anxiety disorders, stress, and relationship problems. He is the author of *Dancing with Fear* and *The Worried Child* and is director of the Center for Anxiety Disorders in Burlington, Vermont. More information about Dr. Foxman is available at *www.drfoxman.com*.

Preface

IF YOU'RE A PERSON with social anxiety, you may very well feel at a loss as to where to turn for help. How do you learn to live comfortably with shyness and social anxiety?

Self-help literature is often the only recourse for many socially anxious or shy people. Since much of social anxiety literature is relatively new, it is nowhere near as vast as the literature on other conditions. That's surprising if one knows the statistics: fifty percent of the population rates itself as shy, a proportion that may be increasing by one percent per year. Thirteen percent of the population suffers from extreme shyness or social anxiety. The books that have been available essentially focus on similar strategies. The approach is often the same: change your thinking; change your behavior. This is called the cognitive-behavioral approach.

As a therapist for over thirty years, a facilitator of social anxiety support groups for fifteen, and an ardent learner throughout my career, I am always on the lookout for good resources. In the course of reading all of the social anxiety literature I could get my hands on, I could not find one comprehensive book on shyness that addresses topics too often missed in others—a book with a variety of approaches clearly organized by topic. It has been my pleasure to fill this gap with the writing of *Living Fully with Shyness and Social Anxiety*.

To name just a few of the benefits of this book, you will learn about both the stigmatized and the positive views of social anxiety. You will discover how the three-part brain works to produce the physical symptoms of social anxiety. Besides learning about the usual ways to physically calm the body through breathing and muscle relaxation exercises, you will be introduced to grounding and self-regulation exercises. For those who blush or have shy bladder syndrome, I include innovative and proven ways to deal with these conditions.

Practical guidelines will teach you how to harness the power of your imagination so you can pursue your dreams. Goal-setting sheets will help you maintain your efforts in the areas of body, mind, and action. You will find out about the intimidating power of eyes and how you can increase eye contact. Specific ways of using body and verbal language to increase your effectiveness at work, play, and in love are described in detail. In short, you will be able to tailor-make an effective plan to gain social confidence.

Social anxiety is a condition that can change. As social anxiety is reduced to a manageable level, shyness also becomes less troublesome. When someone asks me what results I have had with my support groups, I usually respond that the results are varied. I have had people comment that lessons learned in the group have been life-changing. A few people have groaned that it is too much work. The rest of the people are somewhere in the middle, discovering that their lives have opened up in new and exciting ways.

As someone who has grappled with shyness and social anxiety, I have had my share of comments like "Did the cat get your tongue?" or "Erika, you're blushing." Social anxiety has overwhelmed me when making public presentations or speaking in groups. Things are different now. I appreciate my sensitivity, that fabulous quality that often accompanies shyness and social anxiety. It was probably my sensitive nature and interest in people that ushered me into the role of therapist. *Therapy*, after all, means "to attend," and what better quality to help one attend than to be sensitive—capturing nuances, reading body language, and noticing patterns of thinking and being? Certainly, it was my familiarity with social anxiety that led me into this particular area of human fragility. And I am so glad it did. Time and again, I have witnessed the resilience and strength of the human spirit. I have been inspired by how people, in spite of their anxieties, have managed to come out of their proverbial cocoons and flutter their magnificent wings. Michael can finally attend a soccer coaching course. Kerry speaks up at her monthly management meetings feeling calm and centered. John shines in a job interview that he clinches.

A while back, I had occasion to meet, for the second time in our adulthood, my childhood friend Noella. Noticing my social confidence, she asked, "What happened to the shy girl I once knew?" She reminded me how readily I used to blush, how I would decline joining the girls who went to dances, and how I was never outspoken. Those days are long ago. Many of the turning points in my life that contributed to my social confidence have been translated into practical lessons in this book.

I have enjoyed the sweet pleasure of unabashed self-expression, and at times I am still quiet, contemplative, and happily, just a little shy. And it is all okay. On another personal note, I have watched my son, Jordan, once a timid child who spent his first day in preschool blowing out his birthday candles from underneath a table, develop into an outgoing, popular boy in high school, retaining his confidence through his college years. I have no doubt that I have had at least some positive influence on his confidence, sharing with him many of the notions and practices now found in this book.

It is your turn. Accept my invitation to embark on an adventurous journey. If you are determined and make the commitment to apply yourself to even a few ideas in this book, there is no reason why you, too, can't become more confident. You will feel more at home in your body when in social situations. Your mind will discover a myriad of ways to nurture your spirit. And you will experience your fullest sense of self, in voice and in action, in this new world of unbelievable possibilities.

Introduction

IN THE UNLIKELIEST of places—in a sidewalk crack or in a mountainside cranny—a tiny seed will germinate and slowly transform into a scarlet rose or a fragrant pine tree. In spite of obstacles, the growth impulse of life quivers all around us. There is something in each of us that strives to flourish, and when it cannot thrive, uneasiness stirs within.

People with social anxiety or shyness are only too familiar with this sense of uneasiness. They long to express themselves and become the person that lies just beneath the surface of their social anxiety. If life circumstances allow, the growth impulse will prevail. People with social anxiety can and do find ways to become more comfortable with themselves and others. Many people with shyness and social anxiety enjoy satisfying and successful lives.

About fifteen years ago, Kirsten, a thirty-five-year-old office manager, came to see me in therapy about her uneasiness at work. She described how, just before it was her turn to speak up at a management meeting, her cheek would twitch, her heart race, and her face redden. I knew exactly what she was talking about. Except for the twitchy cheek, I had experienced that particular brand of social anxiety in work settings, and sometimes in social settings as well. Life experiences had kindly given me opportunities to overcome some of this social awkwardness. Nevertheless, I was still only a few steps ahead of Kirsten in the journey to self-confidence in social situations.

We tackled her problem from a number of approaches: family systems work, self-esteem work, marital work, and so on. Over time Kirsten felt better about herself, but her cheek would still twitch and her heart would still pound at work meetings. Clearly, she needed something else. Kirsten was the first client to ask if I would consider forming a social anxiety support group. Her request was all I needed. I did some literature research and discovered that group work is one of the most effective ways of learning to manage social anxiety.

It took eight months to gather a total of eight people for my first group. I then approached Kathy Tait, a journalist of Vancouver's newspaper *The Province,* and asked whether she might be interested in writing about social anxiety. Kathy immediately asked whether she could interview the group.

On the weekend that her two-page article on "Fear of People" hit the newsstands, my phone rang off the hook. In fact, it didn't stop ringing for at least a week. During that first year, I ran three separate weekly groups, each containing twelve people.

About three years ago, I phoned Kirsten to see how she was doing. She reported that life was grand. She was especially eager to tell me how she had lobbied the government for a variety of school projects. She reported speaking up at school meetings and speaking freely with the parents at school. She added that she never would have dreamed this possible before she had attended the group, where she had learned valuable lessons.

I have long wanted to capture these valuable lessons in a book that was easily accessible to the general public. Although this book has been gestating for at least ten years, I could not have written it ten years ago. I have learned so much over the years, from many sources: from group members and other private practice clients; from innovative therapeutic approaches; from sage writers about social anxiety and sage writers about life; and from my own miserable and joyful life experiences. I hope I have succeeded, in some small measure, in presenting some of these ideas and experiences in an appetizing and digestible manner.

To start with, I organized the book into four main parts. Part One, "Shyness and Social Anxiety," introduces social anxiety in general. It contains definitions, descriptions, and causes of social anxiety. You will read about ordinary and famous people who have experienced social anxiety. You'll learn the difference between normal and excessive social anxiety and shyness, and explore some of the societal and cultural pressures and practices that can lead to a misguided hatred of social anxiety and shyness. You'll find out that the incidence of social anxiety continues to rise in our society. You'll discover and celebrate the fact that research and mounting clinical evidence point to ways people can embrace their normal shyness and shrink their excessive social anxiety. Very importantly, you'll discover how to look at social anxiety through a positive lens.

Parts Two, Three, and Four are divided into aspects of social anxiety that have to do with body, mind, and action, respectively.

Part Two, "The Body," explains how the brain and nervous systems work to create the physical sensations of social anxiety. You'll learn ways of calming the nervous system through grounding, self-regulation exercises, breathing, muscle relaxation, and through proper nutrition. You'll explore the benefits and risks of taking medication. You'll also look at blushing and bladder shyness.

Part Three, "The Mind," is further divided into two parts: the power of imagination and the power of words. The first section describes the different ways imagination can negatively and positively influence many aspects of life. It examines various theories that explain how imagination works. You'll find guidelines to help you harness and cultivate your imagination in the service of making goals, inducing relaxation, and building confidence in social situations.

Because words hold power, negative self-talk, negative predicting, and negative beliefs and assumptions are exposed and challenged. You will learn how to identify and challenge other mind traps that promote social anxiety. These mind traps include self-focus, perfectionism, enslavement to rules, the wishing trap, and the comparison trap. You'll find out how to foster a ready supply of words that nourish and encourage you, through positive affirmations, gratefulness, and a list of the benefits of anxiety.

Part Four, "The Power of Action," is about follow-through. You'll learn how to expose yourself to anxiety-provoking situations by using a gradual and repetitive approach. You'll begin by making contact with others through body language then verbal language. You can practice how to ace job interviews and presentations. Then you can move into the more intimate areas of developing friendships and dating. The book concludes with a chapter showing you how to keep up your motivation, deal with setbacks, and draw on community resources.

As you can see, this book is a bit like a "soup to nuts" cookbook. Please do not feel that you must absorb every single page to gain benefit from this book. You may wish to read it from cover to cover or you may wish to dip into it, here and there, as you feel the material is relevant. Sometimes it takes only one thing to make a huge difference in one's life. For instance, one former group member reported that learning to focus on others and not on himself opened up a whole new world. Another said that she was more comfortable with herself and others simply because she had learned to accept her shy personality, appreciating the many fine qualities that accompanied her sensitive nature. One fellow was inspired by his imagery work, while another felt that he was finally able to confront the negative self-talk that had formerly restricted him. What one thing will make a difference in your life?

I hope that the personal stories, thoughts, and discoveries of the many people cited in the book will encourage you to think of this book as an adventure—an adventure where you are not alone. Literally thousands of socially anxious people have gone before you in the quest for social confidence, and thousands will follow in your footsteps. Right now, thousands stand right beside you, in the next house, the next neighborhood, the next province or state, the next country, and in the continent beyond. Like you, many are taking measures to manage social anxiety so that they can open themselves to more of what life has to offer. You have lots of company. Enjoy!

PART ONE

SHYNESS
AND SOCIAL
ANXIETY

ONE

YOU, TOO?

The Many Faces of Social Anxiety and Shyness

There are as many borschts as there are Russians.
—ALLA GALTSCHINSKA, my mother

JAKE, A FORTY-FIVE-YEAR-OLD dentist, tells the other members of a social anxiety support group how social anxiety takes control of his life:

> I have no difficulty giving a speech at a professional conference in front of five hundred people. However, terror strikes when I meet a person, one on one. I have no idea what to say. I feel like I am being evaluated. I worry about making a good impression. Even when things are going well, I worry about spoiling a good thing. Informal situations are hell for me. Being myself seems an impossible feat.

Catherine, a mature student taking correspondence classes, clears her throat as she prepares to speak:

> I am the master of avoidance. I will travel to the next town to avoid standing at the cash register of a cashier who has

served me in the past. I have no trouble dealing with a stranger unless I have to deal with him more than once. I worry that he might get to know me and then he won't like me. If my neighbor comes home the same time I do, I will avoid eye contact. If I had planned to do some gardening and I discover that she's already out in her garden, I change my plans and stay indoors. When I used to work as a secretary long ago, I hated my boss watching me writing shorthand, as he'd notice my hands shaking. I would not drink coffee in front of other people, for fear of shaking. I don't go to parties, which disappoints my husband terribly. When I'm in a group, I always feel like I'm on the outside, like I don't belong. It's amazing that I even considered coming to this group, but I know that I can't go on living this way.

What do Jake, Catherine, and others have in common? To one degree or another, they are concerned that people will look at them, evaluate them, and judge them poorly. They fear rejection.

SOCIAL ANXIETY COMES OUT OF THE CLOSET

UNTIL RECENTLY, SOCIAL anxiety escaped the attention of most helping professionals for two major reasons. First, many people did not tell their therapists about their social anxiety. Second, little was written about it in the professional literature. Often people did not talk about their social anxiety because they didn't even recognize it themselves. For instance, one of my group members, Peter, said that it took him a long time to realize that he was suffering from a specific condition. Every year he used to get sick to his stomach on the day he had to go to his company picnic. He figured that it was an interesting coincidence. Peter did not make the connection that this physiological reaction was part of the same thing that he had experienced during high school when he chose to go home for lunch every day rather than eat with his classmates in the cafeteria. Some people don't talk about their social anxiety because they are too embarrassed to do so. Others don't think there is anything they can do about their social anxiety; it's just a part of their personality, so why bother talking about it.

Social anxiety has probably existed since human beings first walked the earth. However, it did not draw any professional attention until the 1960s when British psychiatrist Isaac Marks described a condition in which individuals become anxious whenever they may be subject to scrutiny by others while performing a task. Once an individual is in a particular situation, he is caught up with the idea that he is being watched and that he won't make the grade, that whatever he says or does will be found wanting. He is afraid of being humiliated or embarrassed.

Social anxiety and social phobia are close cousins. When social anxiety becomes so intense and persistent that it affects a person's social and occupational functioning, it is often called social phobia or social anxiety disorder.

WHAT ABOUT SHYNESS?

IN MY SUPPORT GROUPS, I formerly used the terms *social anxiety* and *shyness* interchangeably. One day, Leila, a woman who spoke up easily in one of my support groups, surprised me when she announced that although she experienced tremendous social anxiety in a variety of situations, she never considered herself to be shy. Wow! That was a new idea for me. We can't assume that people with social anxiety are necessarily shy. How about the other way around? Do shy people always experience social anxiety?

Shyness can be divided into two major types. One form of shyness is simply a personality trait whereby people take their time to feel comfortable in social situations. We see this kind of natural wariness in children who take their time to feel comfortable with strangers. This can be a healthy wariness protecting children from people who may be dangerous. Another form of shyness has more to do with concern about being evaluated. This shyness is more closely related to social anxiety. Social anxiety corresponds to feelings of distress related to the fear of scrutiny and judgment while shyness corresponds to the behavioral responses to this social anxiety. These responses include cautiousness and inhibition. According to Christopher J. McCullough, author of *Always at Ease:*

Overcoming Shyness and Anxiety in Every Situation, "Shyness, like a phobia, is not a feeling but a behavior, an attempt to avoid anxiety."

In my experience, most people who consider themselves to be shy often experience social anxiety. Depending on the degree and frequency of their symptoms, people who experience social anxiety may or may not be shy. For the purpose of this book, I will continue to interchange these words, often favoring social anxiety because it is more precise, and more to the point. It is what underlies shyness.

INTROVERSION AND EXTROVERSION

A COMMON PERCEPTION among the general population is that shyness and introversion go hand in hand. The fact is, there are shy introverts and non-shy introverts just as there are shy extroverts and non-shy extroverts. Introverts are people who get their energy mostly from within themselves. They enjoy their inner world of thoughts and reflections. They like to spend time in their own company. A non-shy introvert has no trouble interacting with others. She can keep up a pace of high social energy, but only for a limited amount of time. After a while, she gets tired and needs to find a quieter place where she can be by herself and restore her energy in quiet ways.

A non-shy introvert is likely to leave a party earlier than later. A shy introvert, like the non-shy introvert, also gets his energy from within himself. However, he is not as easygoing when it comes to social interactions. He usually wants more physical space between himself and people he doesn't know well. He often prefers to spend time at home, reading, listening to music, using his computer, or puttering around the house.

A non-shy extrovert gets her energy primarily from other people. She is immediately comfortable in the company of others and likes to hang out with people as long as possible. A shy extrovert also gets her energy from others, but it takes a while before she feels comfortable with people. Once she gets used to her social environment and warms up to people, she usually feels very much at home, talking easily and sensing an increase in energy as the social event progresses. She is often one of the last to leave a social gathering.

The categories of non-shy and shy introversion and non-shy and shy extroversion are not four discrete, self-contained categories. People are not in one category or another. Rather, they have tendencies toward one category or another but, depending on circumstances, can also move in and out of categories, or have mixed tendencies.

HOW SOCIAL ANXIETY SHOWS ITSELF

PEOPLE EXPERIENCE DIFFERENT degrees of shyness and social anxiety depending on their individual personalities and their personal histories.

CONTINUUM OF SHYNESS AND SOCIAL ANXIETY
➤ *Normal*

Most people who experience shyness have normal, garden-variety shyness. They don't experience overwhelming anxiety in the face of social situations. For instance, Roger feels shy when the softball leagues divide up every summer and he has to meet some new teammates. He has come to know that he needs a little time to warm up in the presence of other people. Most people experience normal social anxiety in certain unfamiliar social situations, but like Roger, once they get involved, their anxiety evaporates.

➤ *Mild–Moderate*

There are people whose shyness and social anxiety interfere with their lives only sometimes. Marianne, for instance, is confident at work but feels like she has two left feet when it comes to dancing. Although she has often dreamt about taking dancing lessons, she feels anxious about how she would look to others, and consequently has not even attempted the free dance lessons offered at the local Latino restaurant.

➤ *Moderate–Extreme*

About thirteen percent of the population experience shyness or social anxiety to such an extent that they either avoid social situations or they endure the social situations with intense inner discomfort. When Helena's office mates invite her to join them for lunch or for a dinner party after work, she declines and tells them that she has errands to run or appointments to meet. She is most comfortable when visiting with a few close family members and tends to clam up when too many relatives visit at her family's home.

➤ *Extreme*

At this end of the continuum, people are so afraid of rejection that they avoid people and situations as much as possible, to minimize not only the risk of rejection but also the risk of experiencing anxiety in the first place. Harry spends every single weekend at home. Although he has often thought that having a girlfriend might solve his problems, he takes no steps to meet people. He usually tells himself, "Why bother, no one would like me anyway."

Where do you think your social anxiety falls on this continuum? If normal, then you have no worries. You simply need to accept that social anxiety and shyness are a part of your personality. As you will soon find out, there are many lovely attributes that go along with this degree of social anxiety. If your social anxiety lies somewhere between mild and extreme, please realize that this need not be permanent. People move up and down the continuum, depending on life circumstances and inner strengths and resources. This book will give you lots of ideas about how to cultivate these strengths and resources.

PUBLIC AND PRIVATE SHYNESS AND SOCIAL ANXIETY

LINDA SITS IN the group quietly. Her eyes are downcast as she begins to speak in a soft voice. As she looks up and sees others looking at her, her cheeks flush and she looks away quickly. Linda is publicly shy. Publicly shy people display their symptoms openly. They are often quieter and more cautious in social settings than privately shy folks like Bill. He talks easily in the group. No one understands why he is attending a support group for socially anxious and shy people. He tells the group, "I get this all the time. My friends have a hard time believing that I'm shy. I try to put on a good show, but inside I'm often trembling. I wonder if people will see my lack of confidence. I worry that once they get to know the real me, they won't like me." Privately shy or socially anxious people keep their symptoms to themselves. They often look confident on the outside while feeling shy and experiencing intense social anxiety on the inside.

SYMPTOMS OF SOCIAL ANXIETY

SYMPTOMS OF SOCIAL anxiety generally occur in three areas: body, mind, and action. The following is a list of many of the ways you might experience social anxiety. Check off the ones that apply to you. Add any others in the space provided.

BODY

☐ racing heart   ☐ tight chest
☐ pulse in ear   ☐ tingling
☐ shortness of breath   ☐ headaches
☐ dry mouth   ☐ nausea
☐ tight throat   ☐ dizziness
☐ cracking voice   ☐ too hot, too cold
☐ difficulty swallowing   ☐ sudden need to urinate
☐ loss of appetite   ☐ muscle tension
☐ stomachache   ☐ twitching facial muscles
☐ other aches   ☐ trembling hands/legs
☐ blushing   ☐ stony facial expression
☐ sweating

OTHERS: _____

Mind
Images
☐ imagining some of the physical symptoms mentioned earlier
☐ imagining the worst, sometimes in vivid mental pictures
☐ imagining what you look like to others (usually nervous, inadequate, even weird)
☐ imagining horrible outcomes and consequences

Others: _____

Words
☐ thoughts that are marked with worries, negative assessments, or predictions. Examples: "What if they don't like me?" "They don't like me." "They won't like me."
☐ beliefs and assumptions that are restrictive. Examples: "I must do things perfectly or I will not get approval." "If I succeed, it's because of someone else. If I fail, it's totally my fault."

Others: _____

Mental process
☐ focus on self, obsessing about how you're coming across to the other person
☐ focus on what to say next rather than focusing on what the other person is saying
☐ difficulty remembering what the other person said because it was difficult to pay attention in the first place
☐ difficulty thinking; mind goes blank

Others: _____

Action/Behavior
Avoidance
☑ avoid eye contact
☑ avoid social situations
☑ tend to be passive
☑ hesitate

☐ avoid taking initiative
☐ withhold opinions
☐ procrastinate

Safety seeking
☐ go to familiar places only
☐ stick with old friend(s)
☐ agree with majority
☐ dress low key
☑ take great pains to dress immaculately
☐ tend to be overly helpful
☐ overly agreeable

Nervous gestures
☑ talk too softly, loudly
☐ mumble or stutter
☐ giggle nervously
☑ lips quiver
☐ fidget
☐ become rigid or limp
☑ closed body posture
☑ poor social skills

OTHERS: _____

Lack of social skills has been linked to social anxiety; however, it has been discovered that socially anxious people generally rate their social skills lower than objective observers rate them. Nevertheless, many socially anxious people are not sure how to start conversations, how to keep conversations going, or how to deal with conflict situations. They do not know how to give or accept compliments. They're not quite sure what to say and when to say it.

With which of these three major clusters of symptoms and signs do you identify the most, those that relate to body, mind, or action? Typically, most people state that anxious thinking is what bothers them the most. Still, there are many others who are mostly affected by the physical or behavioral symptoms. Take a moment to figure out how you usually experience social anxiety. This will help you decide where you want to focus your energy and efforts as you begin to take steps in shrinking social anxiety.

EFFECTS ON THE EMOTIONS

Apart from affecting the body, the mind, and the behavior, social anxiety also affects the emotions. While in the throes of social anxiety, anxious feelings are usually the only feelings being consciously experienced. By anxious feelings, I mean nervousness, anxiety, fear, apprehension, and self-consciousness. For instance, as Betty sat down to play her annual audition to determine her part in the school orchestra, she felt the all-too-familiar racing of her heart and trembling in her hands. It was only after she got home that she began to feel furious with herself for having been nervous and for not having played better. It is generally only after the anxiety settles and moves into the background that other emotions come to the fore. Besides feeling furious, Betty might have felt ashamed, sad, depressed, dejected, inferior, and lonely. The reason I didn't include these feelings in the major symptom clusters above is that although we can have direct influence over our body, our mind, and our behavior, we cannot directly change our emotions. Positive emotions will flow naturally once we make changes in our body, our mind, and our actions or behavior.

SITUATIONS

Specific and general social anxiety

Jake, the dentist in our social anxiety support group, is professionally confident but turns to mush when he talks with an unfamiliar person on a nonprofessional basis. He has what is called *specific social anxiety.* Steve, a nature buff, is a good example of someone who experiences *generalized social anxiety.* He describes an all-pervasive self-consciousness that affects him anytime other people are involved.

Types of social situations

To be sure, any social situation can bring on troublesome anxiety. However, a number of situations are popular hangouts for social anxiety. Check off examples below that apply to you. Again, feel free to add your own.

☐ meeting people for the first time
☐ meeting someone you find attractive
☐ talking to authority figures or to people with a lot of status (through wealth, age, or fame)
☐ using the telephone
☐ talking in a group; being the focus of attention in groups, large or small
☐ doing presentations (forty-five percent of the population state that their number-one fear is public speaking)
☐ performing tasks in public: eating, writing, dancing, using the telephone in someone's presence, performing one's job
☐ using public restrooms
☐ writing tests (often considered a type of social anxiety)

OTHERS:_____

Whatever the situation, we wonder whether we will measure up in the eyes of others. Or, more to the point, we worry that we won't measure up!

INCIDENCE OF SHYNESS

IN THE EARLY 1970s, shyness research pioneer Philip Zimbardo and his team surveyed over 5,000 college students. Eighty percent reported that they had been shy at some point in their lives. Forty percent considered themselves to be currently shy. Forty percent reported that they had been shy in the past but were no longer shy. Four percent reported that they were shy all the time, in all social situations, with almost all people. Only seven percent believed that they had never been shy. In other words, if you consider yourself to be shy, you've got lots of company. Consider celebrities who have admitted to being shy or having been shy: Barbra Streisand, Donny Osmond, Carly Simon, Willard Scott, Michael Caine, Terence Stamp, Carol Burnett, Henry Winkler, Orson Welles, Kim Bassinger, Robert DeNiro, Robin Williams, and would you believe—Barbara Walters?

Rising incidence of shyness

By the early 1990s, the percentage of young adults that reported themselves as currently shy rose by about ten percent. The current level of fifty percent is apparently growing at an annual rate of one percent. Researchers speculate that the increase may be due to changes in modern society, including advances in computer technology, automated services, and large corporate practices that value downsizing and productivity over employee satisfaction and security.

In the cyberspace generation, time spent in playing video games, surfing the Web, e-mailing, and online chatting is time not spent in direct contact with people having fun, deepening intimate connections, or working toward a common purpose. Automation is making personal contact in daily transactions not only unnecessary but sometimes impossible. It's now possible to do our banking, pay our bills, and fill our gas tanks without ever having to talk to a real human being. We can open our garage doors with a remote control and don't have to see our neighbors as we leave our car and go back into the house. In the work world, managers are spread thinly across several departments to do the work that was once done by two or three people. Frontline workers are asked to reduce their AHT—average handling time—with customers by twenty-five percent or more. No more time for social niceties. Get to the point, on to the next customer. We're running out of opportunities to practice being social. Even the practice of socializing around the family dinner table is going out the window as family members become entrenched in their individual worlds of computer programs, television reality shows, and personal pursuits. Whew! No wonder shyness is on the rise.

INCIDENCE OF SOCIAL ANXIETY

So FAR, WE'VE been talking about the incidence of shyness. There are no real statistics on the incidence of social anxiety. Since social anxiety is a normal human phenomenon, I would estimate that approximately ninety percent of the population has experienced social anxiety at some time in their lives. This leaves out the seven to eleven percent of people who believe they've never been shy.

Extreme social anxiety or social phobia

According to the current *Diagnostic and Statistical Manual of Mental Disorders,* about thirteen percent of the population suffers from the extreme form of social anxiety called social phobia or social anxiety disorder. Some reports state that men and women are equally affected by social anxiety, and other reports indicate that women are more likely to be affected than men by a ratio of three to two. In either case, men are more likely to seek help than women. Surprised? Men, more than women, may face greater cultural pressure to take initiative. Furthermore, women have an easier time than men choosing to stay home and look after their families.

CAUSES OF SHYNESS OR SOCIAL ANXIETY

WHY IS SHYNESS or social anxiety, for some people, only mildly uncomfortable, whereas for others, it is overwhelmingly distressing? What accounts for the variations in the experience of social anxiety? Why are some people most bothered by their physical sensations, whereas others find their anxious thinking most disturbing?

Why does Jake, the dentist, not have any problem talking to five hundred people but has a meltdown when he talks to a single individual? Why does Steve, the nature buff, get flustered in almost any situation involving people, whether one or five, let alone five hundred? What factors contribute to the development of shyness or social anxiety?

Most researchers and authors agree that no single factor leads to social anxiety. Instead, there is usually an interplay of factors having to do with biochemistry, genetics, early childhood, and later life experiences. People's biochemical response to stress is particularly relevant to those who experience overwhelming physical distress when socially anxious. Over the last few years, a surge in trauma and brain research has examined heightened stress responses. We will explore this in further detail in Chapter 3. It may be that some people experience a "dysregulation" of those chemicals that normally allow our nervous systems to work in an optimal manner. In other words, the traumatized nervous system can become overly sensitive. It goes into overdrive at the slightest provocation.

Family studies and twin studies have revealed that social anxiety can run in families. It is not that people inherit social anxiety per se. They inherit a tendency to anxiety. They are a little more sensitive, a little more reactive to outside stimulation. It is important, however, to remember that genes do not act alone. They interact with the environment.

Environment plays a huge role in whether or not you develop full-blown shyness or social anxiety. There are a host of influences, including the following:

> ➤ infant attachment and response to stress—referring to how your parents or caretakers soothed or irritated your nervous system, training it into a state of alertness or cautiousness
> ➤ messages from family—including positive messages that produce feelings and thoughts in the child of being loved, respected, and safe, and including negative messages such as criticism, neglect, abuse, shaming, or overprotectiveness

that produce feelings and thoughts of being flawed, unworthy, unsafe, inhibited, or inadequate

➤ the shyness label—sending a message that shyness might be "bad" instead of giving the child permission to be who she is

➤ limiting family patterns—setting up adverse situations that produce social anxiety, patterns such as isolated lives; all-powerful adults and children who should be seen and not heard; little or no communication in words or touch, let alone expression of thoughts and feelings; unstable lifestyles; unassertive or shy parents or relatives who model shyness; and excessive emphasis by the parents or caretakers on securing the approval of others

➤ bullying—often occurring in childhood, either by siblings or classmates, often over things one has no control over, such as freckles, weight, wearing glasses, and becoming extra devastating when it becomes group bullying

➤ peer approval—during teenage years in particular, when not fitting in rises in importance

➤ being different—referring to any physical, social, or emotional way that individuals differ, such as being extra short or tall, suffering growths or deformities, being homosexual, or feeling marginalized due to race, poverty, or ethnicity

➤ trauma—during any time of life; also, the reactions of others and internal reactions that lead to shyness or social anxiety

➤ life circumstances—including lack of practice in social situations due to physical isolation (rural life or working abroad), divorce, widowhood, or retirement; or due to new demands such as job changes, relocation, or loss of a loved one or health

The life stories of a few of the members of past support groups may give you an idea of how many factors may come into play. As you read these stories, which I have been kindly permitted to share, take each story in and allow yourself to be moved by the events, and by the durability of our fellow human beings. You may discover themes that resonate with your own story. Or, if you're in a more analytical frame of mind, you may be able to identify factors that seem to give birth to social anxiety, and later, feed and maintain social anxiety.

Thomas

Thomas is a gentle man. He is fifty and speaks with a raspy, kindly voice:

> Growing up there was lots of alcohol and violence in my home. My reaction was to withdraw. I'd hide in my bedroom, under the bed. The more my mother and my stepfather fought, the more I withdrew. My mother met another man, who kicked my stepfather out. We moved to a shack in the woods. My stepfather would come back and harass us. He once shot a bullet through the window.
>
> Ma and her new husband always told me to be quiet. When we moved to a house with a real toilet, I was even afraid to flush the toilet, as it would make a noise. I remember praying to my mother, "I'll be a good boy, just please don't leave me." I couldn't make friends at school. When I got older, my favorite activity was having a pot of tea in the darkness of my bedroom. I thought a lot. I realized I had become a people pleaser. I felt I wasn't important. I remember a cousin was going to teach me how to dance. I was so scared that I took a whole bunch of tranquilizers.

Michael

Michael is in his mid-thirties, a happily married man with three children:

> Primary school was a nightmare. I had difficulty reading, spelling, and doing arithmetic. I was petrified any time I'd have to read in front of the class. It seemed like an eternity as I waited my turn to read. Most humiliating of all was the experience of receiving school

marks at the end of the year. I was always one of the last three. The teacher would start by giving the report card with the highest marks to the highest achievers. By the time he got through the thirty-six students in my class, I was in agony. Everyone was snickering. More than a couple of times, I'd start to cry but then would quickly bump my elbow or something in order to have some stupid excuse as to why I was crying. I never did get the chance to tell the teacher what a bastard he was. I started to blossom in high school, both physically and mentally—thank God! I studied hard and managed to get to be the thirteenth or fourteenth out of a class of thirty-three.

At age seventeen, I was picked up by a semi-professional soccer team. The first game was so exciting. Soon afterwards I was involved in a motorbike accident. I spent five months in the hospital. There was a lot of depression over the following years. The only thing I could do better than anyone else was running, and now that was gone. At age twenty-two, I came to Canada. I started playing soccer at age twenty-six and have been enjoying it reasonably well. I'd like to coach, but I'm too afraid to take the coaching course. Except for my school experiences, I'd say my childhood was a happy one. I was blessed with a great mom and dad who both had a good sense of humor.

Is it any wonder that the events and experiences recounted above may have contributed to the development of social anxiety? Social anxiety is often a normal and understandable reaction to circumstances that are insulting, demanding, uncertain, and even traumatic.

One group member once remarked, "Compared to some of the stories that I've just heard, mine comes from Disneyland." Indeed, although some people with social anxiety have traumatic backgrounds, many others come from supportive and healthy families. As you can see, a myriad of ingredients, in different combinations and quantities, can contribute to the development of social anxiety. Depending on the precise mix of these ingredients, the resulting social anxiety can range from the normal, often helpful type of social anxiety to the extremely unhelpful and even incapacitating type.

NEGATIVE CONSEQUENCES

WHEN SHYNESS AND social anxiety are moderate to extreme, the consequences can be far-reaching. They can influence your social and work lives, not to mention your mood and lifestyle.

➤ *Social life:*

Many people restrict their lives so much that it is difficult to make and maintain friendships and love relationships. Loneliness follows.

➤ *Work life:*

Students may drop out of school, thus reducing their number of job options later in life. There are also people like Teresa and Brad, who work at interesting jobs, but who both passed up opportunities for advancement because they dreaded the prospect of a job interview, and they worried about whether they would be able to keep up with the demands of the new position. Other people, like Sammy, choose to work graveyard shifts in order to minimize their amount of social interaction. Finally, there are the unemployed. Andy chooses unemployment over the unbearable stress of having to work with others; Malcolm would prefer to work but doesn't seem to get the job offers, either because luck isn't with him or because he doesn't present confidently.

➤ *Depression:*

Thirty-five percent of people with social anxiety experience at least one episode of depression in their lifetime. It is difficult to say how much of their depression is a result of the restricted lifestyle associated with social anxiety and how much is due to other factors. If you suspect that you have depression but are not sure, see your family doctor.

➤ *Alcoholism:*

About fifteen percent of people with extreme social anxiety also have problems with alcohol. Many people admit that they "self-medicate" to gain courage while facing the prospect of a social encounter. The irony about using alcohol to cope with social anxiety is that over time, people with alcohol problems can become even more socially anxious. They don't have the opportunity to practice socializing without their liquid courage. Consequently, they can't be confident that they can deal with social situations without alcohol. (A more complete discussion of how alcohol chemically affects anxiety is contained in Part Two, "The Body.")

• *Eating disorders:*

Eating disorders can also accompany social anxiety. I attended a workshop where several women who had previously been anorectic agreed to be interviewed about how fear and anxiety had seduced them into starvation diets. The refrains that these women repeated bore an uncanny resemblance to the refrains I had been hearing from my socially anxious clients. These courageous women described how their inner dialogues used to tell them, "If you're not good, people won't like you. If you show weakness, people will judge you as damaged." These women said that these inner messages were rarely challenged because silence, shame, and secrecy drove them underground. The similarities between social anxiety and eating disorders are inescapable.

THE GOOD NEWS

SOCIAL ANXIETY IS not a fixed state. *It is fluid.* You can change its shape and its quantity. You can definitely reduce it. Indeed, social anxiety is one of those conditions that responds well to active intervention. Once you manage your social anxiety and reduce it to normal or milder levels, you may be delighted to find that social anxiety turns out to be a friend, not an enemy. It has benefits and advantages that can help you succeed in your social and work lives. Read on to see how you can start this new relationship with shyness and social anxiety by first changing your attitude.

KEY REFLECTION POINTS

➤ Social anxiety is the fear of being evaluated and judged poorly in social situations.

➤ Symptoms of social anxiety affect three areas: body, mind, and action.

➤ People can be publicly or privately shy. They can have specific or generalized social anxiety.

➤ The continuum of shyness and social anxiety ranges from normal to extreme.

➤ Currently, fifty percent of the population rate themselves as shy. About thirteen percent of the population experiences extreme social anxiety, called social phobia or social anxiety disorder.

➤ Biochemistry, genetics, and environment contribute to the development of social anxiety.

➤ Extreme social anxiety can lead to loneliness, difficulties in employment, depression and alcoholism. It is often related to eating disorders.

➤ It is possible to reduce extreme shyness. Social anxiety responds well to active intervention.

The one thing I want to remember from this chapter is:

_____

_____

TWO

IT'S A GOOD THING— NO, IT'S A BAD THING

Attitudes about Shyness and Social Anxiety

> I've experienced social anxiety for as long as I can remember. I've always been called a shy person. I would hear that label throughout my life. Whenever I heard that "shy" word, I'd feel down.
> —BILL, group participant

> The more I cloak myself in secrecy, the more anxious I get. I wish I could be like a friend of mine who is open about his insecurities. It's all that holding in that makes for so much nervous energy. A huge weight lifted off my shoulders when I told my friend that I was coming to this [social anxiety support] group.
> —LYN, group participant

DEPENDING ON YOUR background, the word *shy* can describe a gentle, even praiseworthy disposition, or it can describe a shameful character trait. In China, the Mandarin word for *shy* or *quiet* can be translated as "good" or "well-behaved." The word *sensitive* means "having understanding." It is meant to be a term of praise. According to research comparing traits that made children popular, in China, shy and sensitive children are among the first to be chosen by others to be friends and playmates. In Canada, shy and sensitive children are among the last chosen. Why the difference? Why is shyness often considered a social handicap in North America? What contributed to the shame and secrecy of the group participants quoted earlier? The answer is not a simple one. In North America, part of the answer lies in the interplay of economic, scientific, social, and cultural factors. Let's take a closer look at how these factors influence each other and ultimately influence the so-called shy person.

SOCIAL ANXIETY BECOMES A MENTAL DISORDER

TWENTY-FIVE YEARS ago, social phobia, the extreme form of social anxiety, was barely recognized. It was not until 1980 that it was included in the third edition of the *Diagnostic and Statistical Manual of Mental Disorders* (DSM-III). The DSM is considered the North American psychiatric bible, listing and coding diagnostic names and clusters of symptoms of every conceivable psychiatric condition. Many health insurers will not cover the cost of treatment unless the therapist can codify and name the condition being treated according to the classifications of the DSM.

In 1980, the definition of social phobia meant that the person's level of anxiety in a social situation was so high that it compelled him to avoid the social situation altogether. In 1980, this "disorder" was noted to be relatively rare, perhaps affecting two to three percent of the population. Now we are to believe that social phobia is the third most common mental disorder, affecting thirteen percent of the population, or one out of eight people. Extreme social anxiety has now become a common medical condition. What happened between 1980 and now?

In the mid-1980s, Michael R. Liebowitz, director of the Anxiety Disorders Clinic of New York State Psychiatric Institute, criticized the limited definition of social phobia contained in the DSM-III. He argued that many people don't avoid difficult social situations and instead "fight their way through difficult situations . . . at tremendous personal costs." Liebowitz argued that just because these people weren't avoiding the situation didn't mean they weren't suffering terribly. He was concerned that these people would be deprived of insurance coverage if their particular brand of social phobia wasn't also included in the DSM-III. In 1987, Liebowitz sat on the advisory panel that updated the section of social phobia. In the next edition, DSM-IIIR, the definition of "social phobia" now excluded the phrase, "a compelling desire to avoid." It was enough to experience "marked distress" to qualify for the diagnosis of social phobia. Now thirteen percent of the population could expect to suffer from this "disorder"—but at least people's treatment would be covered by health insurance.

Because social phobia is classified as a mental disorder, it joins other mental disorders in carrying some stigma in our culture. Even people who experience milder forms of social anxiety may develop an attitude of shame and secrecy about their anxiety. Few people, including those in the helping professions, realize that the border between what was considered normal and abnormal social anxiety was moved for the benefit of health insurance recipients.

TOTALIZATION OR THE LABELING TRAP

ANOTHER INTERESTING PHENOMENON that contributes to a negative attitude about shyness and social anxiety is that of *totalization*. To totalize means to make into a total. For instance, if I have failed, I may totalize by labeling myself a failure. As soon as I use this label, I'm at risk of thinking of myself as nothing but a failure. In reality, just because I failed on a certain occasion does not mean that I am a total failure.

A number of years ago, before public consciousness was raised about the politics behind naming things, we often called a person with a physical handicap a "cripple." The trouble with this shortcut way of talking was that we missed important parts of the whole person. We didn't stop to think that the "cripple" was, first and foremost, a human being; an individual with dreams, interests, and relationships; a unique personality with talents and abilities.

Fortunately, things change. In the late 1970s, for instance, Rick Hansen did much to help alter Canadians' views about persons with physical handicaps. Rick Hansen was confined to a wheelchair because of a spinal injury he had suffered in an accident during his teens. As a young man, he resolved to make a trip across Canada in his wheelchair to raise public awareness about spinal injuries. Rick Hansen's name became a household word as millions of people in Canada regularly watched him on television, cheering him on, getting to know his personal side through the many interviews during and following his journey. No longer did we see a cripple. We saw Rick Hansen, a man of many outstanding qualities. Around this time, I remember an incident that made an impression on me. I had been driving to work when I saw two men in wheelchairs talking to each other at the corner of a busy intersection. I can vividly recall how different they seemed to me. In the past, I may have seen them as unfortunate souls deserving of my sympathy. Now they were men, possibly heroic men, who were getting through life in spite of personal obstacles.

What about the shyness label? "Don't mind him, he's just shy," says a loving mother about her four-year-old son, who hides behind her leg, his face peeking out just a little. I've heard this well-meaning introduction of children many times; perhaps you have, too. The shyness label seems innocuous enough. But to the child who hears it, especially if he hears it repeatedly, the shyness label can be a significant piece of information as he begins to figure out who he is in this world. Messages from older people, who supposedly know more than he does, will be taken seriously. Fred, an adult who figures he's been shy all his life, remembers distinctly the day his mother first labeled him as shy, to several of her friends. That day, he learned two things. First, he learned that he was shy. Second, he learned that his mother felt she had to apologize for his shyness. To Fred, this meant that shyness must be bad. From then on, Fred lived up to his and his mother's expectations. He would continue to approach the world shyly and on top of that, he would feel badly about himself for doing so.

Allow me to give a word of advice to parents. If you do feel the need to comment on your child's hesitancy in a new social setting, simply say something like, "This is my son, Fred. He likes to take his time warming up to new situations." Avoid using the word "shy." Give your child a reassuring wink or a gentle touch. This way your child is given permission to be who he is. He feels accepted. The door to exploring the world, at his own pace, remains wide open.

People who experience shyness often hide their shyness, at times even keeping it secret from those closest to them. They equate their entire selves with the label "shy." They become over-identified with this label, forgetting there is so much more to them than their shyness. Many self-help books can ironically contribute to that sense of feeling totally inadequate. You can become so focused on your shortcomings, as they are discussed in these books, that you lose sight of your strengths and your unique and delightful personality traits. Your view of yourself can become lopsided.

CULTURAL PRESSURES THAT CONTRIBUTE TO SHYNESS OR CONFIDENCE

There is no conceivable human action [that] custom has not at one time justified and at another condemned.
—JOSEPH WOOD KRUTCH, naturalist

SOCIAL RULES ARE not absolute truths. They change depending on the culture and the values of that culture at a particular time and place. Consider the following contrast. In Japan, people who experience social anxiety are often afraid of making too much direct eye contact, which would be considered rude. Avoiding eye contact by looking downward is considered polite, even "elegant." In North America, avoiding eye contact is considered a hallmark of social anxiety. People who tend to be shy are afraid that they will be judged for making too little direct eye contact. In the case above, what the Japanese and the North American have in common is the fear of breaking the rules of social conduct.

Rules of social conduct in certain cultures can be harsh and exacting. In Saudi Arabia, for instance, social rules are demanding and the consequences for breaking them can be unforgiving. Interestingly, social phobia happens to be common in Saudi Arabia, particularly among men.

One of the primary ways that cultural values get handed down to a society's children is through the parenting practices of that society. Philip Zimbardo, a pioneer in the field of shyness research, has compared the prevalence of shyness in eight countries. Japan rated the highest, with about sixty percent of its population rating themselves as shy; Israel rated the lowest, with only about thirty percent rating themselves as shy. Zimbardo notes that Japanese parents often used shame as a tool to help shape their children's behavior. Children learn early in life that it is important not to bring disgrace to their family. When a child performs poorly, whether at school or in a Little League game, he is personally blamed. Perhaps the child will only have to look at his parents' faces to know they disapproved. If, on the other hand, the child does well during a game, credit often goes to others. The parents might tell the child, "You have a very good coach," or "Isn't it a good thing that Daddy took the time to show you how to do it properly?"

According to Zimbardo, the child-rearing practices in Israel are quite the opposite. If an Israeli boy performs poorly during a baseball game, the blame will often be placed anywhere else but on him. His parents might say something like, "Oh, my goodness, the coach didn't teach you right," or "The competition isn't fair!" If, on the other hand, the same boy makes a home run, he'll get all the credit. He'll probably hear something like, "My boy, I always knew you were a genius!"

Which child is apt to enjoy taking risks; which child will tend to avoid risks? The Israeli child can't lose. He is richly rewarded when things go right. He is absolved from blame when things go wrong. The Japanese child can't seem to win. He gets little credit, if any, when things go right, and he gets all the blame when things go wrong.

WESTERN CULTURE

SADLY, SHYNESS IS currently not admired in our Western culture, particularly in North American culture. Decades ago, those who were extremely shy suffered in silence. Those who were moderately shy were just shy. No big deal. Guys liked shy girls. Girls liked shy guys. People realized that shyness was a package deal. So many admirable qualities accompanied moderate shyness, such as sensitivity toward others, thoughtfulness, and endearing modesty. Shyness was a personality trait that simply meant people took their time to get to know others and to be known by others. Times have changed.

Now shyness is often considered a weakness. According to one source of experts, namely, the hundreds of shy people who have attended my social anxiety support groups over the years, there's a message out there in society that says it's not okay to be shy. According to Michelle Cottle, author of an article in the *New Republic*, called "Selling Shyness,"

> One wonders how much of the nation's social phobia epidemic stems from our growing sense that everyone should be aggressive, be assertive, and strive for the limelight. Forget the life of quiet contemplation. We are a society that glorifies celebrities and celebrates in-your-face personalities . . . For a shot at their fifteen minutes of fame, Jane and Joe Schmoe are lining up to expose even the most degrading or banal aspects of their personal lives to public scrutiny via Jerry Springer, the Internet, and "America's Funniest Home Videos." Increasingly, we have little admiration—or patience—for those who don't reach out and grab life by the throat.

Television shows, movies, and advertising reinforce the notion that the ideal way of being is to go "out there" and be an "in-your-face" kind of personality. As author Phyllis Shaw puts it:

> The action-man, making swift decisions, jet-setting, enjoying a round of parties and having whirlwind affairs with beautiful women, is more commonly found in the media than the librarian who enjoys classical music, goes fishing with his best friend at the weekend, and is faithful to his friendly, garden-loving wife.

Let's face it. If you were a profit-driven movie producer, which kind of characters would you choose to portray, the ones who make the audience reflect about the important things of life or the ones likely to draw the biggest crowd? Businesses are in business to make money. Consequently, we are continually flooded with larger-than-life images of people being "out there." This propaganda pressures us to feel that we, too, should be so bold. It matters little whether this reflects our true nature or not.

JUDEO-CHRISTIAN TRADITION
AND THE BATTLE METAPHOR

I WOULD LIKE to suggest two other factors that have contributed to the notion that shyness is a weakness to be reckoned with. The first relates to the Judeo-Christian influence that permeates our society, and the second deals with the metaphor of battle. In the Judeo-Christian tradition, there is one God and we are made in His likeness. He is all-perfect and it is our job to seek perfection. We must seek good and stamp out evil. This tendency to think in dualities can be a trap for some. For instance, if shyness is seen as less than ideal, less than perfect, it becomes our job to stamp it out.

Add the metaphor of battle to this notion of seeking perfection. The United States won its independence through battle. Its birth as a nation resulted from battle. Its victory in battle is celebrated every Fourth of July. *Battle* is a glorious term. It is a word that has become a part of everyday language. We used to refer to the battle of the bulge (when discussing weight-loss programs) and the battle between the sexes. Now we talk about the war against drugs. Even certain titles of books on shyness promise that the battle of shyness can be won. This only reinforces the idea that shyness is bad and must be eliminated. Look at what your culture dishes out with a critical mind. Swallow that which is nourishing; spit out the rest.

SHYNESS IS NORMAL

SO FAR WE'VE looked at various factors that have contributed to a largely negative attitude toward shyness and social anxiety in our mainstream culture. Let us now look at a perspective that has helped many shy or sensitive people to develop a more compassionate and accepting attitude toward their social anxiety.

> Becky's large blue eyes moistened with tears. "What's going on?" I asked softly. Even more softly, she replied, "I didn't know that I didn't have to stop being shy." Shreds of the single tissue that she had been turning over and over again in her fingers flecked her crimson sweater. Slowly, she repeated, "I didn't know that I didn't have to stop being shy." Then a gentle smile crossed her face. This was a new beginning.

Becky was only fifteen and already she had been convinced that shyness was something to be stamped out, once and for all. The idea that shyness was normal was a new, liberating concept. Perhaps now, she could keep a certain degree of shyness without any shame. Any excess shyness could be worked on, one step at a time. Now, she could reclaim her life, including her shy nature, from the tyranny of negative judgment. Had Dr. Morita been alive today, he would have gladly offered to support Becky's new position regarding her shyness.

Shoma Morita (1874–1938) was a Japanese psychiatrist who worked with socially anxious people. He was of another time, another culture. Sometimes, we are blind to different ways of looking at things because we are so steeped in our own time and culture. What is appealing about Morita's approach is his positive take on the meaning of social anxiety. This meaning is contained within the three fundamental, philosophical premises underlying Morita therapy. According to Ishu Ishiyama, associate professor at The University of British Columbia, they are

> ➤ social anxiety, including shyness, is a normal human emotion
> ➤ social anxiety has a self-actualizing meaning
> ➤ social anxiety can be used as a motivator-facilitator, rather than as an inhibitor, of constructive action

Let's examine these three points more closely. First, social anxiety and shyness are normal. We've already seen in Chapter 1 that only seven to eleven percent of the population reported that they have never felt shy. Morita pointed out that normal shyness is not a problem. People get themselves into trouble when they become *shy about being shy*. This second level of shyness brings with it unnecessary pain—the pain associated with a sense of not belonging, of being flawed.

The second premise underlying Morita's therapy is that social anxiety has a self-actualizing meaning. In Chapter 1, we learned that the usual definition of social anxiety relates to fear of social failure. What this definition lacks is the opposite side of the coin. If we fear social failure, then we must wish for social success. In other words, social anxiety really means that we want to do well. Reframing social anxiety in this positive way can have a liberating effect.

For instance, when my youngest son, Jordan, was six years old and just learning to play baseball, he once took me aside during a break in a Little League game. With an air of concern, he said, "Mommy, when I go up to bat, my arm starts to shake and shake." He looked at me searchingly, as if waiting for a response that would solve this mysterious phenomenon. Had I not known about Morita's ideas, I'm sure I would have slipped into the usual explanation that might have sounded something like, "Well, sweetheart, that's because you're a little nervous, you know, a little shy in front of all those people. Don't worry about it; you'll do okay." I would have felt that I was being supportive. Chances are, however, that these words would have offered little but cold comfort. Chances also are that Jordan would have identified with being nervous and shy and would have worried about whether he could stop worrying. Instead, I told Jordan, "Of course, honey, that's because you want to do well!" His response? An enthusiastic, "Yeah, Mom, I want to do well!" and off he scampered to join his buddies.

When we see social anxiety as an expression of our desire to do well in a social setting, social anxiety is transformed into something honorable. Isn't wanting to do well, after all, an honorable goal? This brings us to the third premise. Social anxiety can be used as a motivator, a facilitator, rather than as an inhibitor of constructive action. If social anxiety can remind us that we are simply human beings wanting to coexist with other human beings in a meaningful and successful way, it can motivate us to stay focused on constructive action. It becomes a green light, telling us to go ahead with whatever task lies ahead, whether it is talking to people, making a toast, or asking someone to dance.

For many, Morita's ideas are liberating. Once the focus is on constructive action, people will notice that any inconvenient anxious feelings that do come up soon run their course and give way to the excitement of achieving a goal. One achievement spurs another. Confidence builds and the way is paved for continued involvement in a variety of social settings.

Granted, people who experience extreme social anxiety may argue that maintaining this positive focus is a lot easier said than done. Of course, this argument has some weight, especially if focusing on negative symptoms and thoughts has become an entrenched habit. In this case, the Morita approach may not be enough. Finding other ways of shrinking the shyness habit will be critical. The approaches described in the rest of the book will provide useful alternatives.

FURTHER CHALLENGES TO NEGATIVE ATTITUDES TOWARD SHYNESS AND SOCIAL ANXIETY

BEFORE WE MOVE on, I would like to share a few pearls of wisdom that have come out of a discussion in a follow-up group composed of graduates of my social anxiety support groups. We meet once a month to discuss anything and everything that has to do with social anxiety and social confidence. The topic on one particular morning was "shyness and secrecy." We agreed that society sends many messages that tell us that shyness is not okay. We agreed that we need to challenge these messages. The following is a synopsis of the key points of the group's challenge.

1. We declare that shyness does not equal weakness. I can be shy and I can still be strong, so long as I do the task that

needs doing, in spite of feeling nervous or awkward. Shyness is independent of strength of character. People can be loud and boisterous, or shy. Shyness does not get in the way of developing strength of character. In fact, it can help, because if I'm shy, I'm used to plowing through feelings of fear and bravely doing whatever it is I need to do.

2. Shyness is normal. A lot of good qualities go along with shyness. There is sensitivity to nuances, to subtle differences. There is empathy for others. These are great qualities for certain life occupations and for solid friendships.

3. We declare that we do not have to buy into society's negative judgment of shyness. It is an arbitrary judgment. In England, shyness is charming. In Japan, shy laughing is elegant. It so happens that in North America, there's a push for that which is big, independent, and showy. People from other cultures would be mortified if they displayed such characteristics. I can choose whether I want to buy into such arbitrary values. I can choose to value that which is closer to my true nature.

4. We declare that we do not have to accept the prejudice of others looking down on those of us who are shy. Some people look down on Albanians, Serbians, Catholics, Jews, Asians, Hispanics, anglophones, francophones, gays, lesbians, aboriginal peoples, people of color, women, computer nerds (unless they're rich like Bill Gates), short people, fat people, people who are too dark, too light, not intellectual enough, not sporty enough, and so on. Power politics will always exist. It's the bigoted person's loss when he looks down on someone. His prejudice is usually a product of a lack of education and exposure, brainwashing, or a mean spirit. I do not have to cooperate with power politics. I do not have to think that something is wrong with me just because someone else may think so.

5. We declare that it may be time to celebrate our shyness, to have a shyness pride parade, to have a shyness coming-out party! I do not have to keep shyness a secret.

So what's it going to be? Buying into the status quo? Or liberating yourself from the influence of external opinions and arbitrary beliefs? As final words of encouragement in this chapter, I would like to quote Viktor Frankl, a psychiatrist who, during his imprisonment in WWII concentration camps, noted that even in the horrible and degrading conditions of these camps: "Everything could be taken from man except for one thing: the last of human freedoms—to choose one's attitude in any set of circumstances, to choose one's own way."

Perhaps it is time to choose your own way. Perhaps it is time to write your own declaration of independence from the influence of cultural, economic, and scientific forces. Is it really necessary to be shy about being shy? Perhaps it is time to appreciate your normal shyness. And finally, perhaps it is time to do something about that extra shyness that gets in the way of having as fulfilling a life as you might like.

KEY REFLECTION POINTS

➤ Depending on your background, the word *shy* can have either positive or negative meanings.

➤ The interplay of economic, scientific, social, and cultural factors determines whether shyness is seen as a desirable trait or as a social handicap.

➤ It is important not to equate the whole person with his or her shyness or social anxiety. There is so much more to a person: his passions, interests, values, and purpose in life.

➤ Shyness is normal. It is when you become shy about being shy that you run into trouble.

➤ Social anxiety means that you want to do well socially. Whether you are temporarily inconvenienced by feelings of social anxiety is not important in the larger scheme of things. What is important is your constructive action.

➤ The sensitivity that accompanies shyness has positive value. People can use this sensitivity to enhance their competence both in their social and work lives.

➤ It may be time to challenge society's negative messages about shyness and appreciate the value in normal shyness and social anxiety. Take the steps to manage excessive shyness and social anxiety so that you can follow through with your hopes and dreams.

The one thing I want to remember from this chapter is:

_____

_____

■ PART TWO ■

THE
BODY

OH GOD, NOT NOW!

The Physical Aspects of Social Anxiety

I started getting really self-conscious in my teens. I was
very quiet. I wouldn't speak up in front of groups. Now,
when I deal with clients at work, I get really nervous. Even
if a client gives me a compliment, I get sweaty and shaky.
I can't concentrate. My face gets really tight. It's difficult
to relax. I'll start thinking, Oh my God, she's going to
know that I have this problem. She'll know that I'm not
confident. She'll think that I'm stupid. I feel really little . . .
insignificant. I often avoid work meetings. I'm so afraid
that if I ask a question, I'll look stupid. I take my lunch
break after everyone else has gone. I don't like to eat in
front of people. I get shaky—what if I spill my food?
—JIM, age thirty-two

JIM'S STORY IS not unusual. His social anxiety is apparent in his physical symptoms, in the way he thinks and in
the way he behaves. It's impossible to talk about one aspect
of social anxiety without talking about the other aspects.
The physical, thinking (cognitive), and behavioral symptoms
of social anxiety are interconnected. Roughly twenty to
thirty percent of the participants in my groups have rated
their physical symptoms as their number-one concern.
They describe their physical symptoms as "excruciating,"

"unbearable," and, if detected by others, "humiliating." The pounding of their hearts, the trembling, the sweating, and the difficulty breathing all take center stage, while everything else recedes into the background. The remaining seventy to eighty percent of group participants also experience physical symptoms but to lesser degrees. If you want to reclaim your body from the grip of anxiety, read on as we explore the workings of the brain, nervous system, and the body.

THE PHYSIOLOGY OF ANXIETY

FOR A MOMENT, imagine that you're sleeping in your warm bed. Your body is completely at rest, limp as the spaghetti you had for supper. Then, in one confusing moment, you find yourself awake, your heart throbbing loudly, your ears and eyes straining for clues about what woke you up. Did you really hear glass smashing? Is someone in the house? Are those footsteps you hear? Do you hide? Call 911? Get the baseball bat and plan on defending yourself? Or do you freeze? The anxiety that you are experiencing is the result of the body's marvelous capacity to activate itself in the face of a possible threat. Mother Nature steps in. In the interest of survival, she plays out a myriad of ploys designed for your protection, as you will soon see.

Anyone who has experienced a strong bout of social anxiety will be familiar with such symptoms as increased heartbeat, increased or difficult breathing, sweating, trembling, and so on. These are the same bodily responses that are activated in an emergency involving some sort of physical threat. In the case of social anxiety, the threat is not directly physical but rather, psychological. The person fears that she might not do well and will be judged poorly. Perhaps at a deeper level, there is fear that such social disapproval could lead to rejection, much like exile from the social tribes of ancient times, which, in fact, would have been a threat to physical survival.

The autonomic nervous system

Let's return to our example of being startled out of sleep by the possible threat of a home invader. The perception of possible danger triggered the brain to send messages to the autonomic nervous system. This nervous system is called *autonomic* because it is involuntary. It operates automatically, according to messages it receives from the rest of the body. Within this nervous system are two subsystems: the sympathetic nervous system (SNS) and the parasympathetic nervous system (PNS).

Sympathetic nervous system

The main job of the sympathetic nervous system is to get the body ready for action, for either fight or flight, in order to survive. It does this by releasing stress chemicals such as adrenalin and noradrenalin from the adrenal glands in the kidney. These chemicals are messengers that energize the body as it prepares for action. When the sympathetic nervous system is activated, different parts of the body begin to do specific jobs.

HEART AND BLOOD
➤ Heart beats harder to speed up blood flow.
➤ Oxygenated blood delivers oxygen to tissues, especially those in big muscle groups such as the leg muscles, preparing the legs to run from the threat or to stay and fight.
➤ As blood feeds large muscles, less blood goes to skin, fingers, and toes, hence the tingling sensations.

BREATHING
➤ Speed and depth of breathing increases in order to increase amount of oxygen going to the tissues that are preparing for action.
➤ This surge of excessive breathing may produce breathlessness, a sense of choking or smothering, and even pain or tightness in the chest.

➤ Another possible side effect of excessive breathing is the decrease of the blood supply to the head. This can lead to feelings of dizziness and confusion.

SWEAT GLANDS

➤ An increase in sweating protects the body from overheating.
➤ Increased sweating also has a protective value: any assailant would have difficulty tussling with someone as slick as a freshly caught tuna fish.

DIGESTIVE SYSTEM

➤ As energy is used up in increasing activity in other body systems, there is less energy for the digestive system, hence the decrease in saliva and the digestive juices, resulting in a dry mouth, nausea, a fluttery or heavy stomach, and even constipation.

EYES

➤ Pupils dilate to let in more light while the eyes scour the surroundings for signs of danger. This can result in sensitivity to light.
➤ Pupils can also diverge in order to access the source of danger. Sometimes they do not return to normal right away (this is called *convergence insufficiency*), and people complain of blurred vision.

ENERGY

➤ Many muscle groups tense in preparation for fight or flight. This accumulation of energy can result in aches and pains, and in trembling and shaking.
➤ Because a lot of energy has been used up in the emergency response, a person usually feels tired and drained afterwards.

It is important to realize that the sympathetic nervous system cannot go on activating the body's arousal system indefinitely. It is stopped in two ways. First, adrenalin and noradrenalin are metabolized by

other chemicals in the body and are reabsorbed by the liver and kid-
neys within a few minutes. Second, after enough activation of the
emergency response has occurred, the parasympathetic nervous system automatically kicks in and slows the body down.

Parasympathetic Nervous System

The main job of the parasympathetic nervous system is to stop
the sympathetic nervous system from going overboard. Left
unchecked, the state of anxious arousal could cause damage. Can
you imagine, for instance, what would happen if the blood flow
never returned to your fingers and toes? If your digestion system
was permanently slowed to almost nothing? The parasympathetic
nervous system restores the body to a relaxed state. It lowers heart
rate, blood pressure, and respiration. It increases the activity in the
digestive system. The activation of the parasympathetic nervous
system is what helps us to feel back to normal.

In cases of extreme stress, where there is no possibility for fight
or flight, the parasympathetic nervous system uses its slowing
effects even more dramatically in order to defend the body from
threat. It will slow things down so much that a person will either
involuntarily freeze or collapse. This response is often seen in the
animal kingdom. The other day, my husband and I witnessed our
ginger cat, Tess, carrying a mouse in her jaws. She'd drop the
mouse and bat it around with her paws as it attempted to scuttle
off and when it suddenly went limp, Tess smelled it a couple of
times, lost interest, and left the yard. Sure enough, within a few
moments, the mouse came to and scurried away. In the book *Social
Anxiety*, Mark Leary and Robin Mark Kowalski cite research
demonstrating that the parasympathetic response patterns are
present in situations where there is strong negative emotion, usually fear, and where there is no possibility of coping.

The parasympathetic nervous system kicks in, not only when
there is an actual impossibility for coping, but also when there is a
perceived impossibility for coping. Hal, a forty-year-old, vividly
remembers his sense of being frozen during a college class twenty
years earlier:

We were sitting in a semicircle around the blackboard when the professor asked me to go to the board and analyze some musical theory. His terminology threw me off. I was used to other terminology. I couldn't figure out what he was trying to say. One of the students tried to help. Then the professor started yelling at me. He screamed. "What's the matter with you?" I froze. I was embarrassed. I felt stupid. Nothing was working. Everything seemed locked. Later a fellow student came up to me at the lockers and said she wouldn't have taken that. She said that she would have yelled back in the professor's face and would have walked out. But that wasn't in my nature.

From Hal's twenty-year-old subjective point of view, there was no possibility of coping with the unexpected and humiliating behavior of the college professor. His upbringing did not teach him that it was okay to challenge a person in authority. To return the rude treatment that he had received from the professor was not an option; it would have gone against Hal's grain to do so. Consequently, at that particular time in Hal's life, even though the sympathetic nervous system may have started to prepare Hal for action, he saw no action possible. The parasympathetic nervous system kicked in and Hal froze. This all took place in a matter of seconds.

Only years later, in therapy, did Hal figure out how he might have handled the situation differently. He realized that he could have used assertive verbal skills that would have supported his gentle and considerate nature. He might have carefully told the professor that he did not appreciate the professor's raising his voice and insinuating that Hal was stupid simply because he did not understand the terminology the professor was using. If Hal did not wish to create a scene in the classroom, he could have met with the professor privately to explain the situation from his point of view. And nowadays, with society's heightened awareness regarding the politics of harassment, Hal might have chosen to report the professor's obnoxious behavior to the proper authorities.

There are other times when the sympathetic and parasympathetic nervous systems overlap. It is not uncommon for a socially anxious person to first experience the sympathetic responses of heightened vigilance, increased heartbeat and tension, and then, even while the heart is beating furiously, to feel faint as the blood pressure decreases.

THE CASE OF THE HAIR-TRIGGER SYMPATHETIC NERVOUS SYSTEM

SOME FOLKS, PARTICULARLY those who have been traumatized in the past, complain that they are almost always on edge. The least little thing can trigger an anxiety response. Even thinking about these triggers can induce physical anxiety. Tricia, a thirty-eight-year-old, describes her workdays as follows:

> I wake up every morning feeling nauseous, afraid to face the people at work. I imagine all kinds of ways I'll make a fool of myself. As I get on the elevator, I can feel my heart do its 'let's beat as fast as we can' number. It doesn't let up even as I walk through the office door. I'm constantly nervous about whether I'm saying the right thing, doing the right thing. Every time I see the manager or one of the secretaries look at me, I feel I'm being judged. By the time I come home, I'm exhausted.

Tricia was brought up in a household of parental abuse, both verbal and physical. Faced with repeated threats of emotional or physical hurt, her nervous system became so used to reacting quickly and intensely that it would automatically go into these intense patterns no matter whether there was a real or imaginary threat, even later in her life. Tricia knew that these anxiety reactions were often overreactions, but she felt like she couldn't help it. It seemed so automatic. Tricia was right. Through no fault of her own, her sympathetic nervous system had learned to spike hard at the slightest provocation; this is called the *kindling effect:* /\/\/\/\ . Other people's nervous systems might react with less intensity, in more modulated patterns: ‿‿‿‿ . Tricia's heart would start racing wildly and she would feel panicky, whereas others might react a little and then get on with the task at hand.

THE THREE-PART BRAIN

FOR THOSE OF you interested in even further explanations about how the body responds when socially anxious, I have saved the best for last—information about the three-part brain. Thanks to recent brain research, the findings of which are steadily seeping into the knowledge base of psychotherapy, we can now further demystify some of the physiological processes of social anxiety. Read on.

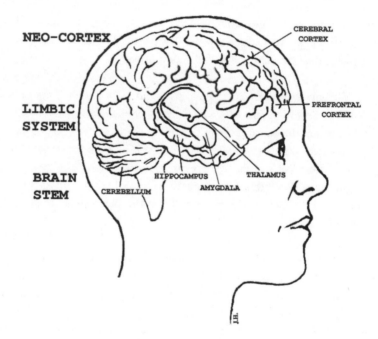

Think of your brain as being divided into three parts. The top third contains the cortex, the thinking part. The middle third is called the limbic system and is the center of emotions and feelings. The bottom third is the brain stem and is in charge of breathing and the autonomic nervous system. When there is a threat, sensory information (sight of an angry face, sound of a growling dog) is sent to the thalamus, which is located in the middle third of the brain.

Thalamus comes from the Greek word meaning "chamber." The thalamus serves as a relay station that sends messages to different parts of the brain. In the event of a threat, the thalamus sends information simultaneously to the cortex, above it, and to the amygdala, beside it, in the middle part of the brain.

The *amygdala* is an intriguing organ. Its name comes from the Greek word meaning "almond," and it is just about the size of an almond. The amygdala's job is to recognize anything that is novel and determine whether it is dangerous. If it decides that it is dangerous, it immediately sends alarm signals to the hypothalamus, beneath the thalamus, also in the middle part of the brain, which, in turn, sets into motion the sympathetic nervous system and triggers the release of stress chemicals such as adrenalin and cortisol. These stress chemicals help to consolidate the memory of the event. This helps the brain and the amygdala to recognize the threat even sooner in the event of a repeat episode.

How does this translate to the world of the socially anxious? It could explain why, if a group of children teased and humiliated you when you were small, any group of people might set off alarm bells in the amygdala, which in turn triggers the stress response and the sympathetic nervous system. It makes sense of the fact that if a parent or teacher emotionally abused you in the past, you might now start sweating and trembling in front of other authority figures such as the police officer, the boss, or the manager.

For people whose mind goes blank when socially anxious, the following information may be interesting. Brain imaging research through MRI (magnetic resonance imaging) has yielded findings that show which parts of the brain turn on or shut down during different events. When people are read descriptions of a traumatic event that they have experienced in the past and they begin to recall this event, there is sometimes decreased activity in the thalamus. As the thalamus, the relay station, shuts down, it is unable to relay messages to other parts of the brain, including parts involved in thinking and in regulating affect or emotions. This brief disconnection between the thalamus and the cortex is the best explanation I have found for why the mind goes blank. Fortunately, when the stress decreases, the thalamus-cortex connection will reset and the person's functioning will return to normal.

KNOWLEDGE IS POWER

HOPEFULLY, ONCE YOU understand the workings of your brain and body when socially anxious, you will be able to take on a researcher's stance and marvel at what is going on, rather than feeling overwhelmed and perplexed. Instead of panicking, you may be able to remind yourself that the activation of the sympathetic nervous system, with all its symptoms of nervousness, will not go on indefinitely. It will run its course and the parasympathetic nervous system will step in and restore the body to a relaxed state.

Let's continue by looking at physical ways of helping to calm the body.

CALMING THE BODY

IF WE WANT to help the parasympathetic nervous system gain dominance, it is critical that we learn to relax. Luckily, relaxation is a physical skill that can be learned.

To begin with, learn to tell the difference between what looks like relaxation and what is really, relaxation. You can do this by checking in with your body and noticing the physical sensations you are experiencing. For instance, many people think watching TV is relaxing. Next time you're watching an action show, a thriller, even a nature show depicting animal survival, notice your bodily reactions.

I once attended a lecture given by trauma expert Peter Levine. During the lecture, he showed a film of a coyote chasing a hare. Imagine this poor, long-eared creature bounding on its huge hind legs, darting this way and that, leaping so high that it seemed to fly, only to touch ground again, narrowly keeping ahead of the determined coyote, which was soon joined by other coyotes. Every thirty seconds or so, Dr. Levine asked the projectionist to stop the film.

He then asked the audience to report on what they noticed going on in their bodies. "My chest is tight," reported one. "I can feel my heart beating," said another. One by one, various people reported the familiar physical symptoms of "fight or flight" preparation. In other words, watching TV or thriller movies can often be stressful, rather than relaxing. If you are truly interested in managing your physical anxiety, you are better off practicing such methods of relaxation as grounding, self-regulation therapy, controlled breathing, and progressive muscle relaxation. I will describe grounding and self-regulation in detail, because they are innovative and effective ways of calming the body. Breathing and progressive muscle relaxation exercises, also effective, can be found in most relaxation literature. You will find samples of each in Appendix I.

Grounding

The following grounding technique is especially effective for those whose physical symptoms are overwhelming, and for those who are unable to calm themselves using cognitive or thinking techniques because their thalamus-cortex connection is temporarily shut down. I learned this particular style of grounding from psychologists Lynne Zettl and Edward Josephs of the Canadian Foundation for Trauma Research and Education. They incorporate this technique in their work with trauma victims. The instructions are as follow:

1. From a sitting position, sense into your feet. The key word here is to *sense* the sensations of your feet resting on the floor or ground. Notice how the soles of your feet feel as they rest in your socks and shoes, or if barefooted, notice how the texture of your skin feels against the texture of the floor. Feel how the floor supports or receives your feet.
2. Now sense into your seat, that is, your buttocks and the backs of your thighs. Notice how your seat sinks into your chair. If your chair is soft, notice how its cushion envelops the backs of your thighs and buttocks. If your chair is hard, notice the sensation of hardness against your body.

3. Next, sense into your hands resting on your lap. Notice all the sensations. Are your hands heavy or light? Warm or cool? Dry or moist? Notice the difference between the texture of the skin of your hands and the fabric of your pants or skirt.

4. Sense into your back. Notice how it feels as your back sinks into the back of your chair. Feel the back of your chair giving your back support.

5. And finally, sense into your breathing. You don't have to do anything about your breath. Simply notice it. Notice the sensation of every inhalation and exhalation. Feel the air as it travels through your nose, down your airway and into your lungs. Notice how your chest and belly rise and fall with every in-breath and out-breath. Notice where your in-breath stops and your out-breath begins. Notice where your out-breath stops and your in-breath begins.

To review, sense into your feet, seat, hands, back, and your breath. Practice this several times a day, first in quiet settings, then in more stimulating settings. That way, when you suddenly find yourself in an anxious state, you'll be prepared to ground yourself immediately. Also, realize that sometimes it's not convenient to ground yourself in a sitting position. Often we can become overwhelmed while we're standing. If that's the case, then by all means, sense into your feet. You can even practice grounding while you're lying down. You can sense into the areas of your legs that are in contact with the mattress or ground. You can also sense into your arms, back, and so on. Grounding is a flexible and portable skill that can help you no matter where you are. I constantly teach my clients how to ground themselves. I constantly use grounding when I'm under stress, any stress. While driving, for instance, I might sense into my hands as they hold the steering wheel. I ground while walking to the trauma room in the hospital, fearful that I might collapse at the sight of a beloved patient who is comatose and struggling to survive after a failed suicide attempt. I ground, feeling the contact of my feet on the ground with every step I make, even while I am talking to a colleague who walks beside me.

Self-regulation therapy

Self-regulation therapy (SRT) is a method of desensitization also taught by psychologists Zettl and Josephs.

Desensitization basically means to become less and less sensitive to something. (Desensitization is explained more fully in Chapters 8 and 12.) Zettl's and Josephs' work has been influenced by a number of trauma specialists, including Peter Levine, who focused on the body and the nervous system. To do justice to the richness of this therapy lies beyond the scope of this book. However, I would like to offer a glimpse into how you can practice regulating your own nervous system using self-regulation therapy.

In a nutshell, you move back and forth between noticing physical symptoms of anxiety and noticing what happens in your body when you draw on a resource, whether it be a memory of something pleasant or the practice of grounding. For our purpose, we will stick with grounding.

First, think about an anxiety-provoking social situation. For example, Ted thought about going to a twenty-year high-school reunion. To start with, he thought about getting ready at home. As this image filled his mind, Ted noticed that his chest tightened and that his heart started to beat faster.

Once you begin to think about your social situation, notice what is happening in your body. If you notice an anxiety symptom, just be curious about it. How tight is the tightness in your chest? How quickly is your heart beating? Once you've noticed these uncomfortable sensations, begin to do parts of your grounding exercise. You might like to sense into your feet on the ground or your seat in the chair. For instance, Ted would focus on his feet on the ground and on his breathing. Then, when he felt calmer, he would think again about the school reunion. This time he'd think about getting ready at home and also getting into his car to drive to the school. If physical symptoms came up again, he would take note, then sense into his feet and into his breathing again. Once he felt calmer, he would continue thinking about his trip to the school. Ted continued going back and forth, back and forth, from distressing material to grounding resources, until he finally imagined meeting and talking calmly with some of his old classmates.

You, too, can continue going back and forth between focusing on your anxiety symptoms as you think about aspects of the social event and focusing on the grounding exercise.

MAKING A COMMITMENT

SOME PEOPLE ARGUE that they don't have enough time in the day to practice calming techniques. If you're one of the folks whose social anxiety is mostly experienced through physical symptoms, my advice to you is, make time. If you suffer from overwhelming physical symptoms, making time to cultivate skills in calming your body, whether through grounding, SRT, breathing, or progressive muscle relaxation exercises, is a good investment, one you can't afford to overlook.

KEY REFLECTION POINTS

➤ The physical, thinking (cognitive), and behavioral symptoms of social anxiety are interconnected.

➤ Most people with social anxiety experience physical symptoms of anxiety; twenty to thirty percent experience these symptoms so dramatically that they describe them as "excruciating" and at times "humiliating."

➤ Many of these symptoms resemble the physical responses people experience when they are faced with a physical threat. These symptoms result from the involuntary activation of the sympathetic and parasympathetic nervous systems. The SNS prepares the body for fight or flight. A mix of SNS and PNS activation triggers freeze or collapse responses (as in fainting).

➤ Certain people, especially those with previous traumatic experiences, have hair-trigger nervous systems that will overreact at the slightest provocation.

➤ Within the three-part brain, containing the cortex, the limbic system, and the brain stem, are the amygdala and thalamus, which play significant roles in triggering the physical aspects of social anxiety. For instance, the thalamus, the relay station for messages to the brain, shuts down under stress. Consequently, some people with social anxiety often complain that their mind goes blank in the face of anxiety-provoking social situations.

➤ You can calm your body through grounding, self-regulation, breathing, and relaxation exercises. Making time for these exercises is vital, if you wish to reclaim your body from the grip of social anxiety.

The one thing I want to remember from this chapter is:

_____

_____

I will translate this one thing into action in the following way:

_____

_____

_____

_____

FOUR

BEET RED

Blushing

At fourteen, Helene was brilliant, clumsy, shy, and far more flamboyant within her fantasies than in a reality where she frequently blushed. Just worrying about blushing would make her feel hot: the humiliating rose color would splash from her chest to her hairline, causing others to stare at her as though the blushing had something to do with them, while she'd shrink further into the curve of her shoulders and try to avoid occasions where she might blush.
—URSULA HEGI, from *The Vision of Emma Blau*

NO DISCUSSION ABOUT the physiology of social anxiety would be complete without including the topic of blushing. Interestingly, it is a topic often ignored or only briefly mentioned in most social anxiety literature. Perhaps, this is because little work has been done on the topic of blushing since 1872, when Charles Darwin called blushing "the most peculiar and most human of all expressions." Darwin observed that women blush more easily than men, that people of all skin colors can blush, that young people blush more frequently than older people, that infants don't blush, and that the tendency to blush seems to run in families. He even noted that the critical ingredient in the making of a blush was the person's awareness of others' focus on them. In Darwin's words, "It is not a simple act of reflecting on our own appearance, but thinking of others thinking of us which excites a blush."

Excites a blush! Not "triggers," "produces," or "results in" a blush but "excites" a blush. I find something life-affirming about Darwin's choice of words. The word "excites" conjures up images of newness, growth, life, adventure. How can something like blushing possibly have any positive connotations? In Chapter 2, I wrote about Morita's compassionate view of shyness. According to Morita, social anxiety is a normal human experience, the meaning of which has to do with a person's wanting to do well in her social environment. It is shyness about being shy that becomes problematic. I believe that it may be the same with blushing. Normal blushing can be an important part of healthy living. Fear of blushing, on the other hand, can become a serious problem.

THE POSITIVE SIDE OF BLUSHING

POETS, WHO ARE in the business of painting images of life with words, capture the life-affirming essence of a blush in the following examples.

Full many a gem of purest ray serene,
The dark unfathom'd caves of ocean bear:
Full many a flower is born to blush unseen,
And waste its sweetness on the desert air.
   —THOMAS GRAY (1716–1771)

Where'er you walk, cool gales shall fan the glade,
Trees, where you sit, shall crowd into a shade:
Where'er you tread, the blushing flow'rs shall rise,
And all things flourish where you turn your eyes.
   —ALEXANDER POPE (1688–1744)

The water hears thy faintest word,
And blushes into wine.
　—JOHN SAMUEL BEWLEY MONSELL (1811–1875)

In Thomas Gray's poem, if a blush is not seen, its sweetness is wasted. To see a blush is to celebrate life's living. In every case, the word "blushing" conjures images of fullness, ripeness, color, and flourishing life. In Monsell's poem, the word "blushes" connotes all these and more. Inspired, water transforms into wine.

It is no accident that young people blush more often than older people. A number of years ago, as I was driving my son home from school, I asked him about a new girl who had been leaving telephone messages for him. He blushed. I noticed but didn't say anything about his blushing. Instead, I kept the conversation going. His blush disappeared and he told me about Susan. How did I interpret his blush? I was excited for him. For me, his blush signaled life. Life was coursing through him. He was obviously interested in Susan and his emotional arousal leaked into the blood vessels of his face. What's not to celebrate? My son was blushing, like a flower that was slowly blossoming. His sexual awareness was budding as it should. Young people are in a period of transformation. It is a new period of discovery, learning, making mistakes, more learning. And often, this period is dotted with moments of blushing. Hallelujah!

Blushing is not reserved for the young alone. People of all ages blush. Blushing serves many purposes. It can mean that you are excited. It can be an important signal to let someone know you're interested in them—another one of Mother Nature's clever inventions. In case you're too shy, too proud, or for that matter, too married to let the other person know you're interested, nature has installed the involuntary mechanism of blushing. Nature doesn't care if you feel a little inconvenienced. Maximizing the chances of survival of the species is the name of the game.

Another thing that blushing can advertise is your embarrassment over an event that you regret. This particular function of blushing can be useful in social settings. The ability to become embarrassed is more important than people usually realize. To demonstrate this point, researcher Rowland Miller asked a group of people to imagine an incident involving a fellow who accidentally spills his soft drink on the head of a colleague's wife, whom he has just met. The poor woman is sitting in a cafeteria chair with dark cola dripping down her face and neck and seeping into her clothes. Imagine that this fellow, who has just spilled the drink, remains calm and unemotional. In a poised manner, he offers his apologies and even insists on paying for the woman's dry cleaning. What would your reaction be if someone coolly offered his apologies to you under similar circumstances? Likely, you'd doubt his sincerity. Probably, you'd prefer not to have any further contact with him. Contrast Mr. Cool with a person whose emotions match his apology. Such a person might blush with embarrassment, be at a loss for words, or apologize profusely when he sees what he has done to you. Whom would you trust, Mr. Cool or Mr. Blush? In fact, when witnesses of such incidents have been asked to rate the likeability of the person spilling the drinks (described in a 1982 article by Gun R. Semin and Antony S. R. Manstead), the person who showed appropriate embarrassment was liked better than the person who remained too calm.

Being able to show embarrassment over our mistakes that may have inconvenienced or hurt others tells people we care about them and we care about staying in their good books. Not everyone who is embarrassed blushes, but certainly blushing is one common manifestation of embarrassment. Blushing can be a signal of goodwill and respect for others. It can reflect our desire to maintain social connections. Blushing, in this sense, can help to maintain healthy social relations. According to Miller, people who are embarrassable tend to be free of psychopathology. They are often less aggressive and more considerate than those who are unembarrassable.

What about blushing that springs from shame? Feeling ashamed and embarrassed occasionally, if we've been caught being less than our ideal self, is not the worst thing in the world. As long as we don't judge ourselves to be flawed human beings, a little shame and embarrassment can motivate us to stick closer to our own standards in the future. Blushing at these times signals acknowledgment that we goofed. Onlookers approve. And life continues.

If you've ever wished that you could permanently wipe blushing from your personal repertoire of emotional displays, I hope you will reconsider. Blushing has many benefits. It lets people know you care about them and you want to belong. Blushing is a reminder that you are a vibrant human being, complete with a rich array of emotions. It's a package deal. We laugh, we cry, we fume, we flame.

FEAR OF BLUSHING, CHRONIC BLUSHING

ALTHOUGH BLUSHING IS often of the benign variety, for some people it evolves into a nightmarish curse. Somewhere along the way, fear enters the picture, and blushing becomes a dreaded event. Fear of blushing actually has a name. It is called *erythrophobia*. *Eruthros* is the Greek word for "red." Not surprisingly, the more one fears blushing, the more one seems to blush. As Viktor Frankl put it, "The fear is the mother of the event." At the extreme, people avoid all social situations to avoid worry about the possibility of blushing. So what is a person to do?

What to do about it

Blushing is usually treated indirectly. The primary focus is on reducing your social anxiety and increasing your social confidence in general. As confidence increases, blushing occurs less frequently. When it does occur, it's not such a big deal! Blushing is just a reminder that you're part of the human race.

More direct ways of dealing with troublesome blushing include paradoxical intention, taking ownership, reframing, cognitive therapy, medications, and in drastic situations, surgery, all of which are explained below.

Taking a paradoxical approach

Paradox has to do with contradictions and puzzles. In other words, doing the opposite of what you might expect to do may accomplish the desired goal. In the case of blushing, rather than instructing a person to try to blush less, the person is told to try to blush even more than usual. In one case study, a man who had been experiencing one long, excruciating blush a day was instructed to practice blushing for ten minutes, three times a day. Months later, he only had an average of two blushes a month. What led to this turnaround? Naturally, the man would have discovered that he could not make himself blush on command. Blushing is involuntary. I don't think this discovery would have changed the amount of blushing.

What I do think may have happened is that the man developed a new relationship with his blushing. For years, this man had probably screamed silently in his head, "Oh no, not again, not now!" every time his blush made its daily appearance. It is as if the blush was an unwelcome visitor that barged in whether or not the host was receptive. In fact, the more this visitor knew it was not welcome and even was feared, the more regularly it would come to visit, in a taunting, mischievous way. Blushing was in control. The man was the victim. One day, this man was told that instead of shielding himself from the possibility of blushing, he should instead invite blushing into his life and do so wholeheartedly. Now who was in control? The tables had turned and the man was in charge. Furthermore, as he became used to this new relationship, he discovered that he was less and less afraid. As the fear of blushing shrank, so did the actual blushing.

Taking ownership of blushing

Closely related to taking charge of blushing is taking ownership. I have not come across any research to support this approach other than my personal experience. In my late twenties, I tried an experiment. I discovered that if every time I blushed I silently said to myself, "I am blushing myself," my blushing faded soon after it began. In contrast, if I silently pleaded, "Oh no, not now," my blushing would intensify. Even though I realized that blushing was totally involuntary, somehow, saying those words, "I'm blushing myself," allowed me to "feel" in control. I was no longer at the mercy of the unwelcome visitor.

Reframing

Reframing has to do with changing your perspective on something, usually by changing the context or meaning of whatever it is you're looking at. For instance, a woman once complained that every time she had just finished vacuuming the house, members of her family would walk right across the carpets, leaving fresh footprints in what had been, just moments ago, a freshly groomed blanket of nylon tufts all standing in order. She was frustrated that her efforts to create a picture-perfect household were so easily smudged out with the "thoughtless" parading of her family through every room in the house. This woman's therapist asked her to imagine a house where the carpets always looked freshly vacuumed. No footprints ever marred the uniform texture of the wall-to-wall carpeting. Immediately, this woman realized that her house would be have to be empty. There would be no children, no husband. Even she would have to tread carefully in her own house. The prospect of an immaculate but lifeless home filled the woman with a sense of utter loss. Footprints in the carpet took on a new meaning. They reminded the woman how lucky she was to be blessed with a family, especially a family that enjoyed being home. Her complaints evaporated.

Think of your blushing as footprints left by the blood surging into the blood vessels under your skin. They symbolize the fact that life is coursing through you. Emotions are traipsing in and out, enriching what might otherwise be an emotionally sterile home. Recently, Lucy, a member of my social anxiety support group, reported that she dreaded blushing when James, a cute fellow from another department, came into the office. She said:

> He walks in and suddenly I realize that I'm blushing. It's instantaneous. My cheeks feel hot. I'm sure he notices it. As I worry, I can feel my cheeks heat up even more. They're on fire. Outside, I go through the motions; inside, I'm wishing I could disappear. Time seems to stand still.

When Lucy finished her story, another group member, Joe, quickly let her know that he loves it when a woman blushes. It makes him feel attractive. He told Lucy that he thought it was great that she blushed, and he hoped that she would always be able to blush, because it made her attractive as well. The following week, Lucy reported, with a huge smile on her face, that she had barely blushed when Mr. Wonderful showed up in the office that week. She further reported that, to her amazement, she didn't really care that much whether she blushed. She thanked Joe for his remarks the previous week and said he had helped her to see blushing in a new light. Since blushing now had a new meaning, it ceased to be an issue.

Changing our irrational beliefs

Blushing, like any symptom of social anxiety, is worsened by negative beliefs and assumptions. Although we will look at beliefs and assumptions in detail when we come to the chapters that have to do with the mind, let's take a moment to briefly review how irrational beliefs can transform normal blushing into problematic blushing. Remember how my son blushed when I asked him about Susan, a girl who had been leaving telephone messages for him? It was a normal blush. No big deal—just a part of life.

Now, imagine by contrast, the following scenario. Joshua, a seventeen-year-old, is taunted mercilessly by friends about his interest in a classmate, Linda. Joshua begins to blush and is utterly horrified that his blush triggers another round of cruel teasing. He feels humiliated and disrespected by his fellow classmates. Because of this unfortunate incident, he begins to build a belief system about blushing based on this one incident. If we were to listen to him talk to himself about his blushing, we might hear something like this:

> I have to look cool, no matter what, especially in front of my friends. If I blush or show any emotion, others will poke fun at me, laugh at me. I'll look like a total idiot. People will hate me. I hate my blushing. People think I'm a weirdo when I blush. There's no way I can blush again, ever.

Poor Joshua. He has just fallen victim to the tyranny of irrational or unrealistic thinking. It's understandable, given the circumstances, that Joshua formed such negative beliefs. But to hold onto such beliefs as if they actually represent the real world, at all times, is asking for trouble. If such a belief becomes a permanent view about blushing in Joshua's mind, he risks cutting himself off from all spontaneous emotional expression to avoid any future embarrassments. Imagine cutting yourself off from your emotions. It would be like living in a sterile bubble all your life. What a loss, not only to Joshua, but also to those around him, who would be denied the pleasure of a fully vibrant Joshua.

To avoid such a loss, he must challenge his beliefs. He needs to know that his beliefs are based on one unfortunate incident. They do not necessarily have anything to do with how the rest of the world would treat him, especially if he felt confident that he had a right to his feelings. Exactly how to go about challenging these beliefs will be presented in chapter 10. Suffice it to say that once the mind is cleared of such awful messages about blushing, blushing once again takes its place at the normal end of the continuum.

Visualization

We can define visualization as the act of vividly imagining yourself in a particular situation. In the case of blushing, for instance, you might close your eyes and imagine that a hot shower or a long brisk walk has created a warm flush in your cheeks. Then imagine yourself splashing cool, refreshing water on your face or sliding a dripping ice cube across your cheeks. Notice how your cheeks are no longer warm, but instead, very cool to the touch. Visualization can be a powerful tool in helping to reduce troublesome blushing.

Medications

Medications can be used to lower anxious arousal. If anxiety is decreased, then the likelihood of blushing usually decreases as well. Certain antidepressants are effective for certain people with symptoms of social anxiety. Minor tranquilizers help reduce anxiety. Beta-blockers reduce the symptoms produced by the autonomic nervous system. Whether someone should take medications is a very personal matter. We'll discuss various views on the subject under the general topic of medication in Chapter 7.

Surgery

Surgery is another form of treatment for chronic blushing. I almost hesitate to mention it, because it is so drastic a measure, especially in light of research that shows cognitive-behavioral approaches to be the most effective way of dealing with social anxiety and its symptoms. Nevertheless, because surgery has become a recent treatment option, one that is readily encouraged by surgeons who advertise on the Internet, it makes sense to at least inform you about this option.

ETS stands for "endoscopic thoracic sympathicotomy." Endoscopic has to do with an endoscope. *Endo* comes from the words for "within" and "scope" originates from the Greek word *skopein,* which means "to observe." An endoscope is an instrument that can examine the inside of an organ. *Thoracic* has to do with the thorax or chest. And *sympathicotomy* has to do with the cutting (from the Greek word *tome*) of the sympathetic nerve. So, ETS has to do with entering the thorax with an instrument and cutting the sympathetic nerve.

Remember the sympathetic nervous system? It activates our fight or flight response in emergency situations. To name just two of its defensive ploys, it can change our blood flow and increase sweating. It comes as no surprise that in this age of technical advances and microsurgery, we have found a way to stop blushing and sweating by cutting into the sympathetic nerves.

There are actually three methods for interrupting the sympathetic nervous supply to the blood vessels in the face: cutting, electrocautery (electrically burning), and clamping. On the Internet, this surgery is promoted as a new procedure for hand sweating and facial blushing. "Uncontrollable, severe facial blushing can now be radically treated—" in only twenty minutes. This sounds too good to be true, doesn't it? Buyer, beware! Although testimonials abound as to how this surgery has changed some people's lives, there is ample evidence that many people regret having had the surgery. A common byproduct of this type of surgery is compensatory sweating. In other words, as sweating decreases in the hands, Mother Nature compensates by increasing the sweating in the rest of the body. The amount of compensatory sweating varies. Some people find it tolerable; others find it bothersome. As far as the face is concerned, it remains pale and dry, sometimes overly dry. Another possible outcome of this surgery is one-sided blushing; that is, blushing on only one side of the face. The percentage of people who experience these side effects varies incredibly, depending on the studies you read. In short, these side effects are far from rare.

Brent, a fellow whose facial blushing had led to depression and anxiety, offered his perspective on the prospect of ETS surgery in an Internet forum. He reported that initially, he had been excited when he read about ETS. His family urged him to spend a year researching the topic before making any decision. He followed this sound advice. He read everything he could find on the topic and spoke to ETS surgeons. He discovered that the rate of compensatory sweating was usually about five to ten percent of patients. Apparently, an experienced ETS surgeon told him that the rate of one-sided blushing after surgery was about ten percent. In the end, Brent stated, "I am not ready to take on something that might magnify the pain I feel to an even higher level."

Whether to have surgery, like the decision to take or not take medication, is a very personal matter. Since I don't have a problem with chronic blushing, I can't begin to advise for or against it. My inclination with most things in life is to stay with the most natural of approaches whenever possible. Remember that when we opt for surgery, surgical trauma is inevitable. We trust that most surgeons will do their utmost to minimize the degree of invasiveness to the body. But cutting into the body *is* invasive, no matter how you cut it! Burning nerve tissue is invasive. Clamping and strangling delicate nerves is invasive. Consequently, my view regarding surgery would be to use it as a last resort. There are so many more natural ways of reducing troublesome blushing that have positive side effects such as increased self-esteem and social confidence. It's true that these natural ways often demand commitment and hard work. Who ever said that life was supposed to be easy? If troublesome blushing persists even after you've given every other option a good and honest, long-term effort—and I doubt that it will—well, then it may be a time to consider more drastic options . . . maybe.

KEY REFLECTION POINTS

➤ Normal blushing can be healthy. Fear of blushing can be problematic.

➤ In poetic writings, blushing evokes images of flourishing life.

➤ There are positive aspects to blushing. Blushing can mean that life is coursing through you; it can signal that you are excited about someone or something.

➤ Blushing can signal embarrassment. A person who shows appropriate embarrassment following a social mistake is more likeable than a person who is too calm and shows no embarrassment.

➤ Blushing can signal shame and embarrassment when we have been caught being less than our ideal self. A little shame and embarrassment can motivate us to do better next time. As we blush, onlookers approve and life continues.

➤ For some, fear of blushing makes blushing worse. Blushing can evolve into a nightmarish curse. Fear of blushing is called *erythrophobia*.

➤ Chronic or extreme blushing is usually dealt with indirectly. Once social anxiety is reduced and social confidence increases, blushing decreases.

➤ Direct approaches include taking a paradoxical approach (blushing on purpose), taking ownership of blushing (feeling in control of the blush), reframing (seeing blushing from a new perspective), changing irrational beliefs (about the impact of blushing on others), and using visualization techniques.

➤ Medications can lower anxious arousal; hence, blushing decreases.

➤ Surgery is used to control blushing as a last resort, because it can have serious consequences. It is preferable to use natural ways of reducing extreme blushing.

The one thing I want to remember from this chapter is:

_____

_____

I will translate this one thing into action in the following way:

_____

_____

_____

_____

FIVE

PUBLIC WASH-ROOMS? NEVER!

Shy Bladder Syndrome

Not being able to use public washrooms
makes my life a nightmare!
—LANCE, fifty-five years old

Y EARS AGO, I received a call from a woman who had
read a newspaper article about one of my support
groups. She said her husband had trouble using bathrooms
in public places. I had read a brief piece about this condition in the social anxiety literature I had been researching
and was uncertain about my capacity to help, but I suggested an initial meeting.

My prospective client was a handsome and distinguished-
looking grey-haired business executive who arrived in an
expensive navy pin-striped suit. He shook hands assertively
and sat down in a confident manner. Nothing about him suggested what he was about to reveal. He explained that he
dreaded going to public washrooms and consequently, his
life was a nightmare. Not being able to relieve himself whenever he wanted led to great physical discomfort. He had
become preoccupied with how and when he could arrange to
go to the single toilet washroom in the basement of the large

corporate building in which he worked. He would calculate when he could enter the elevator without his colleagues or employees noticing where he was going. He refused to go on outings with his wife if he wasn't absolutely sure that he could go to a washroom in absolute privacy. This lovely man further explained to me that he sometimes did venture into a multiple-stall washroom, and if there was absolutely no one else in the washroom, he could manage to urinate. Even so, the anticipation of someone walking in filled him with dread. If someone did walk in, it was impossible to continue to urinate.

At those times, it was as if his bladder ceased to function. Trying his hardest didn't help. He said that even if his bladder were filled to bursting and someone offered him a million dollars to urinate, he would not be able to do it. I was moved by his agony. I also remember my sense of helplessness. I suggested that he work on changing some of his negative self-talk and on visualizing going to the washroom in a nonchalant manner, but my lack of confidence and experience in this precise expression of social anxiety must have shone through; my client never returned.

Thankfully, almost a decade and a half later, shy bladder syndrome is starting to emerge into public awareness. A few newspaper and magazine articles and even a couple of radio shows have addressed this mysterious condition. And in 2001, a book was published by New Harbinger Publications, called *Shy Bladder Syndrome: Your Step-by-Step Guide to Overcoming Paruresis,* coauthored by Steven Soifer, George D. Zgourides, Joseph Himle, and Nancy L. Pickering. If you have the slightest suspicion that you may suffer from this form of social anxiety, I strongly recommend you read this clearly written and informative book.

SHY BLADDER SYNDROME

When urinary retention or the inability to void in the presence of others is connected to social anxiety and not to a medical condition, it is called "shy bladder syndrome" or "bashful bladder syndrome." Its scientific name, *paruresis*, was coined in 1954 by researchers G. W. Williams and E. T. Degenhardt, who discovered a connection between urinary hesitancy and the experience of discomfort when being watched by others; hence the idea that it was a form of social anxiety or social phobia. According to Steven Soifer and his coauthors, a couple of empirical studies reveal that up to seven percent of the population suffers from some degree of shy bladder syndrome. Of those afflicted, ten percent experiences it to such an extreme degree that their lives are seriously affected.

CONTINUUM OF SEVERITY

LIKE OTHER FORMS of social anxiety, there is a continuum of severity of shy bladder syndrome, ranging from occasional episodes of difficulty urinating to being consistently unable to urinate anywhere else other than in the privacy of one's own home, provided no one else is around. Occasional episodes of urinary hesitancy are considered normal and do not qualify for a diagnosis of paruresis. In fact, when I recently mentioned that I was writing about shy bladder syndrome to a few female colleagues of mine, several shared their own strategies to manage bladder shyness. One said that she tries to aim her stream of urine so that it will hit the inside wall of the toilet in order to prevent the sound her stream would have created, had it hit the toilet water directly. Another said that she flushes the toilet to drown out the sound of her stream splashing into the water. This kind of modesty about voiding is probably more prevalent than we think. It is a momentary self-consciousness that has no real consequence. However, when modesty turns into hesitancy and hesitancy leads to a pattern of avoiding public washrooms, life can become difficult.

At the extreme end of the continuum, people often make arrangements to live near work or work from home and only go on brief outings. In short, it's like being under house arrest, except that it is more like neighborhood arrest. Contained within this continuum are variations of experience. John Marshall, in his book, *Social Phobia: From Shyness to Stage Fright,* writes, "Some people are only stricken when other people are within a certain range of proximity, some can urinate in the presence of strangers but not friends and family, some the other way around, some are completely at ease in a stall where there is visual but not auditory privacy, for some the lack of auditory privacy is the great inhibitor, and some are simply unable to use the public restrooms, period, whether or not others are in the room."

CAUSES OF BLADDER SHYNESS

As with any other form of social anxiety, the causes of bladder shyness can be explained from many perspectives. There may be biological and genetic factors. There may be psychological factors, such as thoughts, attitudes, behaviors, and experiences that play a role in a person's inability to urinate in public. For instance, a person may have been taught to be ashamed of his bodily functions. Consequently, peeing in front of others would feel shameful. If toilet training was traumatic, as in the case of a child whose overzealous parent was preoccupied with how much and how often she produced in the toilet, then withholding one's urine may become a habitual involuntary response. Sometimes people can't pinpoint a specific reason for their bladder shyness. All they know is that, in the presence of others, they simply cannot "go," no matter how hard they try.

TREATMENT

Because the causes of shy bladder syndrome can be varied, most therapists use a multidimensional approach. I will not get into the details of cognitive restructuring that has to do with working with thoughts, or relaxation therapy, or support groups as these are more fully explored further along in this book.

Graduated exposure therapy

Soifer and his coauthors suggest graduated exposure therapy as a primary course of treatment. First, the person suffering with shy bladder syndrome must rule out any physical reasons for the problems in urinary functioning. The main idea underlying graduated exposure therapy is that those with shy bladders must expose themselves to the very thing that they fear—gradually, often, and for extended periods of time. In other words, a person with a shy bladder needs to try to urinate in the presence of others repeatedly, first in situations that feel "safe," then eventually in situations that feel more challenging.

Before beginning an exposure session, Soifer suggests that you first load up on fluids. Most people with shy bladder syndrome actually limit their fluid intake to decrease the risk of having to urinate. If you really want to increase your chances for success, you will have to do exactly the opposite. Drink lots of fluid to increase the sense of urgency and, consequently, your ability to urinate. Keep a record of an urgency scale, on a scale of one to ten, one meaning no sense of urgency at all and ten indicating extreme urgency. Soifer suggests that you do not even try these exposure strategies until your level of urgency is at seven or above. Next, you need to solicit the help of a buddy, whether a trusted friend or a family member. Your buddy's job will be to stand at various distances from you while you enter a washroom, starting as far away from you as you like, for instance, way down the hall, and eventually moving closer and closer, according to your instructions.

Once you have your buddy where you want him, begin to pee but not for more than three seconds. Stop your stream at three seconds and wait for three minutes. If you were unsuccessful in urinating, ask your buddy to move away still farther. Try again. If you are successful, then have your buddy stay exactly where he is, and pass three more seconds' worth of pee. The idea here is to repeat the procedure of peeing as often as possible. Once you've successfully peed twice, take another two-minute break and decide whether you're up to asking your buddy to come a little closer. A little closer can mean no more than a few inches closer or it can mean a few feet closer. It's up to you. Your buddy obeys without question. Exposure is a matter of going back and forth, back and forth, from a place of success to a place of slightly greater challenge. Take all the time you want. This kind of exposure will take a number of attempts, because it can only be done when your bladder is full. Eventually, whether it takes hours, days, weeks, or longer, you will be able to urinate successfully two consecutive times with your buddy just outside your door. The next steps involve opening the door, letting your buddy in, and eventually practicing this exposure exercise in public washrooms.

Urinary self-catheterization

Catheterization is the insertion of a tube called a catheter into the urethra, the opening that leads to the bladder, in order to empty the bladder. One of the coauthors of *Shy Bladder Syndrome*, George Zgourides, first recommended self-catheterization as an option in the treatment of shy bladder syndrome in 1996. According to Zgourides, clients report "that it sounds much worse and more painful than it really is, especially in contrast to the alternative of prolonged bladder pain." According to literature on catheterization, even a five- or six-year-old can learn the technique. Some therapists tell their clients that self-catheterization can be a valuable part of the graduated exposure therapy. While the client practices peeing in public washrooms, his anxiety will be greatly reduced in the knowledge that he can always relieve himself with a catheter, if necessary. Or people can actually practice relieving their bladders with the use of the catheter when others are nearby. Once they realize no one cares how they get rid of their urine, then they can begin to practice peeing without the use of a catheter. If you think that self-catheterization is an option worth exploring, make sure you first consult your doctor.

If shy bladder syndrome is one of your challenges, I would again heartily recommend that you read *Shy Bladder Syndrome*. You will find the coauthors' compassionate and straightforward guidance invaluable. Their Appendix C lists ways you can contact each of them. A few offer to work with clients over the phone.

KEY REFLECTION POINTS

> ➤ Shy bladder syndrome, or paruresis, affects about seven percent of the population. Ten percent of these individuals experience it to such an extreme degree that it restricts their lifestyle.
> ➤ As with other forms of social anxiety, causes of shy bladder syndrome include biological, genetic, environmental, and psychological factors.
> ➤ Treatment is multidimensional and can include cognitive, family systems, behavioral, relaxation, and other supportive approaches. Graduated exposure strategies form the mainstay of treatment.
> ➤ Self-catheterization, a method of emptying the bladder with a tube, can provide physical relief to the person with shy bladder syndrome while he or she is learning to become more confident about urinating in public washrooms.

The one thing I want to remember from this chapter is:

_____

_____

I will translate this one thing into action in the following way:

_____

_____

_____

_____

SIX

AGITATORS AND PEACEMAKERS

Nutrition

Tell me what you eat, and I shall tell you who you are.
—Jean-Anthelme Brillat-Savarin (1755–1826)

CERTAIN FOODS WILL help to keep the body calm. Other foods and substances will disturb this calmness and even promote anxiety. The most important nutrients that help to control anxiety and promote calmness are several of the B vitamins, the mineral calcium, and a few amino acids.

THE B VITAMINS

THE FUNCTION OF all B vitamins is to produce red blood cells, to form genetic blueprints, to help the body use energy from food, and very importantly, to keep the brain and nervous system functioning properly.

Vitamin B$_1$, or thiamine

When the level of thiamine runs low, the body experiences increased excitement and nervousness, sleep disturbances, increased levels of adrenalin, and even, in some susceptible people, panic attacks. Natural sources for vitamin B$_1$ include wheat germ, whole wheat, peas, beans, enriched flour, fish, peanuts, and meat. Your recovery may be slow even when you reintroduce thiamine into your diet.

If you're wondering whether your body is thiamine deficient, review your diet. Are you eating plenty of natural foods, especially of the whole-grain variety? And beware: not everything brown is whole grain. For instance, brown bread is not necessarily whole wheat. Molasses and other additives are often used to color bread brown. Labels such as "country-style," "multigrain," or even "stone-ground" don't necessarily mean that the bread is made from whole grains. Biochemist and nutritionist Laura Pollack advises, "If it doesn't say 'whole wheat' or 'whole grain,' assume it's not."

Vitamin B$_3$, or niacin; niacinamide

Another vitamin that plays an important role in maintaining healthy nerve function is vitamin B$_3$. It comes in two forms: niacin and niacinamide. Niacin is a vasodilator. In other words, it can dilate blood vessels, which in turn can cause flushing of the skin. People who aren't fond of blushing, of course, will want to stay away from this form of B$_3$, unless they are being treated for skin problems. The flushing disappears within a few days.

Niacinamide is the B$_3$ usually prescribed to decrease anxiety symptoms. The best natural sources of vitamin B$_3$ are peanuts, brewer's yeast, fish, and meat. Some vitamin B$_3$ is found in whole grains. For anyone who takes vitamin supplements, the general recommendation advises taking niacinamide in the form of a vitamin B complex or a multivitamin, because many of the B vitamins work better when taken together.

Choline

The B vitamin choline does several jobs in the body. Of interest to us is its role in nerve function. It is a component of acetyl-
cholin, which is the primary transmitter of nerve impulses within
the parasympathetic nervous system. As you may remember, the
parasympathetic nervous system slows down the body once it has
been aroused. Therefore, increased choline can help the parasympathetic nervous system do its job of calming the body down even
better. Sources of choline include wheat germ, soybean oil, egg
yolk, liver, oatmeal, cabbage, and cauliflower.

Vitamin B_6, or pyridoxine

Vitamin B_6, or pyridoxine, also plays an important role in
nerve function, in several ways. B_6 helps the amino acids (basic
components of proteins) to do their job of transmitting signals
between nerve cells. B_6 is needed to make serotonin, melatonin,
and dopamine. Serotonin is a hormone that helps a body to feel
relaxed and sleepy. Melatonin is a hormone that helps a body to
sleep. Dopamine is associated with feelings of pleasure. B_6 also
helps in the formation of neurotransmitters (messenger chemicals
in the brain), which regulate mental processes and mood. B_6 is
often recommended as a supplement, in combination with calcium, for women experiencing PMS. Natural sources for vitamin
B_6 are potatoes, bananas, lentils, liver, raisin bran cereal, tuna,
and turkey.

Vitamin B_2, or riboflavin

Vitamin B_2 supports the jobs of vitamin B_1 (thiamine). B_2 is
needed to process the amino acids, which are essential for nerve
function. Vitamin B_2 is found in dairy products, eggs, and meat.
It is also found, in lesser amounts, in leafy green vegetables and in
vitamin-enriched grains.

B-VITAMIN BUSTERS

CAFFEINE, SUGAR, ALCOHOL, and nicotine, consumed in large amounts, destroy thiamine and other B vitamins. If you're addicted to any of these substances, you may experience occasional or frequent bouts of nervous agitation. Consider reducing or eliminating some of these B-vitamin busters from your diet.

The prospect of cutting down on some of these substances can be, for some, a daunting one, as one of my clients once taught me. Allan was a little shy, but mainly he complained of general anxiety. He often felt edgy, irritable, vigilant, and nervous. One day I asked him what he had eaten for breakfast. He told me that he usually had about three cups of coffee in the morning.

"Any more coffee during the day?"

"Yeah, sure, a few cups."

"Any sugar?" I asked.

"Yeah," he replied uneasily, as if I were giving him the third degree.

"How much?" By now, I felt like I was giving him the third degree.

"Just a few teaspoons of sugar."

"Do you eat anything?"

"Right now, my favorite breakfast is a Chinese bun or two."

"What are they like?"

"They're buns filled with a sweet cream."

I told Allan that I had learned that caffeine and sugar were thiamine busters and explained the value of thiamine. I asked Allan whether he'd consider doing an experiment.

"Uh-oh," he whispered.

I asked Allan whether he would reduce his intake of coffee and sugar, at least for a little while, to see if doing so made any difference.

"You know," Allan responded, "the moment you said I should think about quitting coffee and sugar, I could feel this panic build in my chest. 'Oh God, don't take away my coffee or sugar,' I thought to myself." Allan said that he would think about my suggestion, but it wasn't going to be easy to give up his beloved coffee.

Caffeine

According to figures from the National Institutes of Health, four out of five Americans drink at least two cups of coffee a day, making them the leading coffee drinkers in the world. Although the first cup can help people feel alert and ready to take on the day, the second cup doesn't offer greater results. But because caffeine is a psychologically and physically addictive drug, there's a good chance certain people will drink too much. High doses of caffeine have been known to cause nervousness, irritability, and anxiety; and for some people, insomnia, stomach upset, or premenstrual syndrome. Caffeine has also been connected with an increased elimination of calcium from the body, which is one of the most important minerals in maintaining calm.

If you're serious about managing social anxiety, reduce or eliminate your intake of caffeine. In the case of caffeine, one eight-ounce cup a day of coffee (about 150 mg of caffeine) appears to be a safe amount for most people. Decaffeinated coffee, which contains about 4 mg of caffeine, is also an option. Note that chemical solvents are used in some decaffeination processes. These chemicals, along with the chemical pesticides that are used on coffee beans, may have a toxic effect on the nervous system. Other sources of caffeine include black and green teas, which each contain about 80 mgs of caffeine per cup. A twelve-ounce can of cola contains 30 to 45 mgs of caffeine. Herbal teas contain no caffeine.

Sugar

Sugar depletes thiamine and other B vitamins. The average American consumes 120 pounds of sugar a year. Interestingly, sugar was not part of the average diet until the twentieth century. It is found everywhere: in beverages, in cereals, in salad dressings, even in processed meats. It takes different forms: refined sugar, raw sugar, brown sugar, maple syrup, corn syrup, honey, and molasses. Sugars from more natural sources are absorbed more slowly than from refined sources and therefore don't create as much of a sugar rush and sugar high.

Theories regarding the dangers of sugar vary. Most experts agree that refined sugars can cause cavities. Whether too much sugar can cause a dysfunction in sugar metabolism and eventually lead to diabetes is debatable. There is no research that confirms earlier suspicions that sugar causes hyperactivity. What is certain for those who are trying to manage anxiety is the fact that sugar does deplete B vitamins, especially thiamine. Too much sugar, therefore, is definitely a risk factor for people who are prone to anxiety.

Interestingly, for some people, too little sugar can be a problem. These people have a condition called hypoglycemia. When sugar levels drop, these people may experience symptoms such as anxiety, trembling, feelings of unsteadiness and weakness, irritability, and heart palpitations.

In summary, for the majority of people, reducing sugar intake is a wise choice. For those prone to hypoglycemia, maintaining consistent sugar levels is the wiser option.

Alcohol

In Chapter 1, we learned that many people with social anxiety turn to alcohol to help them feel relaxed in social situations. Because alcohol is primarily a depressant, it has a sedating effect on the central nervous system. This accounts for the feeling of relaxation. However, alcohol can also be a stimulant, depending on the individual and the circumstances. If the individual is in a stimulating social setting, low doses of alcohol can disinhibit a person, who will then become talkative, self-confident, and generally more risk-taking. No wonder some people turn to alcohol to help them manage their social anxiety. Unfortunately, certain people have a genetic background that makes them more likely to become dependent on alcohol than other people. Once drinking becomes a chronic solution for social anxiety, serious problems begin to develop.

When consuming alcohol becomes a serious habit, the depressant and stimulant effects become more dramatic. The nervous system tries to balance itself and recover from the initial depressant effects by going into a state of excited agitation. This can feel a lot like overarousal and anxiety. The vicious cycle begins. The person drinks again, to regain a sense of calm. Once calm, it's just a matter of time before the depressant effects wear off and the stimulant effects return with a vengeance. That's why even the person who has a "few" drinks only once in a while, may feel relaxed and ready for bed when the party is over, but in the middle of the night, will wake up, wide awake and unable to return to sleep.

Alcohol is far from the solution to social anxiety that it first appears to be. It destroys B vitamins. It can promote nervous agitation. Alcohol dependency can develop. Once a person is dependent on alcohol, a whole raft of other problems, including very serious physical problems, begins to develop. Excessive use of alcohol can eventually destroy every single organ in the body. Excessive use can lead to damaged relationships with family, friends, coworkers, and self. In the long run, alcohol does not help a person manage social anxiety. In fact, it can make problems worse.

Nicotine

Within seven seconds of inhaling a cigarette, about fifteen percent of the nicotine travels directly to the brain. This quick absorption makes nicotine as addictive as heroin. Once nicotine is in the brain, it triggers the release of a chemical called dopamine. Dopamine is associated with feelings of pleasure. Once again, we have a substance that can be very attractive to the person who experiences social anxiety. Although nicotine is a stimulant, it, like alcohol, can also have relaxing effects. Naturally, the promise of pleasure and relaxation becomes a seductive alternative to anxiety! There's a catch, however. Over time, nicotine decreases the brain's capacity to experience pleasure and so, smokers need more and more nicotine to achieve the same pleasurable results. When nicotine intake is reduced, some of the symptoms that follow include anxiety, irritability, restlessness, sleep disturbances, and difficulty concentrating. Add to these complications the fact that nicotine destroys thiamine. Unfortunately, smoking is so addictive that many people find it almost impossible to quit. If you smoke and have tried to quit but couldn't, consider getting help through counseling.

CALCIUM

CALCIUM IS THE most abundant mineral in the human body and the fifth most abundant mineral in the earth's crust. Ninety-nine percent of our calcium is found in our bones and teeth. The role of calcium in providing us with a strong skeleton is well known. Lesser known is its essential role in nerve function. Calcium serves as a gatekeeper that controls the opening and closing of channels through which pass minerals that carry the electrical currents from inside the nerve cells to outside. Without calcium, there would be no transmission of signals between nerve cells. Where the parasympathetic nervous system is concerned, a lack of calcium would impair the process of transmitting the messages that tell different parts of the body to slow down. Sources for calcium include tofu, dairy products, canned sardines, salmon, and green leafy vegetables. Without vitamin D, the absorption of calcium in the body is impaired.

AMINO ACIDS

AMINO ACIDS ARE the building blocks of protein. There are over a hundred amino acids in the body. We will mention a few, which seem to have a particularly important part to play in healthy nerve function.

Tryptophan

Once tryptophan enters the brain, it is converted into serotonin, which has a sedating effect on the body. Natural sources of tryptophan include pumpkin seeds, sunflower seeds, turkey, and milk. That's why a cup of warm milk at bedtime helps many people fall asleep more easily. Tryptophan may be prescribed by a doctor. It is not taken if one is already taking antidepressant drugs in the group called SSRIs—selective serotonin reuptake inhibitors.

Gamma-Amino Butyric Acid (GABA)

Gamma-amino butyric acid is a neurotransmitter (messenger chemical in the brain) that decreases activity between brain nerve cells. It has a mildly relaxing effect. For this reason, it is sometimes used as a natural tranquilizer, available at most health food stores.

Glutamine

Glutamine is the most abundant amino acid in the body. It is involved in several metabolic processes. In terms of nerve function, it is the only amino acid that can readily cross the barrier between blood and brain, and with glutamic acid, it accounts for about eighty percent of the amino nitrogen in brain tissue. It is found in foods high in protein, such as fish, meat, beans, and dairy products. It is also found in root vegetables such as beets, carrots, and radishes.

For a detailed description of how different foods affect the body in terms of calmness and anxiety, I recommend reading Edmund Bourne's book *Healing Fear: New Approaches to Overcoming Anxiety,* pages 79 to 107, and Douglas Hunt's *No More Fears.*

If you're eating a balanced diet, with plenty of vegetables and fruits, whole grains, dairy products, and some meat or meat substitute, you will be getting most of the vitamins and minerals necessary for healthy nerve function. If you can cut down or eliminate caffeine, sugar, and nicotine, your nervous system will be all the better for it.

KEY REFLECTION POINTS

➤ Certain foods help to keep the body calm; others promote anxiety.

➤ The most important nutrients that help to promote calmness are several B vitamins, the mineral calcium, and a few amino acids.

➤ Caffeine, sugar, alcohol, and nicotine, consumed in large amounts, destroy thiamine, an important B vitamin.
➤ Calcium helps to transmit signals between nerve cells.
➤ Tryptophan, gamma-amino butyric acid (GABA), and glutamine are amino acids that are important in helping to keep the body calm.
➤ A balanced diet, with plenty of vegetables and fruits, whole grains, dairy products, and some meat or meat substitute, will help to ensure that you are getting most of the vitamins and minerals necessary for healthy nerve function.

The one thing I want to remember from this chapter is:

_____

_____

I will translate this one thing into action in the following way:

_____

_____

_____

_____

SEVEN

TO TAKE OR NOT TO TAKE

Medication

Some griefs are med'cinable.
—SHAKESPEARE, *Cymbeline* (3.2.36)

To TAKE OR not to take medication, that is the question. To deal with their social anxiety, some people take medication as a first choice. Many of these people tend to be obsessive, high-achieving professionals who neither care for cognitive-behavioral approaches nor have the time for these approaches. There are others who do better and feel more comfortable with the idea of medication either *while* they are doing other therapy or *after* they have tried other means but with little success. And, of course, there are those who don't even consider medication or choose not to take medication and do very well without it. They learn to manage their social anxiety through many of the means described in this book. Deciding whether to take medication is an individual matter. Personal attitudes and values regarding medication, the severity of social anxiety symptoms, and the weighing of risks and benefits associated with taking medication all deserve consideration.

PERSONAL ATTITUDES

LIKE ATTITUDES ABOUT anything else, attitudes about medication are shaped by cultural influences, education, assumptions, values, beliefs, and personal experience. By "cultural," I refer to all types of mini-cultures as well as to the larger societal culture. We have family cultures, professional or workplace cultures, gender cultures, social network cultures, and broad societal cultures. What do Mom and Dad think about taking aspirins, painkillers, or antibiotics? What do the people at work think about medication? Are they doctors and nurses whose daily trade is in medications? What pressures exist in male and female cultures to take or not take medications? What do your buddies say about medication? Is it just for wimps? Is it the smart, practical choice? What do the people or dogmas of your church, synagogue, temple, or mosque say? Are you advised to put your trust in God alone? In science? In your own efforts? What are the societal messages regarding medication? We know that drug companies promote medications. What do television shows, movies, and newspapers say about medications?

Assumptions shape our attitudes. The less we know, the more we assume. Hence, education is vital if we are to develop a realistic attitude toward medication. Check your assumptions. Do you assume medication will be a quick fix and that social anxiety will disappear once and for all? Do you assume that you will have to take medication for the rest of your life? Do you assume that only really "sick" people take medication? Find out everything you can about any medication you might be considering. Ask your doctor. Read. Search the Internet. Talk to family and friends.

Values and beliefs determine our attitudes. Do you only value natural approaches? Do you believe that chemicals will mess up your brain? Are you open to trying medication? Do you value independence so much that you will go it alone in spite of excruciating suffering?

Perhaps personal experience is the most important determinant of our attitudes. The broader the experience, the wiser we become about the possibilities that exist in the world. My training as a clinical social worker occurred during the early 1970s, the post-hippie era. Hippies had enjoyed a culture of "making love and not war," doing things naturally (sometimes with a little help from recreational drugs), and challenging the "establishment." Some of these values lingered on into the 1970s. It was still important to have as natural a lifestyle as possible. An unspoken prejudice against medication was very much in vogue in the psychotherapeutic community. Training in therapeutic interviewing did not include any education about medication.

Over the years, personal experience has taught me that natural sources are not always enough. When I was anemic, iron saved me from debilitating fatigue. When I had PMS symptoms, Vitamin B_6 and calcium leveled my moods and spared my husband and me unnecessary tension. Working with psychiatric patients for almost thirty years gave me plenty of opportunity to witness the marvels of medication. Depressed people who could barely move or talk became animated on antidepressants. People experiencing manic episodes, unable to sleep, unable to stop talking or stop moving, slowed down on anti-manic drugs. People with schizophrenia were able to decrease their severe symptoms to at least tolerable levels with antipsychotic medication. I developed a great respect for the intricate physiological workings of the human body and for the role medication could play in helping the body restore its equilibrium. I also witnessed poor response to medication, or sadly, on the odd occasion, a worsening of symptoms. In the end, my attitude toward medication is respectful, and both hopeful and cautious. I still favor natural approaches whenever possible, but sometimes, these approaches are clearly not enough.

SEVERITY OF SOCIAL ANXIETY

IT STANDS TO reason that the more severe your symptoms are, the more desperate you will feel and the more likely it is that you will consider taking medication. What is severe social anxiety? It is the type of anxiety that impairs your ability to function in day-to-day living. Psychiatrist Ron Remick considers any condition as severe when it affects two of the following areas: work, love, and play. For example, you feel that you cannot go to the job interview. If you do have a job, you rarely share your ideas or opinions; advancement in your field is but a pipe dream. You dare not answer the telephone. You avoid opportunities to meet new people or a potential love partner. You feel lonely. You don't have fun with others. Even if you do manage to go through all the motions of daily living, you do so at the expense of unbearable personal discomfort, especially when it comes to social situations. Severe social anxiety often leads to depression. Life becomes so restricted that there is little to be excited about. Hope for a better future seems either too distant or altogether impossible. And finally, social anxiety is severe if it persists in spite of long-term efforts at managing it through cognitive-behavioral and other psychotherapeutic approaches.

RISKS AND BENEFITS

Every day is such a chore. I dread going to work and facing all those people. The fear of looking or sounding stupid is constant. I hide this fear behind a blank expression, a mask that I wear day after day after day. Meanwhile, my heart is throbbing and my stomach is churning.
—LILY, thirty-four years old

PRETEND, FOR A moment, that you are Lily. Someone comes up to you and says, "Lily, I have something for you, something that will take away all the fear and pain. The only thing is, however, you must pay me. We won't know exactly what the payment is until after you've accepted my offering and have taken it, as prescribed." How would you respond?

If things are bad enough, chances are, you might take the gamble. Life is meant for living, not for hiding behind a mask. For some people, deciding to take or not take medication can feel like a gamble. Although the financial cost of the medication is certain, the physiological and emotional costs are not. Because of individual differences, people respond differently to medication. Some people experience side effects when they take medication. Side effects are uncomfortable physiological symptoms that sometimes accompany the beneficial effects of medication. A few examples include dry mouth, dizziness, headaches, fatigue, and weight gain. Side effects may disappear after a few weeks for some people and persist for others. Some people decide that side effects are negligible compared to the emotional costs of social anxiety. For other people, side effects may be troublesome and even problematic. These people would sooner experience bouts of social anxiety than these side effects. For still others, there is a risk of medication abuse or dependency. With all this to worry about, why even consider medication? Simply put, it can be good for you. Medication can reduce fears to the point that you finally are able to concentrate and to learn new ways of thinking and being. New coping skills help to solidify any gains people make while on medication so that these gains do not evaporate once the medication is discontinued.

MEDICATIONS FOR SOCIAL ANXIETY

EVEN THOUGH THE U.S. Food and Drug Administration has approved only three medications (Paxil, Zoloft, and Effexor) for treating social anxiety disorders, over the years, physicians have been prescribing a variety of medications that have helped people with social anxiety. These medications are divided into six main groups. They are SSRIs, SNRIs, benzodiazapines, beta-blockers, MAOIs, and RIMAs; don't worry, they will be defined and explained shortly. Because research into drugs for social anxiety is in full swing, this list will likely expand in the near future. These drugs vary in effectiveness, suitability, side effects, and risks for abuse and dependency. Each drug has a generic name and a brand name. The generic name is the chemical name given to a specific class of drugs; the brand name is the manufacturer's name of a drug.

SSRIs (Selective Serotonin Reuptake Inhibitors)

GENERIC NAME	BRAND NAME
sertraline	Zoloft
paroxetine	Paxil
fluvoxamine	Luvox
fluoxetine	Prozac
citalopram	Celexa
escitalopram	Lexapro (not available in Canada)

SSRIs are today's most commonly used antidepressants. They were introduced into the drug market in the late 1980s. Studies have shown that fifty to seventy-five percent of patients treated with SSRIs have shown clear improvement in anxiety symptoms, and consequently, in social functioning. They work by blocking the uptake of the neurotransmitter serotonin into nerve cells. This blocking action raises the level of serotonin in the brain, which leads to relaxation. At the same time, since serotonin is blocked from entering the tiny spaces between nerve cells called synapses, it cannot do its job of transmitting nerve impulses from one cell to another. If it can't, for instance, pass on anxiety messages through the nerve cells, a state of calm is more likely to occur. Although serotonin levels are increased immediately after taking SSRIs, it takes a while for the receptor sites located at the synapses to decrease or to "dry up." For this reason, it usually takes about three to four weeks to feel the benefits of SSRIs when used as treatment for depression. When used for social anxiety, it can take six to eight weeks before noticing any effect.

Limitations

SSRIs have few, if any, limitations. They present no risk of physical dependency. However, people who abruptly discontinue an SSRI or SNRI will usually suffer a withdrawal syndrome— called "discontinuation syndrome"—with features of anxiety, insomnia, vivid dreams, irritability, and electric shock-like sensations. It is critical to consult your doctor as you discontinue your medication.

Side effects

When you read about side effects of any drugs, remember that not everyone experiences side effects. Furthermore, some side effects are common, some are infrequent, and others are rare.

One of the reasons that SSRIs have become so popular is their reputation for fewer side effects than those associated with other antidepressants. Still, the more common side effects include a restless sleep, some loss of appetite, nausea, occasional fatigue, and increased sweating. There may also be headaches, nervousness, insomnia, anxiety, and diarrhea. For some people, sexual functioning may be affected.

SNRIs (Serotonin/Norepinephrine Reuptake Inhibitors)

GENERIC NAME	BRAND NAME
venlafaxine	Effexor XR

Effexor XR belongs to another class of effective antidepressant drugs. Its effects and side effects are comparable to those of SSRIs.

Benzodiazepines

GENERIC NAME	BRAND NAME
clonazepam	Klonopin (Rivitrol in Canada)
alprazolam	Xanax
lorazepam	Ativan
diazepam	Valium
oxazepam	Serax
bromazepam	Lectopam (in Canada)

Benzodiazepines are a particular group of antianxiety drugs, also called minor tranquilizers. They first became available in the 1960s and were considered a safer alternative to the older antianxiety drugs known as barbiturates. When a benzodiazepine enters the brain, it binds to benzodiazepine receptors in the brain. Receptors are single molecules that are attached to a cell, floating on the cell's outer layer, with roots enmeshed in the fluid outer layer and reaching deep into the interior of the cell. These receptors hang around waiting to "receive" chemical messengers that are drawn to their unique chemical structure and fit perfectly into their unique shapes. Once this process of "binding" occurs, information enters the cell. This information triggers a chain reaction of biochemical events, which can cause minute physiological changes, which in turn, can translate into changes in behavior, physical activity, and even mood. In the case of benzodiazepines, as the binding to receptors occurs, the neurotransmitter gamma-aminobutyric acid (GABA) is activated. As you may remember, in the section on nutrition, GABA inhibits activity in the brain cells or neurons that produce anxiety. Usually benzodiazepines are used to treat general anxiety. However, studies have shown that two benzodiazepines in particular, clonazepam (Klonopin, or Rivitrol in Canada) and alprazolam (Xanax), have been effective in reducing symptoms of social anxiety. Because clonazepam is not as quick acting as some of the other benzodiazepines and has a long half-life, it is typically given once a day at bedtime. Physicians have also prescribed some of the other benzodiazepines in the treatment of social anxiety. The quicker-acting benzos include alprazolam, lorazepam, bromazepam, and oxazepam. Alprazolam now comes in a sustained-release form, which needs to be given once or twice a day maximum.

Limitations

A single dose often produces fatigue and drowsiness. Consequently, benzodiazepines are not useful for tasks that demand a mental edge and quick physical reaction time. Until individuals find out how they respond to benzodiazepines, they should exercise caution regarding driving or operating dangerous machinery. When taken regularly, two to four times a day, the body gets used to the drugs, and the side effects of fatigue and mental sluggishness decrease. However, taking benzodiazepines on a regular basis leads to two serious problems. First, because the body adapts to the benzodiazepines, it needs more and more to have the same level of effectiveness. The body develops a physical dependency.

As with any physical dependency, discontinuation of the medication needs to be gradual and under medical supervision, in order to reduce the risk of withdrawal symptoms. The most frequent withdrawal symptom is increased anxiety! Furthermore, abruptly withdrawing from benzodiazepines increases the possibility of a seizure. The second major problem regarding daily consumption of benzodiazepines is the risk of drug abuse. This is especially true of people who have either a personal or family history of drug abuse, substance dependency, or addictions such as overeating, gambling, sex, and so on. (Note: *Dependency* means your body absolutely craves a drug and without it will have withdrawal symptoms. *Abuse* means that you overdo it with a drug, and perhaps get sick, but you do not have withdrawal symptoms.)

John Marshall, psychiatrist and author of *Social Phobia,* defends the use of benzodiazepines for people who suffer serious bouts of anxiety, as long as they have no history of chemical dependency. Marshall advises strict medical supervision when taking benzodiazepines.

Side effects

If taken in single doses, the most common side effects are drowsiness, fatigue, and clumsiness. If taken on a regular basis, side effects diminish; however, they still include fatigue, longer sleeping periods, forgetfulness, impaired coordination, and infrequently, loss of interest in sex. At times, benzodiazepines can worsen symptoms of depression. Individuals who use these drugs should refrain from using alcohol, because these drugs magnify the effects of alcohol.

Beta-blockers

GENERIC NAME	BRAND NAME
propranolol	Inderal
atenolol	Tenormin

Beta-blockers were introduced into the drug market in the 1960s to treat high blood pressure and irregular heart rhythms.

They work by blocking off beta-receptors for the hormone adrenalin.

As you may remember, when the sympathetic nervous system is activated in an emergency situation, adrenalin surges to help trigger the fight-or-flight response. The beta-receptors are located in such organs as the heart and the muscles. If adrenalin is blocked off from these areas, then the heart doesn't get the message to beat faster and the muscles don't get the message to tighten and tremble. The body doesn't get the message to sweat profusely. Everything remains calm.

Remember, too, that in order for the fight-or-flight response to be triggered, the emergency situation does not have to be one of real danger as in the case of a coyote chasing a hare. The danger can be an imaginary one as in the case of a performer imagining that the audience will disapprove of the piano recital, dance performance, or comedy routine. When performers first heard about beta-blockers, it was a dream come true. Finally, they had something that would take the edge off their performance anxiety. Not only did performing artists start taking beta-blockers routinely for their own purposes, but they also started sharing these prescription medications with their performing buddies. This created a bit of a stir, because increasing numbers of performers were taking the drug without medical supervision. Their popularity established, beta-blockers eventually became the drug of choice for people who trembled at the prospect of other types of performances: giving a report at work or a lecture in the community, giving a toast at weddings or taking an oral exam. A single dose of beta-blocker medication, about one hour prior to a performance situation, is enough to block adrenalin and keep the body calm.

Limitations

Beta-blockers are best suited for people who experience high levels of anxiety in limited, specific situations. They are not as useful for people who experience mild levels of anxiety. In fact, in these cases, people often comment how they benefit from the adrenalin rush they experience just as they are about to perform. The added energy gives them the edge and concentration they need to give a peak performance that is full of expression and inspiration. Beta-blockers are also not as useful for people who experience social anxiety in a general sense. It would neither be practical nor healthy to pop a beta-blocker several times a day to cope with the many types of social situations that are part of daily living. Because beta-blockers reduce physical symptoms, they are not suited for people engaged in performances that require a high degree of physical exertion. For instance, a soccer player would not be able to give a peak performance if her edge was gone.

Beta-blockers are limited in their value in a couple of other ways. They are not as effective at reducing fearful thoughts as they are in reducing physical symptoms. And when used regularly, beta-blockers tend to lose their level of effectiveness.

Side effects

Beta-blockers are relatively free of side effects. Two common side effects are a sense of lethargy or fatigue, and light-headedness after standing up quickly. Beta-blockers are to be avoided by anyone with a history of asthma, heart disease, diabetes, or allergies that cause wheezing.

MAOIs (Monoamine Oxidase Inhibitors)

GENERIC NAME	BRAND NAME
phenelzine sulfate	Nardil
tranylcypromine	Parnate

MAOIs were used in the 1950s strictly as antidepressants. In the 1960s, scientists discovered that MAOIs worked more effectively than other antidepressants for a subgroup of people with depression. These people happened to have a tendency to be emotionally overreactive. In the early 1980s, Michael Liebowitz of the New York State Psychiatric Institute (referred to in Chapter 2) treated socially anxious patients with MAOIs in a controlled clinical study. Patients reported an "increased confidence, a higher resistance to criticism, and reduced anxiety during social or performance situations" (John Marshall, p. 185).

MAOIs work by inhibiting the activity of a particular enzyme, monoamine oxidase, which regulates certain neurotransmitters in the brain. Researchers theorize that MAOIs prevent the breakdown of these neurotransmitters, which, in turn, results in higher levels of the neurotransmitters norepinephrine, serotonin, and especially dopamine. As mentioned earlier, norepinephrine helps people to feel alert and awake. Serotonin helps people to feel relaxed. Dopamine is associated with feelings of pleasure—all of which add up to a reduction of social anxiety.

Currently, the MAOI Nardil is the best-established medication for treating serious social anxiety. In several studies, Nardil has consistently helped two-thirds or more of patients with social phobia who have taken it over an eight- to twelve-week period. Sometimes, the effects have been dramatic. The benefits are usually obvious after a few weeks of treatment.

Limitations

Unfortunately, MAOIs can have life-threatening interactions with foods that contain high concentrations of the amino acid tyramine. These interactions can cause a sudden rise in blood pressure, headaches, vomiting, and most seriously, a stroke or even death. Consequently, people who are considering taking MAOIs must be prepared to follow a strict diet. They should make sure to obtain specific food restrictions from the prescribing physician. In general, the foods to avoid include those that are aged, spoiled, fermented, or pickled. All foods, especially meat, fish, or poultry, should be eaten only when fresh. Canned meats may only be used immediately after opening. Some specific foods to be avoided are certain sorts of aged cheese (you can eat mozzarella and ricotta), sausage, certain alcoholic beverages (avoid beer, red wine), marmite, and fava beans. Certain prescription drugs and over-the-counter drugs such as decongestants must also be avoided. If dietary restrictions are followed religiously, even mild high-blood-pressure reactions are rare.

Side effects

Apart from the serious but uncommon risks mentioned above, common side effects include fatigue, drowsiness, dry mouth, light-headedness (when standing up suddenly), weight gain, and occasionally, difficulties with sexual functioning. These side effects typically do not start until one to three months after starting the medication and, unfortunately, they often persist.

RIMAs (Reversible Inhibitors of Monamine Oxidase)

GENERIC NAME	BRAND NAME
moclobemide	Manerix

Manerix is a relatively new antidepressant. It inhibits the same enzyme as MAOIs do, but not as completely. Its advantage over MAOIs is the absence of dietary restrictions. However, its effectiveness in treating social anxiety is not as impressive as that of the other MAOIs. Nevertheless, this class of drugs offers promise. Research continues and we may be hearing more about RIMAs in the future.

Two other medications that are sometimes used for social anxiety include the older tricyclic antidepressant, imipramine (Tofranil), and the anticonvulsant, gabapentin (Neurontin).

TAKING MEDICATION

TAKING MEDICATION IS a decision usually made in consultation with a physician whom you trust. Depending on your symptoms and medical history, your physician will suggest which medication best suits your needs. Each person has different responses to medications, so it may take some time to find the right medication for you. In other words, you need to be patient.

It is true that many people who suffer from social anxiety report dramatic changes with medication. Some people would call these changes astounding, nothing short of personality changes. I worked briefly with a painfully shy teenage girl whose mother decided to take her to a psychiatrist. The psychiatrist prescribed Prozac, an SSRI, and the mother reported that the daughter has not looked back since. Almost instantly, she became confident and outgoing. Similar anecdotes can be found in the social anxiety literature. Typically, however, the results of medication tend to be modest. For the most part, medication will not cure an excessive need for approval. It will not automatically change habits of negative thinking. It will not resolve the underlying roots of low self-esteem. Medication is rarely the perfect solution, nor should it be a long-term solution. Medication can, however, still the heart long enough to provide relief. Without the distraction of anxiety symptoms, concentration increases, and it is possible to focus on new ways of thinking and new ways of being. Commitment to a program of natural approaches can reduce the need for medication. The changes in thinking and behavior that occur as a result of genuine effort outlast the changes that occur through medication. Consequently, once medication is discontinued, usually at six to twelve months, the typical return of symptoms is minimal. Even if fears return, new coping skills and memories of successful social encounters help to keep fears at a manageable level.

KEY REFLECTION POINTS

➤ Your personal attitudes and values regarding medication, the severity of your social anxiety symptoms, and the weighing of risks and benefits will all need consideration as you decide whether to take medication.

➤ The six groups of medications that are used in the treatment of social phobia are SSRIs, SNRIs, benzodiazepines, beta-blockers, MAOIs, and RIMAs. Each has its benefits, limitations, and side effects.

➤ Taking medications can be an excellent option for those who suffer from extreme social anxiety. Medications will help calm the body so that concentration improves and it is easier to focus on learning skills and strategies that help you manage anxiety and gain confidence.

➤ Gains made through a program that addresses body, mind, and action will last longer than those made through medication alone.

➤ An honest discussion with your doctor should help you to make the right decision about whether to take medication.

The one thing I want to remember from this chapter is:

_____

_____

I will translate this one thing into action in the following way:

_____

_____

_____

_____

■ PART THREE ■

THE
MIND

EIGHT

JUST IMAGINE . . .

The Power of Image

The vision always precedes the realization.
—Lilian Whiting, poet, 1847–1942

MOST OF US associate "mind" with thoughts. When we were babies and toddlers without language, our first thoughts came in the form of images. These images are the result of activity in the right side, or hemisphere, of the brain. Later, as we acquired language, our thoughts also took the form of words. These words are the result of activity in the left side, or hemisphere, of the brain. Since images came first, it seems only natural to first examine the power of images in relation to social anxiety and social confidence.

IMAGES FLOW AND THE BODY OBEYS

IMAGINE THAT YOU are going to a party. What is it that you see, in your imagination, as you approach and walk through the host's door? What do you imagine happening, as you see yourself entering a room full of party guests? These are questions I ask members in my support group. Kevin, a twenty-five-year-old auto mechanic, summed up the typical response when he replied:

> I see myself shaking as I knock on the door. As soon as the door opens, I see myself walking quickly across the room, with my eyes down. I head for the armchair in the far corner of the room. I see myself sitting in the armchair, turned a little sideways from the crowd. No one comes up to talk to me. I feel lonely and I wonder why I ever came.

I then asked Kevin, "So what happens, once you're actually at the party?" He responded: "That's exactly what happens; I walk over to the chair in the corner, I sit down, and nobody talks to me. I feel really self-conscious and I can't wait to get back home."

I thanked Kevin for sharing with us a wonderful example of just how powerful images can be. In Kevin's case, his imagination became the blueprint for action. As if hypnotized, he followed, almost to the letter, the actions described in his imagined party scene. As if that wasn't enough, there was another layer of hypnosis occurring at the same time. The actual image of Kevin's closed-in body told people that he was not available for conversation. He looked unapproachable and so, no one approached him.

Be aware of the images you entertain in your mind. Some of them will affect you positively; others will affect you negatively. The following are a few examples of how imagination can have a positive and dramatic impact in a person's life.

Image as director of physiological responses

There is no shortage of documentation regarding the power of imagery in producing physiological changes. Studies have shown that in the process of imagining, people experience changes in muscle activity, oxygen consumption, blood flow, and blood pressure. There are films that show people of Eastern cultures poking swords through one cheek and out the other without any bleeding.

Balinese children learn, from example, how to walk through burning coals without blistering.

If anyone doubts the connection between image and body, I ask you to do the following experiment. The next time you catch yourself having a sexual fantasy, take note of any sensations in your body, especially in your lower body. See what I mean? Sexual fantasies are nothing but images which tantalize our sexual appetites and set in motion any number of sensual bodily reactions.

Image as evoker of emotions

Have you ever caught yourself shedding a tear as you imagine the death of someone you loved? Perhaps you've burst into laughter at the vivid memory of a funny incident. Maybe you have felt your blood boil with rage as you recall an injustice. Images, recalled or fantasized, produce emotional responses. Wouldn't you like to use your imagination in such a way that inspires excitement at the prospect of a certain social situation rather than dread?

Image as healer

Imagery can also help the healing process. There is plenty of documented and anecdotal evidence of the power of image in healing. Although still considered an alternative approach, the use of imagery in the healing of cancer and other illnesses has increased; so have the number of personal stories of triumph over illness.

Image as performance enhancer

For years, athletes have included imagery work or visualization in their training programs. Psychologists are now also working with artists in the performing arts, using imagery work to help artists achieve what is called a peak performance. Members of my social anxiety support groups have found imagery work invaluable in helping them do things they formerly found daunting.

For instance, Liz, a fifty-two-year-old who had been afraid to invite her sister-in-law to lunch, began to practice imagining phoning her sister-in-law and inviting her to a cozy café down the street. In her imagination, she could even smell and taste the pasta with Alfredo sauce that she planned to order. Before long, Liz actually asked her sister-in-law out and the two had a lovely time. Liz became so encouraged with the power of her positive images that she applied this practice to many other situations in her life. To her surprise, she started speaking her mind in situations that previously intimidated her. She confronted her ex-husband when he tried to take advantage of her. She talked to her son about a touchy family issue. She began to feel good inside her skin, instead of shrunken like a shriveled prune, afraid to stand up in the world. She fed her unconscious a diet of encouraging messages and images; her body obeyed.

IMAGINATION AND WILL

IN THE EARLY 1900s, a French physician by the name of Emil Coué wrote about the beneficial influence of imagination on the healing of physical ailments. Most of his ideas are commonly accepted in today's literature on imagery. One idea I found particularly fascinating and unique was Emil Coué's comparison of willpower and imagination power.

First, let's define *will*. The dictionary defines will as the faculty of determining one's actions. Will is also defined as moral strength and energy, and as determination. Now suppose that you are determined to do one thing but your imagination pictures you doing something else. Which do you think would win—will or imagination? Without exception, imagination will always triumph over will. If you imagine that you'll be socially anxious and awkward, you will be socially anxious and awkward.

Insomnia is an interesting example of imagination's power over will. If you've ever had trouble sleeping, perhaps you've noticed that the more you want to sleep and the harder you work at trying to sleep, the less likely it is that you do fall asleep. In your mind, you may see an image of yourself "trying" very hard. Guess what happens. You continue "trying" very hard. Or you may see yourself continuing to have trouble falling asleep. So you continue to have trouble falling asleep. Imagination provides the blueprint. The body obeys.

GUIDING IMAGINATION

An imagination gone wild can be trouble. Coué likens imagination to a torrent of water. If a huge torrent of water runs loose, it wreaks havoc, ruining farm crops, homes, and possessions, even killing people. If, on the other hand, we were able to capture this torrent of water and alter its course, we would be able to transform its fantastic power into useful sources of energy such as movement for turbines or electricity for cities. The same holds true for imagination.

If our imagination runs wild with images of disastrous consequences of some action, we suffer terribly. We become anxious, even to the point of physical distress. If, on the other hand, we learn to harness the power of our imagination and guide it in such a way that is constructive, we benefit enormously. We feel in control and at ease.

HOW IMAGINATION WORKS

RESEARCHERS OFFER NO definite explanation about how exactly imagination influences the body and actions. There are only hunches. These relate to communication networks in the body, energy patterns, the gullibility of the unconscious, and the influence of future images on the present. Let's take a brief look at each.

Communication network

Candace Pert, in her book *Molecules of Emotion*, proposes a network of communication, where chemical messengers carry information from cell to cell and from organ to organ. There is an interconnectedness among all body systems. If this is true, then once the visual system gets stimulated by images, even in imagination, the chemical information network goes into action and within moments, the body responds.

Energy patterns

Some people believe that everything in the universe, including thoughts and images, is composed of different forms of energy. Edmund Bourne, author of *Healing Fear*, states that energy travels in different patterns of waves. He contends that the energy of a certain thought or image will line up, or "resonate," with similar energy forms. This may explain why once you imagine a certain goal, all sorts of events, sometimes called coincidences, come into play to help that goal come true.

Gullibility of the unconscious

The dictionary defines the unconscious as the area of mental activity which escapes our mental awareness. According to Coué and others, the unconscious is gullible. It cannot tell the difference between what is imagined and what is real. Its only concern is to run the show according to the messages it receives. John Kehoe, author of *Mind Power*, says the unconscious will "manifest failure, ill health and misfortune just as easily as success and abundance. It works to reproduce in our life according to what seeds we have nurtured within it."

Future determines the past

Most of us have been brought up with the idea that the past influences our present. And certainly, this is true. However, it is also true that our vision of the future can also determine our present.

The late Milton Erickson was a well-known psychiatrist who often used hypnosis when working with his patients. Whenever he felt stuck with people, he would hypnotize them and ask them to visualize future scenes, whether with the family or at work. He would say something like "It's now a year after our therapy began. Give me a report about successful therapy. What worked? Tell me what was most helpful. What kind of changes do you notice in your life?" Then Erickson would hypnotically induce amnesia. When these clients returned for an appointment two weeks later, they reported all the changes they had made, just as they had described in their trances. Unconscious imagination was the blueprint. Once again, the body obeyed.

HARNESSING THE POWER OF IMAGINATION

IF YOU CAN remember what a spoon looks like, then you can imagine. Nevertheless, some people find it difficult to see pictures in their mind. If this is your situation, do not despair. Check out the guidelines in Appendix II. These can be enormously helpful in cultivating your skills in imagery work. If you still find imagery work difficult, do not worry. There are plenty of other ways to manage social anxiety.

USES OF IMAGERY FOR SOCIAL ANXIETY

IMAGERY CAN BE used to help manage social anxiety and increase social confidence in several ways. The most common uses are to imagine goals, to increase relaxation, and to rehearse social interactions. We can also use imagery to help us deal with specific situations such as facing authority figures and preparing for job interviews. We can even use imagery to increase our self-esteem.

Goals

Because goal formation is a cornerstone in managing social anxiety and gaining social confidence, Chapter 9 is entirely devoted to goals. You will find rich details about how imagination and goals work together for your benefit.

Relaxation

Relaxation is a key to reducing social anxiety. In Chapter 3, we covered the effectiveness of grounding and breathing techniques. Using images of relaxation is another way of altering your body chemistry and enhancing your general well-being. Examples of relaxing imagery work include the following:

A walk on the beach

Breathe out a few times. Close your eyes and imagine that you are walking on a beach. Feel the warmth of the sun shining on your skin. See the surface of the ocean sparkling under the late afternoon sun. Hear the waves crash against the craggy rocks over to the right. Smell and taste the salt air. Feel the hot dry sand under your bare feet, and so forth.

Your favorite place

Alternatively, you can remember from past experiences or create in fantasy a place where you feel completely at ease. Remember to include all your senses when you imagine visiting this favorite place.

A relaxed body

Starting from your head down to your toes, imagine every single part of your body becoming more and more relaxed. Feel the tension drain away from your face. See your lips part in relaxation. In your imagination, feel your shoulders drop, sense your breathing slowing down, deepening a little. Feel your body sinking into the bottom of a soft but supportive chair. Imagine droopiness, softness, heaviness. Feel the relaxation.

Rehearsal

Once you have decided on your goal and you have achieved some level of relaxation, you can use imagination to practice or rehearse achieving your goal.

Rehearsal using systematic desensitization

In 1958, Joseph Wolpe, a Philadelphia psychiatrist, was the first to describe *systematic desensitization*. To become sensitized to something means to become very sensitive to it. If, for instance, you have ever experienced high anxiety while giving a talk, it would be likely that you will feel high anxiety the next time you give a talk. In other words, you have been sensitized.

Desensitization involves weakening the association between a particular situation and anxiety. This can be accomplished in a "systematic" way. The system is to *expose* yourself very gradually to the situation that intimidates you. We will go through this in detail in the following chapter.

Variations of rehearsal imagery

Not everyone has the time to mentally rehearse weeks in advance of an anticipated event. Sometimes, you have only a week to prepare, or only a day, or even only a few minutes. In these cases, adding other images to your main scene images may be useful. Let's look at a few possibilities.

Borrowing from a real-life hero

When I first started giving public speeches, I was a nervous wreck before, during, and after each speech. These nervous images of myself were all I had to go on before the next public speech. Naturally, the nervous images only served to reinforce my nervousness the next time I prepared for a speech. Then one day, I found myself totally inspired by a speaker who also spoke about mental health issues. The speaker was Virginia Satir, a well-known family therapist at the time. Satir was visiting from the United States to give a talk to an audience of at least a thousand people at the University of British Columbia. I was mesmerized by her powerful and confident display of words and gestures. She wore a red dress, and as she moved across the stage, her whole body spoke with energy and purpose.

From then on, every time I mentally rehearsed for a presentation of my own, I would imagine Virginia Satir entering my body, like a ghost might do in a television show. She infused me with her energy and verve. I would see myself in a red dress, taking huge, confident steps across the stage, speaking clearly and loudly, opening my arms dramatically toward the audience. What a difference these energetic images made! Confidence and excitement replaced my usual anxiety. And even though my images were exaggerated and larger than life, my actual presentation was done in a more subdued, professional, but energetic style.

I highly recommend borrowing from other people's confidence. Who are your real-life heroes? They can be family members, teachers, friends, acquaintances, movie or sports celebrities, spiritual, political, or community leaders.

Borrowing from a fantasy hero or fantasy guide

Heroes can be from fantasy. They can be mythical gods and goddesses, heroes from novels, television, and movies. They may even be cartoon characters or private heroes from your imagination. As described in Appendix II, one of the guidelines in doing imagery work is to keep an open mind. In imagination, anything is possible.

Borrowing from past successes

Another effective way to mentally rehearse for a social event is to remember images from past successes. A while back, a regional mental health director asked me to present the key points of a recent mental health conference to about a hundred colleagues at an upcoming regional meeting. I was happy to do so. However, about three minutes before my presentation, I felt my heart start to pound furiously. Without warning, my sympathetic nervous system started to do its thing. I thought, "Oh no, not again, not now!" Instantly, as if my unconscious were offering me a gift, I found myself remembering the talk I had given at my fiftieth birthday party. It was the first speech I had given to a large crowd without having prepared it in writing. I had been feeling especially confident that night, surrounded by family, friends, and acquaintances. I had spoken from my heart, with energy and calm.

As I sat waiting to be called to do the mental health talk, I imagined wearing the blue dress I had worn to my party. In my imagination, I could feel the soft blue fabric caressing my shoulders and torso. I could see the acceptance and love in people's familiar faces. I could feel the warm glow of my birthday night travel through my body. Still waiting to give my mental health talk, I noticed that my heart rate was back to normal. When my name was called, I was ready. The speech went well. I was relieved and delighted.

Images of past successes—big or small—are a great way to short-circuit any anxiety cycle that threatens to take over. Too many times, people minimize their successes, eventually forgetting them altogether. Treat each success, even the smallest, as a treasure. If you can't remember anything recently, then dig back into the past. Remember a time when, in spite of feeling nervous, you went ahead and followed through with some form of social engagement. You were the first to smile at someone. You asked someone a question. I remember, as a child, what an accomplishment it was to ask the clerk in the Wal-Mart store where the girls' skirts were. Perhaps you went to a party. Maybe you didn't stay long, but at least you went!

Imagining a support network

Receiving support and encouragement from others often gives us strength. There are so many stories that support the idea that when we feel in connection with others, we feel stronger.

During the process of writing this book, I have regularly done imagery work. One of the things that I imagine is diving down into an underwater cave where I briefly meet with my support network. For the longest time, I was simply meeting with an imaginary wise man who would give advice and encouragement. One day, standing beside him, were three authors: Steven King, whom I saw interviewed on television and who said that he writes five hours a day, seven days a week; James Michener, who apparently had written more books after the age of eighty than before; and Natalie Goldberg, who wrote a wonderfully encouraging book about the process of writing. Each day I'd visit these people and they'd wave to me and cheer, "You can do it."

Then my son told me that John Grisham, author of so many best-selling thrillers, sets a goal of writing only one page a day. The next day Grisham appeared in my underwater cave. Before I knew it, other people also joined my underwater gang: Habata, an African student I taught in Africa thirty years ago; my editor, Elizabeth Lyon, whom I met at a writer's conference and who was tremendously encouraging; even Oprah Winfrey, successful talk show hostess, avid reader, and patroness of writers. Every day, all of them would send me home with messages of "You can do it."

I marveled at my growing imaginary cheering section and suddenly realized I hadn't included my husband, my sons, my colleagues, and very importantly, so many members of current and past social anxiety support groups, all of whom had been encouraging me about this book. My cave started looking pretty crowded. I can't tell you what a treasure I have, knowing that I can draw on the encouragement of all these folks, whether my connection with them is imaginary or not.

How about you? As you prepare to face the challenge of a particular social situation, who would you like to imagine standing beside you, encouraging you?

Specific situations

Imagery can be used in creative ways to deal with a variety of specific situations. Here are a couple of examples.

Authority figures and imagining new dimensions

What kinds of images come up for you when you picture meeting with your boss, the doctor, the professor, the bank manager, or the police officer? Are you a tiny tot, while he is the unfriendly giant? A little squirrel facing a pit bull? Whatever the image, it is sure to relate to size and power. Let's borrow from *Alice in Wonderland* and explore new dimensions.

Imagine that you are preparing to meet with your boss (doctor, bank manager, etc.). You have dressed yourself and now you are giving yourself a last-minute check in front of the mirror. You are a little shocked because the reflection you see in the mirror is of a four-year-old swimming in clothes that are way too big. You plop down on the floor and sit while contemplating this image.

You notice a hunger beginning to grow in your belly. On the oak table, beside the mirror, is a loaf of cinnamon-scented bread. You reach for the bread and notice that it is still warm from the oven. You take a bite from the end of the loaf. The spicy taste fills your being with utter delight. As you chew the morsel of bread, you notice that the reflection in the mirror is changing. It is getting bigger and bigger, looking older and wiser. You look down at your own body and notice that, indeed, it is growing and growing. Your head is nearly touching the ceiling. You marvel at how strong and robust you look. Your clothes fit remarkably well. It is time to meet with your boss.

You are invited into his office and take a seat in front of his desk. But a very strange thing has happened. You notice that it is now your boss who looks about five years old. He looks a trifle misplaced in this huge office filled with large pieces of executive-style furniture. As you look into the eyes of your boss, you sense in yourself, a feeling of parental concern toward this little mite of a human. Even as the little tyke begins to puff out his chest, you see past his show of strength to the little boy's eagerness to do his job well. You give him a smile of encouragement.

With your bigger body, you have bigger eyes, and with these eyes, you recognize the soft spot in the middle of your boss's being, that vulnerable spot that makes him every bit as human as you and everyone else. In a relaxed and self-assured way, you begin to talk about your job (or your academic questions, your diagnosis, your request for a bank loan, your traffic ticket, etc.). The conversation goes well. Before you know it, you're shaking hands. You're at each other's eye level, both standing, both about the same size.

Job interviews and memories of the future

Job interviews can also be intimidating. This time, let's use imagery work that jumps to an imaginary future, lying beyond the anticipated social event. Instead of rehearsing for something that will happen in the future, imagine that the event for which you are preparing has already happened in the past and has been successful.

John, a member in one of my groups, announced that he had a job interview in five days. He felt completely prepared as far as knowing his "stuff" was concerned. Besides coming to my social anxiety support group, he had also been attending a Toastmasters group, learning to improve his speaking skills. He wondered what else he might do to prepare for the interview and to not feel so nervous. I told John that he had done a good job in terms of left-brain activity. He would not have a problem with "words." He knew the technical jargon, the policies and procedures connected with the job he was after; he knew basic interviewing skills. I suggested that he now focus on right-brain activities; namely, on images and sensations. I proposed that he focus on the future, that he imagine having succeeded at getting the job he wanted. Here's the scenario I proposed.

Imagine that you've just received a telephone call. The voice at the other end says, "You got the job." Let the news sink in. Notice what you are feeling. Perhaps you have a mixture of feelings. Relief? Excitement? Sense the exhilaration as it rushes through every muscle fiber, every bone in your body. Perhaps you want to jump up and down, and scream, "Right on!" You may prefer simply to sit down and enjoy the glow of your success. Imagine breaking the good news to your family and friends. Let their happiness for you soak in, as they offer their congratulations. Imagine yourself celebrating in some fashion. Whatever the celebration, smell, taste, see, hear, and feel whatever it is that you're experiencing. See yourself at your new job, being welcomed by your boss and coworkers. Imagine yourself enjoying the novelty of the new job, appreciating the challenges, or the extra time, or the meaningfulness of what it is you are doing. If your paycheck is larger than formerly, think of all the ways you'll make use of the extra cash. Now look back at your interview, which landed you this job. Recall how you sailed through it. Your confidence was contagious. You inspired your interviewers. Within the first couple minutes, they knew you were the one for the job. At some level, you knew it, too. Now it all seems so long ago.

John practiced these imaginary scenes religiously, three times daily. He reported to the group that it was a marvelous experience to be preparing for his interview in this way. "It's really amazing. Each time I do my visualization, I can't help myself, I get all revved up and head for my desk to prepare a little more for the interview. The use of this kind of imagery as a motivator is unbelievable." John realized that the employers may have already picked their man and were simply going through the motions of interviewing. All the same, he felt he had no choice but to do his best. Practicing this imagery work motivated him to prepare for the interview as much as he possibly could. John told the group that even if he did not get the job, the process of preparing for the interview and actually going through the interview would help him for the next job interview he might have. He couldn't lose! In fact, John did cinch the job he wanted. I phoned John three years later to see how he was doing. He said that he was as busy as ever. He was still at his new—now old—job and enjoying it.

Self-esteem

As already mentioned, not everyone who experiences social anxiety has low self-esteem, but certainly many do. Let's see how imagery work can help boost self-esteem.

Visit to the nursery

This exercise may be easier for those of you who are parents, or who have a soft spot in your hearts for children. Even among clients who have difficulty seeing themselves as lovable when they were young, few can resist the miracle of a newborn baby.

Imagine that you are at a hospital nursery, peering in through the window at a few rows of newborn infants, swaddled in pink and blue. The infant closest to you, just beneath your nose, happens to have your name on the nameplate at the end of its clear plastic nursery bed. You realize that through some magic of time travel, you are able to see yourself just hours old. Watch with amazement how this little darling breathes with its tiny nostrils, pushing air in and out, as its stomach gently rises and falls. Marvel at her wee fists with fingers curled, like blossoms yet unopened in the early dawn. Now hold this treasure in your arms so that you can see her face. Smell the fragrance of her baby skin. Hear a cooing sound rise in her throat. Coo back, just as gently. Rock your baby back and forth and whisper in her ear. Tell her how thrilled you are that she is here. Let her know how blessed the world is, to have a little treasure such as herself come into being. Tell her that you will be there to support her as she grows, that you will stand by her side whenever she needs help. It is almost time to go. Know that you can come back to this imagined lovely self whenever you want to. For now, tell her, "I love you." Remind her that you will hold her close to your heart at all times.

There you have it, a smorgasbord of possible imageries that can help you gain social confidence. Some will fit and some won't. Don't even imagine that you need to try them all. Hopefully, you'll find one or two that you find useful.

KEY REFLECTION POINTS

➤ The power of imagination is formidable. It can direct physiological responses in the body, evoke emotions, heal and save lives, and enhance performance.

➤ Imagination is so strong that in a contest between imagination and will, imagination will always triumph.

➤ No one knows for sure how imagination works. Possible explanations relate to an intricate communication network connecting mind, body, and action; energy patterns resonating with similar energy patterns; the gullibility of the unconscious, which accepts any images as true; and finally, the fact that images of the future can determine the present.

➤ To use your imagination constructively and effectively, it is useful to follow guidelines (Appendix II).

➤ Most common uses of imagination to help manage social anxiety are to imagine goals, to increase relaxation, and to rehearse social interactions.

➤ Variations of rehearsal imagery include borrowing from a real-life hero, borrowing from a fantasy hero or guide, and borrowing from past successes. Also, you can imagine a support network.

➤ Imagery work can be useful in managing social anxiety in a variety of situations, such as dealing with authority figures and preparing for job interviews.

➤ Imagery work can help boost self-esteem.

The one thing I want to remember from this chapter is:

_____

_____

I will translate this one thing into action in the following way:

_____

_____

_____

_____

NINE

WHERE DO I START?

The Value of Goals

Tell me not, in mournful numbers,
Life is but an empty dream!—
For the soul is dead that slumbers,
And things are not what they seem.

Life is real! Life is earnest!
And the grave is not its goal;
Dust thou art, to dust returnest,
Was not spoken of the soul.
—HENRY WADSWORTH LONGFELLOW,
"A Psalm of Life" [1839]

LONGFELLOW WAS RIGHT: Life's goal is life itself. To be fully engaged in living is a goal that fits well with nature's design for us. A fellow therapist once told me to imagine, for one moment, that living one's life is like sitting in a concert hall. Try it. Imagine that you can choose to live in a fulfilling way so that, at the end of your life, when you look back at your experience of the concert hall, it is with satisfaction that you remember all the dramas, the comedies, the music concerts, the operas, the ballets, and the jazz dances that took place in the hall. You also remember the rising and falling of those sumptuous, velvet curtains, many, many times before the last curtain call. The price of admission was well worth the show. Or you can choose to live your life so safely and carefully, with as little risk as possible that, at the end of your life, as you look back at your experience of the concert hall, you realize that you're still sitting there in your seat, waiting for the show to begin.

In the previous chapter, you learned that one of the key ways you could use your imagination was in goal formulation. Let's look at how imagining goals is the first step in ensuring that you get a good seat in the concert of life.

OVERALL GOAL AND MINI-GOALS

MY SOCIAL ANXIETY support groups take place weekly for ten weeks. During the first session, I ask people to imagine and write down what they would like to accomplish, in a social sense, by the end of the ten weeks. I ask them to be realistic. If, for example, they are lonely, it would not be realistic to choose, as a ten-week goal, a steady mate, a marriage, and a baby on the way. The following are a few examples of realistic and worthwhile goals. Mary would like to organize a birthday celebration for herself, inviting two or three people to her house for dinner. Tom would like to feel more confident in job interviews. Kerry would like to speak up at the monthly management meetings that she attends.

At the first meeting, Mary, Tom, and Kerry all agree that these goals seem too big, too difficult, and too scary, but maybe, just maybe, they will be able to accomplish them within ten weeks. I then ask what tiny steps they might take to help them reach their larger goals. For instance, Mary, who has difficulty initiating social contacts, is going to work on initiating tiny social interactions on a daily basis. Her first week's mini-goals consist of being the first to say hi to one person a day, and making telephone calls to two friends that she hasn't called in over a year.

IMPORTANCE OF SETTING GOALS

JANICE, A THIRTY-YEAR-OLD dental receptionist, often complained that she had a boring and uninteresting social life. She wished she had a more exciting life, but she had no ideas about how to create one. She certainly had no goals or plans. It's not unusual for many of us to have wishes like Janice's and then do nothing about it. We may wish to have a better job, go traveling, or become more socially confident, but then nothing else happens. Why not? Because we have no specific destination! Without a destination, there's no movement and no motivation.

Donald Liggett has a lovely story to tell in his book, *Sport Hypnosis*, about his meeting with a group of female gymnasts ranging in ages from nine to thirteen. He asked each girl to name a specific trick she was working on. Every girl but one named one or two specific tricks. The remaining girl simply said that she wanted to be a better gymnast. When the coach overheard her reply, he realized why she had seemed so unmotivated during their practice sessions. The coach and Liggett then helped the girl choose two specific flips to add to her routine. Within only one week of focusing on and practicing these routines, this girl's attitude improved dramatically. She was keen and motivated. The simple act of setting specific goals gave her the boost she needed.

From the above anecdote, you can see why setting goals can be so important. Goals serve several functions:

Goals provide focus and direction

Energy and attention that formerly had no place to go can now be channeled.

Goals provide images and words that inform the body

Once you have a goal, it often takes the shape of an image in the right hemisphere of your brain. Or, it may take the shape of words in the left side of your brain. As we've already learned, once the message is there in vivid detail, the body obeys, and what was merely a wish eventually becomes a reality.

Goals provide motivation and mobilization

Once you have a goal in mind, you often feel excited and energized. Energy begets energy.

Goals provide opportunities for learning and development

If your efforts at the mini-goals are not as successful as you might like, there is usually something to learn. You learn to develop new strategies. You learn that your goal was too big to start with, and you need to do something more modest but achievable. You learn that perhaps it was just a bad hair day and you need to take a break from goals.

Goals provide opportunities for success and reinforcement for continued efforts

When goals are specific, they are measurable; that is to say, you know when you've accomplished them. Once Mary has said hi to seven people during the week, she knows she's accomplished her first mini-goal. Achieving goals reinforces your desire and efforts for continued success. This is why it is important not only to have overall or long-term goals, but also the short-term or mini-goals, which are easier to accomplish.

Goals raise consciousness about resources and possibilities

Have you ever noticed that once you have your mind set on a goal, your awareness is drawn to all kinds of things that can help you achieve your goal? For example, if you decide on a goal of becoming more confident in job interviews, your ears perk up when you hear about programs focused on interview skills.

WARNING:
GOALS CAN BE DANGEROUS TO YOUR LIFE

HAVING DESCRIBED THE benefits of setting goals, I hasten to add that goals can also have a serious drawback. Although they are meant to help you live life more fully, they can also distract you from living life fully. Ironically, goals that are meant to be at your service sometimes end up making you their slaves. Unfortunately, some people get addicted to goal setting. Every goal accomplished becomes another feather in their cap. Feather collecting becomes an obsession at the expense of enjoying the journey along the way.

I remember traveling in Maui with my mother and two young sons. We drove down the coast on the road to Hana, which consisted of six hundred curves and fifty-four bridges in a thirty-mile stretch through a luxuriantly green rain forest. The road was sometimes treacherous, and the scenery was always beautiful. Especially impressive were the many exotic forms of green foliage that waved to us from above our open-roofed car. It so happened that at the end of the road were the Seven Sacred Pools, lovely pools of fresh water, a couple of which you were allowed to swim in. I remember reading tourist information about the Sacred Pools. The information included a mild chiding to tourists who considered the Seven Pools to be the final destination, for, from the Hawaiian point of view, the entire road to Hana was to be enjoyed and admired for its own wondrous sake.

When goals become the be-all and end-all in a person's life, that person risks losing sight of everything that is happening between point A and point Z. I had one client in my group who, because he had been such a casualty of goal obsessiveness, made it a point to not make any goals during the course of the ten-session social anxiety support group. He was, in fact, making one goal: to sit, participate, and soak in all the information and experiences that the group had to offer. I thought his was a good decision based on his unique needs. By the end of the group sessions, he was, indeed, more relaxed and more socially confident.

For the majority of folks who would like to gain social confidence, however, setting goals is an important first step. But like the road to Hana, the road to social confidence can be bumpy, smooth, treacherously close to the precipice, or comfortably tucked in the emerald jungle. There is always something to discover—places to breathe and relax and places that require you to be alert and prepared.

FIGURING OUT YOUR GOALS

SOME PEOPLE HAVE no trouble formulating a goal; others wonder where to begin. The following suggestions should help you get started.

Identify which social situations trigger anxiety.
EXAMPLE: "I have difficulty accepting invitations to parties."
Write your own: _____

_____

_____

Then convert these problem areas into positive overall goals.
EXAMPLE: "I want to accept invitations to parties."
Write your own: _____

_____

_____

Now, begin to formulate mini-goals in the service of these overall goals, by identifying the signs and symptoms of your anxiety in these situations, in areas of body, mind, and action.

BODY
EXAMPLE: "My chest tightens."
Write your own: _____

_____

_____

Convert symptom into positive, specific goal:

EXAMPLE: "I will practice grounding three times a day for one week."

Write your own: _____

_____

_____

MIND

EXAMPLE: "I worry that I will be miserable at the party, that no one will want to talk to me, and that even if they did, I wouldn't know what to say."

Write your own: _____

_____

_____

Convert into positive, specific goal:

EXAMPLE: "I will identify my distorted thoughts and replace them with realistic, positive, and compassionate thoughts. I will sit down and do this twice a day for a week."

Write your own: _____

_____

_____

BEHAVIOR/ACTION

EXAMPLE: "I look down and avoid eye contact."

Write your own: _____

_____

_____

Convert into positive, specific goal:

EXAMPLE: "I will practice holding up my head and looking directly into people's eyes for one to two seconds, saying silently, 'I welcome you.' I will do this at least twice a day."

Write your own: _____

_____

_____

It is important to follow your own pace. If you want a convenient way to keep track of your goals under the headings of body, mind, and action, you may find the goal recording chart in Appendix III useful. An empty recording chart is also available. For suggestions on possible goals for the week, see Appendix IV.

GUIDELINES FOR SETTING EFFECTIVE GOALS

Make sure the goal you set is under your control.

When I asked Leah Pells, a Canadian finalist runner in the 1996 summer Olympics, what tips she might have in terms of goal setting, one of the things she mentioned was that she made sure her goals were under her control. Her goals were related to her performance and not to the performance of others. In her words,,

> I compete only with myself. There is always someone faster, and always someone slower . . . so I focus on my own gains. This way I do not get caught up in little jealousies with people. I focus on what I do . . . and I can be happy for my competitors when they run fast . . . because I know that whether they run fast or slow, it has no bearing on my performance.

Making sure that we only set goals over which we have direct control makes sense.

Make both long-term and short-term goals.

It's easy to get overwhelmed by goals that seem too large or too far in the distance. When Leah Pells runs a 1500-meter race, she doesn't aim for the 1500-meter mark. She breaks the race into portions, running her absolute best to the first 20-meter mark. Then she runs her absolute best to the second 20-meter mark, and so on, and so on. She feels that she can remain at her peak longer this way. To run her absolute best for the total 1500 meters would be too overwhelming. It is easier to stay motivated and feel in control in shorter spurts than in prolonged situations.

In terms of social anxiety, a long-term goal might be to invite someone to your home for dinner. This is equivalent to the racer's 1500-meter marker. A short-term goal may be to practice saying hello to people in your office when you first arrive. This would be the first 20-meter marker. Little by little, the incremental growth in confidence will allow you to finally reach the 1500-meter marker and feel triumphant when you actually invite a friend over for dinner.

Have one-shot goals *and* repeatable goals.

Occasionally, a member of my group will say that his goal is to do one thing that week. For instance, Calvin might want to initiate one conversation with one person during the week. This is an honorable and worthwhile one-shot goal, but what is happening during the rest of the week? Is he waiting for things to happen? Is he avoiding? I usually recommend that people also form goals that they can practice on a regular basis. For instance, Calvin could visualize initiating a conversation on a daily basis. Regular and consistent efforts will bring you to your destination sooner.

Make your goal specific and measurable.

Telling yourself, "I will be more friendly this week," is not as useful as saying, "I will say hi to at least one person every day, and I will ask Mary to join me for lunch." Specific goals are easier to imagine. Remember, images are powerful messages to the body. At the end of the week, it is far easier to measure whether you have greeted seven people and have asked Mary to lunch than to measure how friendly you've been.

State your goal in definite terms.

"I *think* I will *try* to . . ." is not as effective as "I will." As soon as you use such phrases as "I think," "I guess," "I'll try," you reduce your chances for success. These words conjure images of hesitation. When talking about goals, I tell people to throw the word "try" out the window. If you are doubtful that you can achieve a certain goal, you're better off changing your goal. Choose a goal where you are "almost" guaranteed to succeed—small and easy enough to be doable, big and difficult enough to provide a challenge.

State your goal in positive, doable terms.

"I will be less nervous" is less effective than "I will be calmer." Notice how the words "less nervous" still evoke an image of nervousness, though less so, whereas the word "calmer" creates an image of peace and quiet. Furthermore, although "I will be calmer" is positive, it's still too vague. Translating the image of calm into an actual task is even more effective. "I will be calmer; I will practice grounding twice a day and muscle relaxation once a day, all week," gives you something you can actually do and accomplish.

Have a time frame, and choose "sooner rather than later."

Pinning down a time frame or a deadline for your goal helps strengthen your commitment to that goal. Have you ever noticed that when friends who haven't seen each other for a while bump into one another, they might enthusiastically end their conversation with "Let's get together some time"? There's jovial agreement. Then both friends walk away, get busy, time passes, and neither bothers calling the other to make a date. It's important to pin down a date right then and there. I'll usually say to my friend, "Okay, let's get our date books out and see when we can have lunch." We agree on a time and place, and look forward to seeing each other again.

It is also important to accomplish your goals sooner rather than later. For example, many members of my social anxiety support groups agree to phone at least two members of the group during the week. When they report how they did with this particular goal for the week, a few will inevitably say they were nervous about making the calls, so they left it to the end of the week, and by then it was too late. They couldn't reach anyone. As Ian, a group member, once said, "Procrastination has its own momentum." The more he put off doing something, the easier it was to continue putting it off. The longer he put off accomplishing his goal, the more his anxiety mounted. One way to shrink the tendency to procrastinate is to expand the habit of doing things as soon as possible. For this reason, members who have tended to postpone making phone calls, begin including a "sooner rather than later" clause in their goal statements. They will say, for instance, "I will make two calls by the end of three days" rather than "by the end of this week."

Record your goals.

Writing down your goals is another way to increase your commitment to your goal. For most people, a written contract carries more weight than a verbal or mental commitment. The physical act of writing paves the way to other physical acts, namely the achievement of the goal.

Track your progress.

Research has shown that when you write down your goals and record your progress, the rate of progress increases. Recording your progress may take the form of keeping a journal of what exactly happened and what you learned and how you feel about what happened, or it may involve simply placing a checkmark beside your goal once you've accomplished it. As you look back at your checkmarks, you are reminded that you are actually making headway. This tangible evidence encourages you to keep going.

Revise your goals.

Once your time limit is up, it's important to review your goals. Were they too easy, too ambitious, or just right? Did you learn that they weren't quite on target, after all, that something else might be more to the point? Goals are just aids. Revise them as needed.

Share your goals.

Every week, members in the group share their goals and report on their progress. Everyone looks forward to this experience, because they are eager to find out how their new friends have done. When there are successes, the whole room fills with inspiration. If things didn't turn out as well as people had hoped, there is discussion, learning, encouragement, and hopes for a better outcome next time. This kind of accountability to each other goes a long way in motivating people to take risks they might not otherwise take.

When I finally decided to take time to write this book, I made sure to tell a lot of people about my plans. I didn't do this to brag. I did it because I was afraid that if I kept this goal to myself, it would simply shrivel up in my mind and evaporate completely, as so many ideas can do. I thought if I told enough people, there was no way I would back out. I would have to keep my word and follow through with my plans. Not only did sharing strengthen my commitment to this project, it opened up opportunities for shared ideas with others. One member of a former group told me about a writers' conference, which I subsequently attended. At one of these workshops, I met my editor; at another, I met my agent. Other people gave me other ideas, and mostly, I received encouragement. Although it may not always be practical to share your goals, do so whenever you can. Perhaps you can tell your family or a few close friends. Letting others in on your goals helps to reinforce your own commitment and, believe it or not, helps to inspire others with their aspirations.

KEY REFLECTION POINTS

➤ Forming and achieving goals can help you manage shyness and social anxiety so that you can have a fulfilling life.
➤ Goals serve several functions:
   ■ Goals provide focus and direction.
   ■ Goals provide images and words that inform the body.

- Goals provide motivation and mobilization.
- Goals provide opportunities for learning and development.
- Goals provide opportunities for success which reinforce motivation for continued efforts.
- Goals raise awareness about resources and possibilities.

➤ Goals can be unhealthful if you become addicted to them and lose sight of the journey along the way.

➤ One way to figure out your goals is to identify the social situations that you find challenging and identify the symptoms of anxiety that accompany these situations in the areas of body, mind, and action. Then convert these problem areas into specific, positive goals.

➤ Guidelines for setting effective goals are the following:
- Make sure the goal you set is under your control.
- Make both long-term and short-term goals.
- Have one-shot goals as well as repeatable goals.
- Make your goal specific and measurable.
- State your goal in definite terms.
- State your goal in positive, doable terms.
- Have a time frame and "sooner rather than later."
- Record your goals.
- Track your progress.
- Revise your goals.
- Share your goals.

The one thing I want to remember from this chapter is:

_____

_____

I will translate this one thing into action in the following way:

_____

_____

_____

_____

TEN

WORDS THAT BURN

The Power of Words

Thoughts that breathe, and words that burn.
—THOMAS GRAY (1716–1771)

T HE THOUGHTS AND words that visit or live in our minds can soothe our spirits like a warm balm on chafed skin. They can encourage us, embolden us, inspire us, and propel us into action. Thoughts and words can also tyrannize us, like secret police watching our every move. In response to the brutal words we hear in our heads, we can cower in fear, hide in shame, and shrivel in despair.

In this chapter, we will learn how to recognize and challenge the thoughts and words that discourage us. We will also look at how to cultivate thoughts and words that help us to feel more comfortable within our own skin and more confident in our ability to interact with people.

CORE BELIEFS ABOUT SELF
AND ASSUMPTIONS ABOUT THE WORLD

Like little sponges, toddlers absorb the words that surround them. These words may be neutral or they may be emotionally charged words that mean "welcome" or "danger."

For a moment, pretend that you are a little child who is hearing the following from a caretaker, whether one of your parents, a relative, a teacher, or a friend.

> What a sweetheart you are! Now tell me, how ever did you come up with that wonderful idea? Sometimes, you have the most amazing thoughts! Can you tell me about that painting (drawing, hobby) you're doing? It looks very interesting. You sure are a creative, curious little soul, aren't you? Really? Tell me more. It's fun being with you.

How would you feel if you heard these words? What kinds of beliefs about yourself would you start forming? Would they be, for instance, "I'm lovable, I'm a good person, I'm interesting, I have important things to say, I'm worth listening to, I'm fun to be with?" What assumptions would you have about the world? Might they be something like, "People are friendly and they like me. People think I'm okay, more than okay. People accept me for who I am. Things usually turn out right. The world is a friendly place"?

Now, contrast this with another experience. Pretend that you are another child of the same age and that what you hear from your caretaker is the following:

> What's the matter with you? Haven't I told you enough times that that's not the way to do it? You spilled your milk. Go sit at the pig's table. Don't tell me that. You don't know what you're talking about. Don't bother; it won't do you any good anyway. How do you expect people to like you? Sometimes, I feel like giving up (on you).

Think of yourself as that little sponge, absorbing these critical words. You have no breadth of experience, no knowledge of other realities. As a small child, you have little choice but to believe what your caretaker tells you. They're bigger; they must know better. You will likely begin to tell yourself, "There's something wrong with me. I'm no good. I can't do things right. I deserve to be punished. I have nothing important to say. I might as well not try, it won't amount to anything." You will assume, "People can't be bothered. People don't care about me. People think I'm a slob. People don't want to hear from me. The world has no place for me. The world is a dangerous place. I might get hurt."

Sometimes we get these messages much less directly than described in the above examples. One fellow, Mike, told me that he knew his grandmother loved him just by the way she looked at him. However, Mike was not convinced that he was worthwhile because the overriding message he received at home was that he was not worthy enough to hold people's interest. At least that was his interpretation. Mike came into the world under unfortunate circumstances. While his mother was pregnant with him, she was diagnosed with a serious degenerative disease. Naturally, Mike's mother was distracted during the first years of Mike's life. She never said anything outright, but her lack of enthusiasm registered deeply in Mike's being. He translated this negative impression into such words as "I'm not interesting enough. I must do everything right or else I will be found not good enough. The world expects me not to make a fuss. There are too many other, more important things going on. I don't deserve to have my needs met." How can Mike feel socially confident if he doesn't feel the right to exist?

As you may recall, sixty to eighty percent of the members of my social anxiety groups felt that thoughts played a major role in their social anxiety. That's why most social anxiety literature focuses on cognitive behavioral therapy; that is, therapy that involves paying attention to one's thinking as well as to one's behavior. Let's explore a couple of ways we can attend to our thinking, learning to recognize and challenge those thoughts that hurt us.

VOICE THERAPY

ONE OF MY favorite ways of challenging negative inner thoughts, particularly negative self-judgments, is through voice therapy, a method designed and studied by psychologist Robert Firestone. Voice therapy simply means paying attention to our inner self-critical voice.

I mentioned that a child is like a sponge that absorbs the words that are directed at it. By the time the child reaches twenty, thirty, forty, or fifty years of age, he will have forgotten the origin of these words. Having repeated the negative messages so many hundreds and thousands of times to himself, he will find that the words have embedded themselves in every cell, every fiber of his body. He will have come to believe that these words represent who he really is.

Firestone found a way to help people examine these negative messages, discover their source, and realize that they do not represent reality. He found that it was indeed possible to stand up to these negative voices and find one's own voice. Voice therapy can be done intellectually or emotionally and dramatically. Your emotions may get stirred up, and if you have difficulty tolerating emotional pain, this work is probably best done with the support of a therapist. If you are comfortable with your emotions and trust that you will survive temporary uneasiness, this work can be invaluable in finally getting rid of the negative messages that make you feel small and insecure. There are two main steps. First, you must externalize your negative judgments about yourself. Then, you must stand up to them.

Externalizing the negative voice

To externalize your negative voice, you must first be aware of what this voice is saying. For some people, this is easy. The messages are clear. For others, it is a little more difficult as the messages are not so much in words as in feelings. "I kind of feel uneasy with people. I think they won't like me." Don't worry. Just start somewhere, even if this somewhere is vague. Say the words out loud in the second person, as if someone is saying these things to you. In other words, use the "you" word. "You are so uneasy with people. You're not likeable." Then just keep it going. Exaggerate, if it helps. See what comes up. Listen to the negative voice of Michelle, an attractive, articulate, young woman whose social anxiety keeps her from speaking freely to her coworkers. Michelle often thinks people will think there is something wrong with her. When she spoke her negative voice out loud, this is what came up.

> What's wrong with you? You're so odd. You're not like everyone else. You're making me feel uncomfortable. You've got negative energy. You're insecure. You're weak. I don't like you. I'd rather not talk to you. I'm not interested in you. You don't matter. You disgust me. You're a loser. You're a nothing.

When I asked Michelle if this voice reminded her of anyone in her life, she immediately responded that her grandfather had often treated her in a punitive way, as if she had done something wrong, and yet she could never figure out just what she had done wrong. Once, for instance, when she was about five years old, her grandfather slapped her because she was daydreaming at the kitchen table. Michelle remembers being shocked and humiliated. Since it was often difficult to figure out exactly what she had done to merit the belittling remarks and gestures of her grandfather, she simply assumed that there was something seriously wrong with her, that she was fatally flawed.

Challenging the negative inner voice

Once you've externalized your negative voice, the next step is to challenge it. I have found that it is often easier to do this first indirectly, then directly. For instance, in Michelle's case, I asked her to imagine entering the kitchen and witnessing a grandfather berating his granddaughter for daydreaming. I asked Michelle to pretend that she was the granddaughter's fairy godmother, a good aunt, or a social worker. Michelle then was to speak to the grandfather and let him know what she thought of his behavior. Here is what Michelle said.

Who do you think you are? How can you do that to a small child? How sadistic and frightened you must be to pick on a small, frightened, and sensitive child. Have you no compassion? Obviously not! Were you thinking at all? How you talk to her is going to affect her for the rest of her life. She'll doubt herself. She's helpless. You're not. Which makes you irresponsible with the power that you have. You don't deserve to take care of her. If you keep talking to her like that, I will take her away from you.

As you can see, Michelle's verbal stand reveals several important points. First, her grandfather is held accountable. Michelle spells out exactly how his behavior is destructive and irresponsible. By doing this, she makes it clear to herself that it was her grandfather who had a problem, not the child. The second important thing that happened in this short confrontation was that Michelle gave her grandfather an ultimatum. Either he stops his destructive talk or the little girl leaves. After Michelle confronted the grandfather's voice indirectly, she accepted my invitation to confront him again, but this time, directly, from her own point of view, on her own behalf. This is what this second challenge sounded like.

What you're doing disgusts me. Leave me alone. Get out of my face. Let me be who I am. Stop your rage. You have a problem that has nothing to do with me. It is not my fault. I'm nothing like you. You don't understand me. You don't deserve the likes of me. You've betrayed the sacred trust of caring for me. I am sorry for your insecurity, but still, that doesn't give you the right to dump on an innocent. If you continue, I'm out of here. I deserve better than this. It's all your problem. There's something wrong with you. There's nothing wrong with me.

Can you hear the justified anger in Michelle's words? This time, she is even more emphatic about how she is not the problem. She separates herself from her grandfather. She draws a distinct line between him and her. His outrageous behavior is reflective of him—not her. This is so important to understand. Think about your own situation. If you've had the misfortune of being treated poorly as a youngster, can you see that this mistreatment is a reflection of people and circumstances outside of yourself? Please believe that you were, as every little child is, a wonderful human being, delightful in your own right, and full of promise. Unfortunately, because of direct or indirect negative messages, you lost sight of your wonderfulness and came to believe you were, somehow, not good enough. It's time to reclaim your place in the world as a lovely human being, deserving of respect and welcome.

It's your turn. Take a moment and think about any negative inner voice that you may have. I recommend writing these negative messages down on a piece of paper or in your journal. Alternatively, you might like to record them into a tape recorder. There are two reasons for this. When you write down the negative messages or say them out loud, you are moving them from inside your head to outside on paper, or into the air. Symbolically, this can be a very freeing experience. Otherwise, the thoughts are apt to continue rolling around and around in your head. Furthermore, if you write or speak out loud, you are using your body, which helps to strengthen the new messages you wish to cultivate.

Once you get good at *catching* your thoughts, *recording* them, and *recording* the challenges in a physical way, it will be easier to carry on mentally whenever the thoughts return for a surprise visit.

STEP ONE: Record your negative messages in the second person: "You are: _____

_____

_____

_____ "

STEP TWO: Challenge the voice from your own point of view, reaching inside to that place that contains your inner life force and strength. You may wish to do this in two stages, first indirectly, as if you were a benevolent adult stepping in on behalf of a child, and then directly, from your own viewpoint: _____

_____

_____

_____

Sometimes this work is so powerful that it only has to be done once to have lasting effects. Other times, it has to be repeated. After all, a voice that has lived in your mind and body for so long is not necessarily willing to leave lickety-split.

One more thing: sometimes people tell me that they feel guilty about challenging one of their parents, particularly if they now have a good relationship with that parent, or if that parent is now old and weak or has had a traumatic and difficult past. I immediately clarify that this exercise is not meant to be parent-bashing. First, it is not our parent (or grandparent, teacher, or other caretaker) that we are challenging. It is our parent's voice that we took into ourselves a long time ago. Second, it is important to remember that whatever negative message the parent might have given, this message is not necessarily reflective of the entire parent, just one aspect of the parent, at a certain time in his or her life. And it is that aspect that we are challenging. Although some parents are sadistic and mean, most parents are usually well-meaning, even loving, but because of their own unfinished business of the past, they may slip up and act out their problems on their children. We can continue to love our parents, appreciate all that they have done for us, feel compassion for their own struggles, and at the same time refuse to accept what has been toxic to our mental and emotional health.

FLAWS IN THINKING

NOT ONLY CAN your mind entertain misguided, negative thoughts about your core value as a human being, your mind is also ingenious in supporting this core view of yourself, through numerous ways of flawed thinking. The key pioneers in identifying and changing destructive thought patterns were Albert Ellis and Aaron Beck. Over the last thirty decades, therapists have continued teaching their clients how to challenge this kind of negative thinking.

Mind reading

When it comes to social anxiety, mind reading must be number one on the chart of flawed thinking. There is usually some projection involved. For example, Terry has a negative view of himself. Then he projects this view onto a stranger, as if this view were coming from that stranger. Imagine that someone yawns or appears distracted while you're talking and you automatically think, "I'm so boring," or "He knows that I'm shy and have a hard time talking." You believe you know what others are thinking. This is mind reading. But we can never be certain unless we ask the person outright what she is thinking. Next time you catch yourself mind reading, just stop. Realize that if you are a normal human being, like the rest of us mortals, you simply cannot know what others are thinking. If a person yawns while you talk, there are so many other possible explanations. Perhaps she didn't sleep last night. Perhaps she breathes shallowly and from time to time has to yawn to get an adequate amount of oxygen. If the person is distracted, maybe she has something to be distracted about. Perhaps she's still thinking about the fight she just had with her spouse. Or she is trying to remember whether she left the bean soup simmering on the stove. Mind reading can lead to unnecessary suffering.

Predicting a negative outcome

> Don't paint the devil . . . for the devil will appear.
> —A Russian saying, as told to me by my mother

Negative predictions must be number two on the chart of flawed thinking. People who are socially anxious tend to overestimate the likelihood that they will do poorly in a social situation. They also tend to overestimate the negative consequences that might follow. Telling yourself that things will turn out badly is tantamount to casting a spell on yourself. You feed your unconscious a negative message and your unconscious obeys. "Aye, aye, my captain, one poor performance coming up." If you're going to cast a spell on yourself, why not a more encouraging one? "Ah," you ask, "but can I believe the encouraging spell?" With a little work, you can learn to think more realistically and optimistically. Remember that predicting a negative future, like mind reading, is usually based on your core belief that you are somehow not worthy. We've already discovered how this basic premise is false. Let's look for some hard evidence that will challenge a negative prediction. Look to the past and discover instances where you were successful. Suzy, for instance, was afraid that no one would talk to her at the party. Then she remembered how she, in fact, had talked with an interesting man about parasailing, at the last party she had attended. With a little work, Suzy's thinking transformed from flawed and impoverished to realistic and encouraging.

As mentioned earlier, people with social anxiety also tend to overestimate the negative consequences of their predicted negative outcome. Think of a typical consequence you might predict if your voice trembled while talking to a group of people. "Oh my God, my voice is trembling. Now they know I'm anxious. They'll think I'm weird." This is where people usually stop thinking any further. The idea of being thought of as weird can be so horrible that it is enough to stop a person cold. But the trick is to go on and flesh out your thinking. Ask yourself what would happen next. "If they thought I was weird, then they'd stop talking to me." Then what? "Then I'd be all alone." Then what? "Then I'd cry." Then what? "Then I'd really make a fool of myself." Then what? "Then nobody would ever want to talk to me again." Then what? "Then I'd have to leave town." Then what? "Then I'd have to start a new life." Now it's time to ask yourself, "Would I really move from town, leave my family, and start a new life just because my voice trembled?"

Try it. Flesh out your thoughts. Too often, we don't bother tracking our thoughts to see where they might lead. If we took the trouble to do so, we'd discover that our worst-case scenario is often rather dramatic, even preposterous, at the very least, comical. We would put our imagined consequences into perspective. Hopefully, we might even laugh.

Overgeneralizing

This is another popular mind trick that feeds social anxiety. Look out for such words as "always," "never," and "everyone." As soon as you hear these words, you know there is a huge flaw in your thinking. When Kenny said to himself, "Everybody knows how to have a good time except me," he was being unrealistic. He painted himself a picture of extremes. Everyone else was totally confident. He was the only one completely at a loss. How could he not feel like an outsider? This is sometimes called black-and-white thinking. The world simply does not work this way. Realistically, some people at the social gathering will be confident; others may look confident on the outside but be shaking on the inside; still others will experience various degrees of caution and uncertainty. There are many shades of gray between the extremes of black and white.

Labeling

Watch out for noun words, especially negative ones. Such noun words might include "loser," "wimp," "failure," and "freak." Negative adjectives can also be used in labeling. These might include "stupid," "not good enough," "useless," "boring," and so on. In a way, this is a form of overgeneralizing. For instance, suppose you have just made a mistake. Then you call yourself a failure. You have just made a giant leap, concluding that because you failed at one thing, you are a total failure. This is a gross exaggeration and therefore flawed thinking. Please realize what an unkindness it is to label yourself.

When we use verbs instead of adjectives and nouns that label us, we are less likely to lose sight of our wholeness. When we tell ourselves, "I made a mistake," "I didn't know what to say," or "I tripped and felt embarrassed," we use verbs which help us keep perspective. Just because I made a mistake or I didn't know what to say doesn't mean that all of me is somehow defective. It simply means that one of the thousands of actions I performed today didn't go so well. But I'm still me, mostly sound and mostly good. Do watch out for those labels.

Focusing on the negative

Negative focus has to do with the perennial "empty glass" question. People with an optimistic view of life will usually see the glass as half-full; those with a pessimistic view will tend to see the glass as half-empty. Whichever focus you use to see the world will have a profound effect on the rest of your thoughts, feelings, and behaviors. The following is a wonderful example of how focusing on the negative can ruin your day. Ted is a socially anxious person who has also fought depression much of his adult life. One day, Ted told me about his week, starting with a report about his cat. Notice how you feel as you read Ted's rendition of the week.

> My cat was in for surgery. He had an infected paw. The whole week was terrible. I had fever, skipped my guitar lessons, skipped teaching a few classes. When I'm physically ill, it's hard to feel emotionally strong. I had gastric pains that reminded me of ulcers. I'm still chasing after the lawyer. It's taking so long for all the documents to come in.

Can you feel the heaviness and discouragement? I asked Ted if he was willing to try an experiment. I asked him if he'd describe the week again, but this time through a positive lens, as if he could only see the bright side of things. The following is his new account of the week, interspersed with a few prompts of my own.

> TED: "My kitty's okay. I'm really happy he came through the surgery. He's a lot more energetic. He came out of the chair and walked over to see me."
>
> ERIKA: "So you took your kitty for surgery; you weren't negligent of your cat. What does this say about you?"
>
> TED: "I'm taking care of things. I'm being responsible and caring."
>
> TED: "I also got a PhD student out the door. She did marvelously. She'd been trying to get her dissertation done for the last seven or eight years. This time, at her presentation, she was in command of everything. Her proposal went off better than I expected. I was happy for her."

ERIKA: "What does this say about you?"

TED: "I care about my students. I want them to do well."

ERIKA: "What else happened this week?"

TED: "I called my lawyer. That was a big load off my mind. Also, I had given some thought to how I'd talk to her about my expectations. So I'm looking out for myself. I'm clarifying expectations. I'm realizing I deserve respectful treatment. I deserve attention from someone whose services I'm hiring."

After Ted finished recounting a couple more incidents of the week, I asked him to let this story of his week really sink in. Then I asked him what he noticed. Ted said that his week felt lighter, that he felt lighter. He explained,

I realize that I'm satisfied. Even if things seem like they're falling apart, I'm still accomplishing things. Sometimes I'm afraid of burnout. But when I look at what I've just described, I realize that I am taking care of myself, taking care of things. This exercise tells me that I've been viewing the world in a depressive and negative way. It's sort of a habit I've developed. There are other ways of looking at things. This isn't particularly news to me, but it's a dramatic illustration.

Insightfully, Ted added that this habit of seeing the world negatively offered him familiarity. Also, it offered an escape from having to engage in new things. In other words, seeing life through a negative filter kept life safe and cozy, free from risk-taking. No wonder people who are afraid of social risks find it difficult to drop this habit. But what is the cost? Lack of energy? Isolation? Lack of opportunity to build confidence?

Discounting the positive

Related to negative focusing is the habit of discounting the positive. Discounting the positive means to reject good things, for one reason or another. For instance, if someone just finished giving you a compliment, you might say "Thank you," but inside, you might think, "Oh, they're just being polite. They feel sorry for me and want to make me feel better." Some people are so good at discounting the positive that they don't even notice or hear the positive comment in the first place. It's as if they are living inside a bubble that protects them from the penetration of a positive comment. The comment doesn't even register. It's as if they are tone-deaf. But rather than being deaf to musical tones, they are deaf to anything positive.

Shinichi Suzuki, founder of the popular Suzuki Method of teaching music, had an interesting viewpoint about tone deafness that illustrates my point. It was Suzuki's five- to ten-year-old Japanese violin students who moved us to tears when we watched them play Mozart and Bach on the Ed Sullivan variety show about forty years ago. Suzuki insisted that these children were not geniuses, as we westerners thought them to be. He explained that the reason they played so well was that they had been immersed in music practically since infancy. Suzuki did not believe that anyone was born tone-deaf: "On the contrary, a baby absorbs perfectly any out-of-tune pitch of its mother's lullabies. It has a marvelous ear. That's why the child will later sing in the same way."

I believe that, similarly, a child who has heard mostly negative messages has difficulty hearing positive ones. But there is hope. With awareness and practice, it is possible to train oneself to hear and absorb the positive. Suzuki managed to train so-called tone-deaf students to hear and reproduce tones perfectly. How did he do this? Through repetition. According to Suzuki,

> If they have learned the wrong fa (do, re, mi, fa) by hearing it five thousand times, one must make them listen to the right fa six thousand or seven thousand times. [Eventually] the ability to produce the correct fa acquired by listening to it six thousand times begins to take precedence over the ability to produce the wrong fa that was acquired by listening only five thousand times.

I have noticed so often in therapy that clients initially have difficulty hearing any positive comments from me. However, over time, something finally goes BING! Thankfully, it doesn't take six or seven thousand times. The lullabies you heard were not on key.

However, with repetition, you can eventually learn to hear the good stuff, let it in, and allow it to warm your soul as would any good piece of music.

Taking things personally

Have you ever been with a person who looked grumpy and you assumed that you must have done something wrong? That's taking things personally. This is a little like mind reading, but the accent is on the fact that somehow you feel responsible for having caused a person to feel badly. Perhaps the person is grumpy because she just missed winning the lotto by one number. Maybe she has a mood disorder. Maybe she just stubbed her toe. You can always ask and check things out. Don't assume that everything is your fault. As tiny children, we often assumed that the world revolved around us and that if something bad happened, it had something to do with us. As adults, we sometimes get trapped into feeling the same thing. But we need to realize that we simply don't have that much power. The truth is, we are not at the center of other people's moods.

CHALLENGING FLAWED THINKING

THINK BACK OVER the last day, week, or month. What typical automatic thoughts have you had that are negative and likely to prove flawed? Draw a vertical line through the middle of a sheet of paper; on the left side, record these thoughts. On the right side, challenge these negative thoughts with thoughts that are more realistic, compassionate, encouraging, and positive.

Here are a few examples from people in my social anxiety support groups:

FLAWED, NEGATIVE THOUGHTS	REALISTIC, ENCOURAGING, POSITIVE THOUGHTS
I won't be able to do this.	I've been able to do other things that I've set my mind to. I can do this. I just need to take one step at a time.

| They think I'm boring. | I can't be sure what they are thinking. A few of my friends have told me that they like talking to me. Possibly these people might also like to talk with me. If I think I'm boring, maybe it's time to do interesting things, so I have something to talk about. |
| I'm such a clumsy idiot. | Nonsense! I do some things very well. Either I give myself permission to not have to be perfect at this, or I find out how to improve and start practicing. Even if I am not great at this, I am still a good and wonderful person. |

Keep track of your thoughts for at least a week or two. Be patient and kind to yourself. Remember that it took a while to learn patterns of negative thinking. It will take a while to unlearn them and replace them with realistic ways of thinking.

AFFIRMATIONS

THE PRACTICE OF saying affirmations has been popular for some time. Basically, an affirmation is a positive statement, a declaration that something is fact. Affirmations, like images, send powerful messages to the body. Affirmations use the left side of the brain, the side concerned with language. Affirmations are not magical. They are simply communications to yourself—positive communications that have a positive impact.

Members in my support groups often tell each other how such positive statements make a big difference in their lives. Nora, who used to think of herself as a "scaredy-cat," hesitant to venture into anything new, started telling herself, "I can do it." That's all she said. "I can do it." Several times a day, she would remind herself, "I can do it." Before long, she reported to the group that she was doing things that she never imagined she'd be able to do. She confronted a rude relative. She went to a company picnic. She offered to drive a couple of church members home. Each time she followed through with a challenge, she collected new evidence that she could indeed "do" it. This fueled her enthusiasm to continue repeating her affirmation, "I can do it."

Designing affirmations

The best affirmations are tailor-made to fit your needs. One way to identify your needs is to look at your hopes and desires. If you want to be more outgoing, your affirmation would be something like, "I am reaching out. I take initiative. I phone my friends." If you want to feel more courage, you can say, "I am confident. Courage inspires me. I take risks."

Another way to figure out your needs is to listen to the negative messages that you tend to give yourself, and then to invent an antidote, a completely opposite message. For instance, if you say things like, "Oh, no, I'm shaking," then you need to remind yourself that you can relax. Your affirmation might be, "I am relaxed." or "I am calm." If you tend to say, "They'll think I'm weird," your affirmation might be, "They think I'm okay," or "I enjoy these people" (taking the focus off yourself). The following are sample affirmations:

FOR THE BODY
I am relaxed.
I am calm.
I am breathing calmly and evenly.
This is just adrenalin passing through my body. This will pass.
I am grounded.

FOR THE MIND AND EMOTIONS
I enjoy myself with others.
I am interested in others.
My good humor is shining through.
I have something important to say.
I have a right to my opinions.

I have a right to express my thoughts and my feelings.
I have a right to make mistakes. I learn from them.
I am a worthwhile person.
Life is an adventure, and I am a courageous
   person partaking in life.
I deserve respect.
I have unique qualities.
I accept my shyness.
There are many good qualities that accompany sensitivity.
I am flexible.
I can cope with changes.
I am delighted with surprises.
It is okay to be vulnerable.
I am human.
I belong.

For Behavior and Action

I form goals easily.
To yourself: Good morning, honey, time to get up. It's a good
   day for action.
I achieve my goals effortlessly.
I can do it.
I can figure out what needs to be done.
Sounds like a good plan.
Do it now.
It's okay to just *be*.
I deserve a rest.
One small step at a time . . .
Little by little . . .
I celebrate my successes.
Good for me!

Believability of affirmations

Some people ask, "How can I repeat something that I don't
believe?" They say that they get so distracted by how untrue the
statement feels to them that they can't repeat the affirmation with

any hope or conviction. One part of their mind is saying the positive affirmation and another part is simultaneously saying that the opposite is true. My suggestion is to start with something that feels more neutral. Go over the list above and check off the affirmations that feel either neutral or possibly true. With time, and with some social successes under your belt, some of the more daring affirmations will seem more and more believable! For guidelines on how to create effective affirmations, check Appendix V.

Tending to the mental garden

What you've probably noticed about these methods of challenging thoughts is that it's not enough to simply stop thinking these negative thoughts. What would happen if you pulled the weeds out of your garden and did nothing more? You'll have prepared the soil for yet more weeds. Instead, take the time to cultivate new plants, hearty flowers, bushes, grasses, and shrubs. As these new plants take root and flourish, there is less opportunity for the weeds to return and thrive.

KEY REFLECTION POINTS

- ➤ Thoughts and words can either encourage and embolden us or shame and inhibit us.
- ➤ Young children are like sponges absorbing whatever words come their way. If these words happen to be critical, the child develops a core belief that she is somehow flawed and the ground is set for social anxiety, the fear that one won't measure up.
- ➤ Voice therapy is an effective way of challenging negative inner messages about oneself.
- ➤ There are numerous patterns of flawed thinking that support one's negative core beliefs. These include mind reading, predicting a negative outcome, overgeneralizing, labeling, focusing on the negative, discounting the positive, and taking things personally.

➤ Once you recognize these patterns of flawed thinking, it is possible to refute them and replace them with realistic, encouraging, and compassionate thoughts.

➤ Affirmations are positive statements that nourish the mind and have a positive impact on your confidence. Keep affirmations short; word them in positive terms and in the present tense; repeat them often and with gusto (see Appendix V).

The one thing I want to remember from this chapter is:

_____

_____

I will translate this one thing into action in the following way:

_____

_____

_____

_____

ELEVEN

IF ONLY . . .

Other Mind Traps

Fraternity is born more easily on the road of error
than on that of perfection.
—MARIA MONTESSORI

JUST AS A variety of weeds can hamper the growth of
a beautiful garden, there are numerous mental processes
that can restrict the cultivation of social confidence. These
mind traps include: excessive focus on self, perfectionism,
difficulty with making mistakes, post-event autopsies, rules,
comparisons, predictability and control, the wishing trap,
misguided concepts of courage, and lack of appreciation
for the benefits of anxiety. Let us examine each in its turn.

SELF-FOCUS

IF YOU ARE like most people who experience social anxiety,
your attention during a social interaction is on yourself and
how you are coming across to other people. You worry
about how you look and what others are thinking about
you. It's natural to want to make a good impression. After

all, we are social beings who want to belong. However, when our focus on ourselves and how we are doing becomes all-consuming, we're in trouble. Our self-absorption leads to self-consciousness which, in turn, leads to feeling distracted, nervous, and not part of what is going on. Of all the mind traps, I think this is the single most dangerous one. So what is the solution?

Focus on other

Some people make "focusing on other" a practice goal. Their job is to draw others out and really focus on what the others are saying. Many state that learning to focus on other has been the most important factor in learning to be less socially anxious and more confident. If you don't have a support group and feel that asking questions of others is too big a leap at this time, there are other ways you can train yourself to focus your attention outside yourself.

The fascinated observer

Remember how thrilling it used to be going to the zoo, in the days before we appreciated animal rights? What made going to the zoo so fascinating? Wasn't it the intrigue of unfamiliar species, some of which were docile, and some of which were ferocious, even dangerous? Are we human beings any less intriguing? I don't think so! Each of us is a unique and formidable creature. Each of us has our own idiosyncratic habits. Sheila slips a strand of hair between her lips and quietly sucks on it for a moment, especially when she's concentrating on her math homework. Tom's laugh is so loud you can hear it a block away. Frieda's fuzzy red hair looks positively electric under her bright blue hat. The human zoo is full of fabulous sights, sounds, smells, and textures. It is a world of drama, comedy, and mystery. If you want to train yourself to focus your attention away from your concerns about how you look to others, there's no better place to start than in the human zoo immediately around you.

Pretend that you're a rookie detective. Notice details about other people, their clothing, physical characteristics, mannerisms, and so on. Be an objective observer. Do not judge. This is an exercise to help you develop an interest in the people around you so that you're more likely to want to focus on them even further. You may surprise yourself and find your curiosity about people growing. You may truly want to know what makes different people tick, what makes them similar or different.

Focusing on other in social interactions

Once you have developed your observational skills, it becomes much easier to begin engaging with others. Based on your observations, you can make comments, ask questions, and offer opinions. For instance, if you notice that Susan looks a little blue, you might comment, "I notice that you look a little down. Is everything okay?" Or, if that feels too personal right now, stick with the less personal. "Say, that's a lovely jacket you're wearing. I haven't seen it before. Is it new?" More tips on conversation skills will follow in the section on action. For the time being, the point is to appreciate how critical it is to move one's focus outwards, away from concerns about oneself.

Focus on purpose

Another antidote to self-focus is focus on purpose. I remember preparing to give a talk on shyness and dating at a Singles Fair. I had done my imagery work, my breathing exercises, my affirmations. I had sung loudly in the car just to loosen up further. I knew my material. I was confident and ready. "World, here I come." Suddenly without warning, as I walked by the hall where I would soon be talking to three hundred people, I was overtaken by anxiety. My heart pumped furiously and I panicked. Luckily for me, within moments, I heard my inner voice remind me, "Erika, this is *not about you*. This is about the audience in there . . . a lot of shy people are waiting to hear some useful information." That's all I needed. I barely noticed that my heart rate returned to normal. I was too busy focusing on my purpose: to share something worthwhile with an expectant audience. Know your purpose and keep it close to your heart.

PERFECTIONISM

ANOTHER COMMON MIND trap that people with social anxiety often experience is perfectionism. There's nothing wrong with striving for excellence. In fact, it is often sadly noted that many of today's products lack the craft and perfection of yesteryear. But there is something wrong with the perfectionism that enslaves a person to ideals and principles that cannot be reached. Sonya, a shy seventeen-year-old, would often hesitate as she spoke. In her words, "I'm thinking about how I can tell you what I want to tell you in perfect sentences." She was afraid that if she did not speak perfectly, she would be judged. Perfectionism is acted out in other ways. People might procrastinate. They postpone or avoid projects and activities to avoid the possibility of doing something that is "not good enough." In fact, perfectionism and procrastination are very close buddies, often traveling hand in hand. Perfectionism is the thought and procrastination is the action, or more accurately, the lack of action.

In her book *Addiction to Perfection: The Still Unravished Bride*, Marion Woodman declares, "It is easier to try to be better than you are than to *be* who you are." I say that it is often easier to strive to be perfect than to be who you really are, because to accept who you really are is to accept that you can be not only loving, but also hateful; not only generous, but also miserly; not only kind, but also mean; not only happy, but also desolate; not only bold, but also shy . . . for this is the human condition. Each of us contains opposing qualities, to some degree. Each of us is human, and that's all there is to it. The sooner we let go of perfectionism, the more human we will become. When we accept our humanness, there is no more need for constant worries about every little thing we say, do, or think. The critic and judge move out of the way to make room for spontaneity, for reality. And, as a woman in one of my groups insightfully said, "It is easier to love and feel tender toward a person who is vulnerable and imperfect than a person who is strong and perfect."

MISTAKES

IF YOU THINK that making mistakes is to be avoided at all costs, you are stuck in yet another mind trap. This trap is closely related to perfectionism; however, the stress is on avoiding mistakes rather than on achieving some idealistic standard. To some people, mistakes are enemies, telling tattletales, showing the world that they are inadequate and somehow flawed. To other people, mistakes are just mistakes. These people see mistakes as friends that teach them how to do better the next time.

I remember, when I was in high school, there was a science teacher who asked Geraldine, a mild-mannered student, to answer a question. When Geraldine gave the wrong answer, the teacher gave her what we called "the look" and vehemently spit out the words, "I have never seen such a disgusting display of intelligence!" Those words seared themselves into my brain and heart, and decades later, I still remember them, even though they were not directed at me. We all loved Geraldine and her gentle ways. Her humiliation was ours. In those long-ago days, talking back to your teacher was not an option. You can imagine how Geraldine felt about mistakes. At a physiological level, her brain would have registered that making mistakes was dangerous. It would be understandable that people with similar experiences would be reluctant to answer questions, let alone offer comments, for fear of making mistakes. Mistakes have become dangerous.

For those who have learned to associate mistakes with danger, making a turnaround and greeting mistakes as friends can be a monumental challenge. It would mean letting down one's guard, which would go against one's sense of survival. But making this transition is crucial if one is to feel at ease in life. Mistakes are a part of life. Maria Montessori reminds us, *"It is well to cultivate a friendly feeling towards error, to treat it as a companion inseparable from our lives, as something having a purpose, which it truly has."*

The purpose of mistakes is to teach us, not because we are stupid, but because we can't possibly know everything. Thomas Edison, when asked about the thousands of failures he had before he succeeded at inventing the light bulb, insisted that he did not consider his previous attempts to be failures. On the contrary, these so-called failures taught him thousands of ways of not creating a light bulb. Albert Einstein said, "Anyone who has never made a mistake has never tried anything new."

Hopefully, with time, you will learn to be grateful for your mistakes and see them as friends, teaching you something useful, surprising, creative or even lifesaving.

POST-EVENT AUTOPSIES

ANOTHER POPULAR MIND trap is that of the post-event autopsy. This occurs when we go over and over a particular, past social event with a fine-tooth comb. We filter through bits and pieces of the event, picking out the bad parts and obsessing about them, sometimes for days and even weeks. We scold ourselves, saying things like, "Why did I say this?" "Why didn't I say that?" "I should have . . ." "I shouldn't have . . ." "I could have . . ." Furthermore, we will often mind read and catastrophize other people's reactions: "They probably think I'm stupid. They don't like me. They're not going to want to talk to me again. They pity me for acting so pathetically." Clients have told me that they have wasted entire days doing postmortems on past events. There's nothing wrong with having regrets that motivate you to do better the next time. But if your postmortems only add to your steadily rising mountain of self-criticisms, then these sorts of regrets are useless, and worse, dangerous.

One antidote to this specific mind trap is asking yourself whether you would ever treat a child who has been discouraged about some event in the same way you treat yourself. Would you relentlessly nag and scold her about what she did or didn't do? Most people say, "Of course not!" And why not? Because it would shame the child. To shame the child would be to inhibit her. She'd be afraid to express herself again, for fear of further criticism. Recognize just how hard you're being on yourself when you get into the autopsy trap. Be kind to yourself. Ruthless self-criticism kills the spirit! Think of ways you would be encouraging to a child, ways you would inspire her spirit. Why treat yourself any less lovingly?

RULES

PEOPLE WHO EXPERIENCE high degrees of social anxiety often fall into the rule trap. They believe they'll feel at ease in the world once they have all the rules down pat. They believe that there is a right way to do everything, but they're not always sure what that right way is. Steve described how he would puzzle over the way he should act when hiking in the forest. He told us,

> I love hiking alone. But every time I hear people approaching from behind or in front of me, I duck into the forest and hide behind a tree until they pass by. I'm never sure at what point I should say hi to them. Is it when we're fifteen feet apart, ten feet, five feet, right in front of each other? I figure it's easier just to hide rather than look like a fool by saying hi too soon or too late.

Harold noted that he, too, often wondered about whether he was doing things the right way or not. We had just finished watching a video about negative inner voices, and he commented that he noticed his inner voice was asking him, "Is it okay for my legs to be crossed while I sit in this group, or should I uncross them while we discuss the video?"

Social conventions do exist and dictate how we should interact with each other. People who are exposed to these conventions take them for granted. Others, like the fellows mentioned above, may feel at a loss as to what is expected of them. If you also happen to feel at a loss about rules, take heart. There is no big rule book that tells us the one right way for every little thing we might do in the company of others. Basically, the main rule is to be considerate of others. That's why we say thank you, why we return people's phone calls, why we help each other with our coats, and why we call a friend to wish him a happy birthday.

Many rules are arbitrary. They change with time and they change according to the culture in which you live. Rules can range from stringent to casual to practically nonexistent, according to culture and historical period. If you want to find out what everybody is doing in your neck of the woods, you simply have to observe or ask. For instance, I recently went to Seattle to attend a conference. I was sitting at the airport waiting for the hotel shuttle bus to arrive and pick me up. When the bus arrived, a man who had been sitting nearby joined me on the bus. After the bus had dropped us off at the hotel, I told him that I thought I had noticed him give a tip to the driver. He agreed that he had done so. I further asked him what would be the normal amount expected. He replied one or two dollars. So, after the conference was over, on the return trip to the airport, I gave the bus driver two dollars. One can watch and discover what the locals are doing and take their lead. Furthermore, it wouldn't have been the end of the world if I had not given the bus driver a tip. Maybe I would have been judged as cheap, but so what? Sometimes I am cheap!

The other important thing to remember about rules, at least in middle-class North America, is that there is room for flexibility and rebellion. In contrast to the rules in such countries as Japan and Saudi Arabia, our rules are casual or nonexistent. For instance, in Japan, it is customary to keep your business card in one of your upper pockets. Why? If your business card is in your back pocket, you might sit on it. To sit on a business card that will later be offered to someone is considered offensive. In fact, when the business card is given to a business acquaintance or friend, it is graciously offered with both hands and a bowing gesture. In Western countries, business cards are exchanged much more casually, with no particular business card etiquette.

Chances are, there are no rules for many of the behaviors you're worried about. Whether your cross or uncross your legs while sitting in a group is of little concern to anybody. Mainly, if you are generally kind to people and don't do anything that offends your own sense of decency, you'll probably fit right in with everybody else.

COMPARISONS

A TROUBLESOME MIND trap is that of comparing ourselves to others and often coming up short. If this is one of your pastimes, you know how much unnecessary suffering you've put yourself through. You tell yourself, "Jim is smarter, more successful, taller than I am," or "Sheila is prettier, more confident, and more outgoing." People with social anxiety tend to magnify other people's good points and minimize their bad points. At the same time, they tend to minimize their own good points and make a big deal of their shortcomings. People in my groups have shared how they sometimes feel bitter and resentful when others seem more confident than they are. If this resentment turns into envy, then suffering mounts. Envy can poison our hearts, distract us to no end, and get in the way of constructive action.

Steven Gilligan, a psychotherapist from California and author of *Therapeutic Trances; The Cooperation Principle in Ericksonian Hypnotherapy,* told a delightful story about comparisons at one of his workshops. The story is of Queen Malika, one of the first converts to Buddhism and a contemporary of Buddha himself. One summer evening, Queen Malika and her husband were sitting out on the veranda. The king sidled up to Malika and asked, "Whom do you love the most?" Being a Buddhist, she replied, "I love myself the most." Initially, the king was taken aback. Then he said, "Come to think of it, me too, I love me the most." They were intrigued and went over to their neighbor, Buddha, and asked him what he thought. He replied, "You're on to something. . . . When you love yourself, you stop exploiting yourself, prostituting yourself. You don't have to monitor yourself, hoping that people won't judge you." In other words, you stop bending yourself out of shape in efforts to please others. Buddha went on to explain that in order to practice self-love, you must first give up the idea that you are superior. In order to do that, you must give up feeling inferior. And to do that, you must give up feeling equal. At that point, you give up comparing yourself to others altogether, and you enter into connection with others. When you're no longer concerned about being superior, inferior, or equal, you realize there's more about human beings that connects them to each other than sets them apart.

THE PREDICTABILITY AND CONTROL TRAP

We go uneasily avoiding unfamiliar activities by hiding out in routine patterns of behavior aimed at ensuring the protective approval of other people. As a result, we may feel secure but our timid lives are terribly dull. We worry so much about what might happen next that, in the interest of avoiding shock, we end up sacrificing the pleasure of surprise.
—Sheldon Kopp, *Raise Your Right Hand Against Fear: Extend the Other in Compassion*

Jake, the dentist, has no trouble talking to an audience of five hundred people because he knows exactly what he is going to say, but he trembles at the thought of talking with a single person he has just met because he has no idea what will come of their meeting. Many successful actors and actresses claim they are extremely shy in social situations where there are no scripts to go by, no prompts to rely on. Members in my groups have occasionally asked me to describe in detail what we will be doing the following week, even though I have already given out course outlines. The prospect of unpredictability is unnerving. Why is it so important to be in control and leave nothing to chance?

Generally, we take control when we want to protect ourselves from disappointment or hurt. We make hotel or camping reservations ahead of time to avoid the disappointment of seeing a "No Vacancy" sign when we reach our destination. Exercising control by planning ahead can be a healthy thing. However, exercising control by personally pinning down every single detail of an event before it happens, in anticipation of people's judgment and approval, is something else. This excessive control can rob life of its luster and excitement. There is little chance for moments that are spontaneous, delightful, and unexpected. Once you recognize that you may be one of those people who needs to be able to predict how everything is going to turn out, you can realize and appreciate that this need for control, likely a useful survival mechanism in the past, is no longer so useful. The next step is to allow yourself to take tiny risks into the unknown. Practice your grounding and see if you can rediscover a childlike delight in surprises.

THE WISHING TRAP

"IF ONLY I had a million dollars." How many times have you wished for a windfall that might lift you out of your current situation into a more promising one? If not wishing for more money, you might wish for more confidence, more friends, a better job, a bigger apartment. There's nothing wrong with wishing. It's often the first step toward the goal you seek. However, for many, wishing is the first and last step. It becomes a mind trap filled with fantasy thoughts and images that lead nowhere: "If only I weren't so scared of taking chances"; "If only I had a partner, like everybody else seems to have"; "If only I could be like Dana, who breezes through job interviews." People who find themselves stuck in "if only" fantasyland often face feelings of hopelessness and helplessness.

To move out of this particular trap, you need to do two things. First, you need to accept the reality of your situation rather than idly wishing for something else. Instead of saying, "If only," substitute, "Given this reality," More specifically, you might say, "Given the reality that I'm scared of taking chances," or "Given that I don't have a partner," or "Given that I tend to avoid or stumble through job interviews . . ." Once you've accepted whichever reality you're dealing with, the next important thing to say is "What needs to be done?" or better still, "What do I need to do?" Now, you see, wishing has become only the first step and not the final step. A world of possibilities opens up:

> If I don't know what to do next, where do I find out? Go to the library? Talk to friends? Talk to family? If I want to start taking risks, maybe I can make a plan to take one small risk and see what happens. For instance, I can take a new route to work rather than

the old familiar way. If I want to have a partner, perhaps I need to get out more, look at the community papers, and see what's going on in town. If I want to be more successful in job interviews, perhaps I can read Peter Desberg's *No More Butterflies*, or rehearse questions and answers using my tape recorder.

Options and possibilities often lead to even more options and possibilities. Instead of feeling hopeless, you'll notice that you start feeling excited. Sure, there will be twinges of apprehension along with the excitement, but that's to be expected anytime you are trying something new. And now, instead of feeling stuck in a vat of inertia, you're moving, learning, and participating in the process of life, and all because you said, *"Given this reality, what do I need to do?"*

COURAGE IS A FEARLESSNESS TRAP

ANOTHER MIND TRAP worth mentioning is the notion that we must be fearless to be courageous. It is important to realize that a courageous and confident person is not necessarily a fearless person. Nor is he or she necessarily free from all anxiety. Susan Jeffers, in her book, *Feel the Fear and Do It Anyway*, writes that no matter how much her confidence grew, she continued to feel anxious each time she tried something new. She realized this was true for nearly everyone. Sure, you will finally feel unafraid once you've mastered a particular situation. But as long as you continue to grow and put yourself into new and unfamiliar situations, you are bound to feel at least a trifle anxious while you are still getting your bearings and figuring things out. The next time you are feeling anxious in a new situation, it may help to remember that this anxiety is really just life coursing through your body. You are challenging the unknown, trading the familiar for the unfamiliar. You are being courageous.

Osho, a spiritual leader of the twentieth century, writes in his book *Courage: The Joy of Living Dangerously*, that "Life is not a mechanical process; it cannot be certain. It is an unpredictable mystery." He adds, "Readiness to remain in uncertainty is courage." He also states that the only difference between a coward (pardon the label) and a courageous person is that the coward listens to his fears, whereas the courageous person, who shares identical fears, puts them aside and goes ahead. He accepts life as an adventure.

Once you get used to the idea that fear and anxiety are a normal part of life, life becomes less fearsome and anxiety provoking. You may still be fearful and anxious about new situations, but at least you are less afraid about being afraid. Remember, being fearful or anxious does not necessarily mean that people are lacking in courage. On the contrary, people who experience social anxiety and still go through with their social encounters can be considered very brave indeed!

APPRECIATING ANXIETY

As YOU FIND your way out of these mind traps, you increase your ability to see anxiety in a new light. Instead of dreading anxiety, imagine being grateful for it. When I ask members in my groups to list the benefits of anxiety, many look at me as if I'm crazy. But after a little brainstorming, they discover a variety of ways anxiety can be beneficial:

Anxiety protects you from danger.

Your body is geared for survival. Any time you perceive danger, even unconsciously, you will become anxious. Your sympathetic nervous system is activated and your body prepares to fight or to flee.

Anxiety means you want to do well.

You wouldn't get anxious about your midterm exams unless you wanted to do well. You wouldn't fret about the dinner you're putting on tonight unless you wanted everything to go well. Anxiety is a reminder that you belong to a community and that you wish to do well in that community.

Anxiety motivates you to prepare.

If you're anxious about a math test next week, you'll skip going to the movies and stay home and study. If you're anxious about not having anything to talk about at the party you're going to, you'll make sure to watch the news and remember three interesting news stories. Anxiety is an excellent reminder that we may need to prepare for an event to reduce anxiety once the event takes place.

Anxiety helps you to focus.

As long as your anxiety isn't going overboard, it can help you concentrate on the task at hand. Musicians and performers often state that they prefer to be a little anxious rather than too calm before a performance. The anxiety gives them the edge they need to play with focus, energy, and passion.

Anxiety gives a shine to success.

If you've been anxious about how your date was going to turn out, you'll be doubly pleased when, after the date, both of you agree to see each other again. If you've been anxious about your presentation on blue lizards from Africa, you'll be all the more thrilled when your audience applauds loudly and asks you to return next year. The contrast between the joy of a successful event and the anxiety that preceded it makes success all the sweeter.

Anxiety reminds you that you're human.

Anxiety can remind you that you are a feeling human being and not an unfeeling robot. Anxiety is one of many normal emotional experiences.

Anxiety keeps you connected with others.

People who are well acquainted with anxiety can empathize with others when they feel anxious.

Anxiety can be a signal that you're sitting on something that needs to be dealt with.

Perhaps one of the most important benefits of anxiety is that it can be a valuable clue, telling us that we need to pay attention to something that is escaping our conscious awareness. We may be avoiding dealing with something or someone that arouses our anger, sadness, or fear. The energy spent in pushing away these feelings might leak out as anxiety.

Eight ways anxiety can be of value to you! Is it possible that you might consider anxiety a friend and not an enemy—not something you need to conquer but something that you need to channel, manage, and at times, even listen to? Most people in my groups are relieved as they begin to develop a new relationship with their anxiety. As they begin to appreciate the positive aspects of anxiety, they begin to accept their own anxiety. And guess what happens when you stop fighting anxiety. It doesn't fight back. It usually stays at a manageable level, ready to be at your service.

KEY REFLECTION POINTS

➤ Focusing on self during social interactions is a mind trap that increases social anxiety. The antidote is to focus on the task at hand and to focus on other.

➤ Perfectionism that drives people to measure themselves against impossible standards also feeds into social anxiety and procrastination. The antidote is self-acceptance.

➤ Seeing your mistakes as opportunities for learning will help to change your attitude toward mistakes from one of horror to one of appreciation.

➤ Post-event autopsies or dissecting past social events and dwelling on what went wrong shrinks confidence. Focus on what went right and learn from the rest.

➤ Social rules vary in strictness across cultures. In most Western cultures, simply being considerate of others will pave the way to smooth social interactions.

➤ Comparing yourself to others feeds anxiety. Don't compare.

➤ Needing to predict exactly how things will unfold in social events reflects the fear of not being able to cope otherwise. Taking small risks into unknown territory helps to develop confidence and an appreciation for the many surprises that life has to offer.

➤ Wishing for a different life and not taking steps to change your life increases anxiety. Ask yourself what needs to be done; then do it.

➤ Courage is not fearlessness. As long as you are learning and treading into new territory, there will be anxiety and fear. Many socially anxious people are extremely brave even as they feel anxious.

➤ Anxiety has numerous benefits. For instance, it helps you prepare for danger, it motivates you to do well, and it sometimes is a signal that you are sitting on a stressful emotion that needs attention.

The one thing I want to remember from this chapter is:

_____

_____

I will translate this one thing into action in the following way:

_____

_____

_____

_____

PART FOUR

THE POWER
OF ACTION

TWELVE

LET'S DO IT!

Exposure, Exposure, Exposure!

You gain strength, courage and confidence by every
experience in which you must stop and look fear in the
face . . . you must do the thing you think you cannot do.
—ELEANOR ROOSEVELT
(former first lady and once a very shy person)

WHEN YOU DARE to do what you're afraid to do,
you learn that taking action is less frightening than
anticipating taking that action. You gather evidence that
action brings success. The root of the word "succeed"
means to follow through. As we've heard many times
before, ideas are a dime a dozen. It's the following through
on an idea that makes the difference between "just a
dream" and a reality.

HIERARCHY LISTS

IN CHAPTER 9, you learned about the value of goals and
recording your goals. So you already know how important it
is to begin with small steps. As you feel more confident, you
gently move through the more difficult, challenging steps.
One way of organizing these steps is to make a hierarchy list.

This is a list of actions or situations, ordered according to the level of difficulty, starting with the easiest and moving to more challenging ones. This list can be based on time and distance, on a theme, or on separate events. Let's look at each.

Time and distance hierarchy list

This list is particularly useful for people who are hard-hit by the physical symptoms of social anxiety. Let's imagine your friend is giving a dinner party. She has invited you and a few other friends, including Terry, a person you find attractive. You feel excited at the prospect of finally having the chance to actually talk with him. However, anxious thoughts and memories squelch your excitement. You remember how paralyzed you felt the last time you and Terry were in the same business meeting. You recall how you looked away each time he glanced in your direction. The following are chronological scenes, according to a hierarchy of easiest to most challenging, building up to actually meeting Terry, face to face.

1. Getting ready for the dinner party.
2. Leaving the house to go to the party.
3. Knocking on the door of the host.
4. Giving your coat to the host and looking around to see if Terry has arrived.
5. Spotting Terry.
6. Smiling at Terry and giving direct eye contact.
7. Walking up to Terry.
8. Extending your hand and saying hello to Terry.
9. Initiating a conversation, by asking who else Terry knows at the party.

Imaginal Exposure

Remember, a key factor in gradual exposure is to approach the situation, even in imagination, in a relaxed state. First, choose one of your favorite calming methods. Once relaxed, imagine the first scene, getting ready to go to the party. Don't forget to include all the senses in your imagined scenes, so that they feel real. If you begin to get anxious, then slow down and focus on your breathing. Once you're relaxed again, imagine that first scene again. When you feel ready, move on to the second scene. Keep repeating this process, relaxing, imagining, and stopping whenever you feel anxious. If necessary, feel free to return to an earlier scene, and make sure you're calm again before you proceed to the next scene. Depending on your comfort level, you can work through just a few scenes at a time, or you can work through all the scenes, working forwards, backwards, and forwards again, as many times as you need to, regaining your sense of calmness before going on to the next scene.

Ordinarily, it is suggested that exposure sessions last at least an hour, enough time to feel the rise and fall of anxiety symptoms. When it comes to imaginal exposure, as in imaginal rehearsal, I suggest instead that you practice for as long as it takes to experience the dissipation of anxiety symptoms. For some people, this may mean a few minutes, several times a day; for others, it may mean an hour or so. In either case, practice every day and keep track of your progress.

If you find that you have a hard time getting through all the scenes, see if you can identify the stumbling blocks. Perhaps negative thoughts are distracting you. Possibly you're telling yourself, "This will never work." If you are, then take a break and do some work on clearing out those unrealistic, limiting thoughts by using the strategies described in Chapter 10, "Words that Burn."

Real-life exposure

When it comes to real-life exposure, sessions that last only minutes are usually not long enough to experience the decrease of anxiety symptoms. Prepare to set aside at least one hour, so that you can discover that anxiety symptoms will indeed abate in time. Start at the first scene, getting ready for the party. Relaxation is the main focus through all the scenes. Perhaps you've exercised earlier in the day, or you've had a hot bath with some relaxing music playing in the background. As you get dressed, you continue to practice grounding. You may repeat affirmations such as, "I am relaxed; I am confident and calm at the party."

You move on to the second scene and leave for the party. While you're driving, you focus on remaining calm. If you feel your heart starts to race at the thought of Terry, notice this sensation and use an affirmation. You might say, "This is just adrenalin passing through my body. I'm understandably excited." Now focus on your breathing or grounding. Notice the sensation of your feet on the floor, your buttocks on the seat, your back against the car seat, your hands on the steering wheel, and your breathing in and out.

Now you arrive at your friend's house and park your car. If you need more time to relax, take the time. You may wish to imagine how confident you are as you walk up the steps and knock on your friend's door. You get out of your car. You take a moment and focus outwards, noticing the smell of the flowers in the front garden. You ascend the steps, feeling the sensation of your feet as they hit the steps, one by one. You knock on the door (the third scene). So far, so good.

Now to the fourth scene. Your friend opens the door. You give her your coat and chat in front of the closet door. You take a look around and see that Terry is already there, standing by the fireplace in the living room (the fifth scene).

You notice your heart beating faster again. You remind yourself that this is simply natural excitement. You do some grounding. You make a point of staying in the living room as you continue to tell yourself that all is well. You notice a friend that you haven't seen for a while and start a conversation with her, catching up on each other's news. When your attention returns to thoughts of Terry, your heart predictably starts beating faster again. You remind yourself that this is excitement, you're fine, and everything is all right. You concentrate on your friend again, asking her a few questions. At some point, Terry passes by. You catch his eye, give him an "I welcome you" look and smile (the sixth scene). Bravo! You've made it all the way to the sixth scene.

Most experts would advise you to keep on going. It's up to you. At this point, you may decide that this has been a great triumph, and for the time being, you don't want to push yourself any further. Or you will nudge yourself just a little and actually initiate a conversation with Terry. Whatever you do, stay focused on your success. Too many people will discount their success by saying things like, "I didn't manage to talk to Terry, after all. I'm such a wimp." Nonsense! I keep reminding members in my groups that even moving ahead in baby steps is a lot faster than not moving at all. Little by little, you will achieve your goal. Keep exposing yourself to those social situations that make you nervous, and you will get to your destination eventually.

Theme-related hierarchy lists

Another way of arranging action goals is to figure out the theme of your goal. Suppose your goal is to become more comfortable with someone who attracts you. Depending on your sexual orientation, you may have to adapt the following story to suit your needs. For now, we will assume that you're a heterosexual male who becomes anxious in the presence of most women, more so in the presence of an attractive woman. And to you, attractive means someone who is a little plump, dark-skinned, and confident. You don't have your eye on a particular woman. You would like to, but the mere sight of an attractive woman sends you into retreat mode. The theme, then, is "approaching women."

Now make a list of tasks, ranked from easiest to most difficult. This gives you a hierarchy list. For example:

Practice having an open and friendly face in the presence of
     any females—young or old, big or small, dark or light.
Practice smiling at these women.
Practice saying hi to women.
Initiate a short conversation with a grandmother type, then
     an aunt type.
Smile at all kinds of women, including plump ones.
Smile at attractive plump women.
Say hi to plump women.
Say hi to attractive plump women.
Start a short conversation with one.

Start a five-minute conversation with one attractive plump
woman.

Challenge yourself with one type of exposure at a time. For
instance, for the first three days, you may focus on practicing having an open face with all kinds of women. If, by the end of three
days, you've accomplished this goal, move on to the next step; that
is, practice smiling at all kinds of women. Then the next three
days can be taken up with actually greeting all kinds of women.
Don't forget, you may be using imagery work, positive affirmations, breathing, relaxation, and grounding techniques anywhere
along the line, to help you stay calm. Each time you succeed in
accomplishing your goal, you move on to the next scene. If you
notice that you're having difficulty moving past a certain step in
the exposure hierarchy, it's time to take a break and identify stumbling blocks. Is it negative thinking, poor self-esteem, or too big a
leap to the next step? Once you have cleared out the negative
thinking, restored your self-esteem, or adjusted your goals, then
you're back on track and can proceed again. As you continue with
this method, you'll notice your confidence growing.

Hierarchy of events

Another type of exposure hierarchy is listing all the types of
social events that trigger social anxiety, ranked according to the
degree of challenge or difficulty. This is useful for those who feel
overwhelmed in more than one type of social situation. Try it.
First, list all the social situations that typically evoke social anxiety
or shyness. For instance, Karl listed the following:

Talking to the manager, Mr. Brown (9)
Talking to the supervisor, Mr. Black (8)
Reading in front of a group (7)
Playing piano in front of strangers (7)
Asking someone out for a date (10)
Talking on the telephone in someone else's presence (5)

Going out with friends to a club (5)
Accepting invitations to parties (6)

Go over the list and give each event a value according to the degree of anxiety that particular event would trigger. Give each event a value of 1 to 10, one signifying the least disturbing level of anxiety and 10 signifying the most disturbing. Reread Karl's list and notice the values he assigned to each event. Now rewrite your list according to the assigned values, beginning with the lowest value, or the least disturbing event, and moving to the highest value, the most disturbing event. Karl's new list would look like this:

1. Talking on the telephone in someone else's presence
2. Going out with friends to a club
3. Accepting invitations to parties
4. Reading in front of people I don't know
5. Playing piano in front of a group
6. Talking to the supervisor, Mr. Black
7. Talking to the manager, Mr. Brown
8. Asking someone for a date

Now you have your starting point. For example, Karl's first overall goal will be to remain calm on the telephone at work as he deals with complaints from customers, even if someone else comes into the room. His mini-goals, in the body domain, may be to practice grounding just before he gets on the phone, or to focus on his breathing every time someone else enters the room. His mini-goal in the mind domain may be to do imagery work that focuses on talking on the phone as others walk by, possibly eavesdropping. He may imagine himself remaining calm and relaxed no matter who walks in and how much attention they pay to him. He may say affirmations like, "I am totally focused on the individual on the other end of the line. Everything else is a blank. I am being of service to this client. That is all that counts right now." In the action domain, Karl's mini-goal may be to practice key sentences that he has been trained to use when dealing with complaints.

Hierarchy lists help you to figure out what action or situation you want to deal with first. Your goal charts (Appendix III) help you stay focused and motivated.

GUIDELINES FOR EXPOSURE STRATEGIES

USE THE FOLLOWING guidelines to get the most out of your exposure sessions:

Small, gradual steps; slower is faster.

No step is too small, as long as it takes you out of your comfort zone. All exposures will bring on at least mild anxiety; otherwise, they're not worth doing. If you take little steps consistently, you'll usually end up accomplishing your goal sooner than if you take too large steps which may result in overwhelming anxiety.

Stay with it until anxiety level drops.

Stay in the exposure situation until the level of your anxiety starts to drop, as it inevitably will. If you quit while your sympathetic nervous system is on full blast, with your heart racing and your breath speeding, you don't get to experience the relief of anxiety reduction. You don't have the opportunity to develop the trust that things will work out.

Exposure, exposure, exposure.

It stands to reason that the more often you repeat your exposures, the more successful you will be in learning to cope with your anxiety. Each success paves the way to further successes.

Review, revise, and celebrate.

As with goals, exposure strategies must be reviewed, evaluated, and revised. Note your progress. When successful, celebrate. When movement slows down, identify stumbling blocks, address them, learn from them. You can't lose. There is always something to celebrate. You are always learning, from your successes and your misses.

Let's move on to the road of social interaction!

KEY REFLECTION POINTS

➤ When you dare to do what you're afraid to do, you discover that taking action is less frightening than anticipating taking that action.

➤ Translating goals into action begins with small steps.

➤ Exposure means deliberately exposing yourself, in graduated steps, to the very situation that provokes anxiety.

➤ A hierarchy list based on time and distance refers to a chronological ordering of action steps. Each graduated step moves through time and comes closer and closer to the object that is feared.

➤ A hierarchy list based on theme consists of ordering action steps moving from contact with more general, less intimidating forms of the object feared (all sorts of women) to contact with the specific form (an attractive woman).

➤ A hierarchy of events orders different types of social events according to the degree of challenge (using the telephone, reading in front of people, asking someone for a date).

➤ The best way to do exposures is to practice in your imagination first, then practice in reality as often as possible, one step at a time. Stay in the situation, using all your skills related to body, mind, and action, until your anxiety level drops. Record your efforts (as in goal charts), review, revise, and celebrate.

The one thing I want to remember from this chapter is:

_____

_____

I will translate this one thing into action in the following way:

_____

_____

_____

_____

THIRTEEN

HERE I AM!

Social Interaction through Body Language

When the sun rises and shines,
not all the lotus buds
in the lakes and ponds bloom;
only those that are ready do.
The rest have to bide their time.
But all are destined to bloom,
All have to fulfill that destiny.
There is no need to despair.
—SATHIYA SAI BABA

FOR THE LONGEST time, social anxiety may have enticed you into hiding. By shrinking your body, lowering your eyes, and keeping your thoughts and your feelings to yourself, you have protected yourself from others. Like the turtle whose head disappears into its shell, you may have found ingenious ways to remain invisible and unnoticed. Jill hides her face behind long black hair. Sherry talks in a quiet monotone. Mary wears large, nondescript shirts and pants. Harry stands in the background, his hands in his pockets, his head bowed down. The only trouble is, once you're so well hidden, it's hard to get found, and the world feels like a dull and lonely place. It's time to come out of hiding and make contact with the world.

NONVERBAL COMMUNICATION

DEPENDING ON THE study cited, nonverbal communication—that is, "looks" and "sounds"—makes up anywhere from sixty-five to ninety-five percent of what we communicate to each other, especially when we first meet. Nonverbal communications include facial expression, eye contact, body posture, gestures, movements, how far we stand from each other, touching, and even qualities of language such as tone of voice and timing. Through each of these means, we constantly send and receive messages to and from each other. These messages signal varying degrees of friendliness and approachability. Let's explore various components of body language.

Facial expression

The human face is the most expressive conveyer of body language. The face is like a stage where the players, such as eyes, eyebrows, lips, teeth, and wrinkles around the eyes, all act in concert to produce displays of emotion. One recent night, as my husband and I flipped through television channels, an opera singer by the name of Cecilia Bartoli caught our attention. Her eyebrows would lift in the center, her brow furrow, her lips narrow and broaden, and then her face would do something altogether different in a matter of seconds, and then again and again and again, all in sync with the ever-changing mood of the music. The spirit that quivered, stomped, rushed, and wandered through Bartoli's face and body held us riveted. The audience went wild. They gave her standing ovations after every piece. Bartoli signaled love to all by holding her hands close to her heart and then throwing them open to the audience with a huge, welcoming smile. The audience swooned.

What about the socially anxious face? Typically, in sharp contrast to the energy flow of Bartoli's face, an anxious face may communicate inertia. One of two different processes may be involved. In the first, the socially anxious person voluntarily hides her feelings from others; her face looks as if it's lifeless. In the second process, the socially anxious person's involuntary defense mechanisms kick in so that his face actually *becomes* lifeless. Let me explain the first process with an example.

Gregory hints at some of what lies beneath his neutral, no-tales-told face as he describes his experience attending an orientation session for a Wilderness Leadership course.

> I worry that the speakers might judge me by the neutral expression on my face. Oh, if they only knew what was underneath that expression. I am so anxious about being with all these people. It feels as if there is a battle going on inside me. One side of me wants to appear normal and the other side savagely mocks me. The neutral expression on my face is my best attempt to hide what is going on inside me. Inside, I feel so much pressure, like the pressure of mounting steam in a pressure cooker, and like the clasps, which secure the lid on, my facial expression holds the pressure. The neutral expression is locked onto my face. It is unable to change, because of the high pressure. After a while, time steps in. The intensity of the battle dies down, but the damage is done. Like a dog that has lost its fight, I run to escape further injury. I decide I won't pursue this Wilderness course. I leave the meeting.

In Gregory's case, his blank expression is a tense shield that prevents anyone from discovering the intense anxiety pulsating within. Other times, blank expressions are void of all tension and all life. Over-activation in the sympathetic nervous system can trigger the parasympathetic nervous system to slow everything down to the point of apparent lifelessness. Blank expressions are the result.

Whether your blank expression is a voluntary or involuntary response to an anxiety-provoking social situation, it is a good idea to do something about it, not only for your own sake but for the sake of others. You see, one effect of a blank face that is often overlooked by the socially anxious person is the discomfort it causes in the other person. Have you ever talked with someone who gives you absolutely no clue as to what they are thinking or feeling about what you've just said? As you desperately look for some type of response, any response, and find none, what happens? If you're like most people, you'll feel uneasy. Don't forget: we're all human. We're social animals. It's in our makeup to look for signs signaling "friend" or "foe." Registering no signals, people, in their uneasiness with you, will move on.

As with work on blushing, an indirect approach will often result in the changes you're after. As you continue to work on the different aspects of social anxiety by relaxing and regulating your sympathetic nervous system, engaging in a healthy lifestyle, cultivating realistic and compassionate thinking, and actively participating in social interaction, your face will soon reflect the calm energy that courses through your body.

Using a direct approach can certainly help the process along. You can learn how to consciously improve your facial expressions and eye contact.

Open face

Somewhere between opera singer Bartoli's facial drama and Gregory's closed screen is the average human face that freely expresses whatever it needs to express. A frequent goal of many of the members in my groups has been to practice having an "open face." An open face is just what it sounds like. Rather than being closed, turned away, it is open and available. Try this experiment. First, lower your head and your eyes. Notice what you feel like. Now lift your head and your eyes. Notice the difference. Usually, when we bow our heads, we feel more introspective, more focused on ourselves and on our feelings. When we simply lift our heads, our attention is drawn up and outwards, into the world. An alertness and an excitement follow. Now add a smile. A gentle one will do. Notice the difference between smiling and not smiling. Rowland Miller, author of *Embarrassment: Poise and Peril in Everyday Life*, cites evidence that pulling back the corners of one's mouth, even by pronouncing the letter "e" will make one feel happier. If smiling is unnatural for you, you may need to practice.

David Burns, in his book *Intimate Connections,* tells how he spent hours in front of the mirror practicing how to smile. One thing that might help is to smile from the inside out. If you're simply plastering a smile onto your face, it will feel and look phony. See if you can look at yourself in the mirror with a twinkle in your eye and tell yourself that you're not half bad looking, that you are good enough for the friends you hang out with. Joke with yourself a little; dare to make fun of yourself. If smiling is still difficult, don't fret. See if you can think "soft." Soften your brow, your cheeks, your chin, your mouth. Add eye contact and voilà, you have an open face.

Rebecca, an office worker and former member in one of my groups, could not wait to tell us what happened when she had practiced her "open face" the previous week.

> I couldn't believe it! Usually when I come into the office in the morning, I just silently and quickly go to my desk without ever looking at anybody. This week, I made sure that when I came into the office, I looked at people with an open face. All kinds of people said hi to me. I couldn't get over it. I had always thought they didn't care, that they were snobs.

The excitement in Rebecca's voice was contagious. An open face can be the gateway to many a wonderful human connection.

The power of eyes

An eye can threaten like a loaded and leveled gun, or can insult like hissing or kicking; or, in its altered mood, by beams of kindness, it can make the heart dance with joy.
—Ralph Waldo Emerson

Eyes have long had the reputation of being able to arouse or intimidate. Is it any wonder that a hallmark of social anxiety is avoidance of eye contact? Psychiatrist John Marshall states that the common thread running through the stories of his socially anxious patients is concern about the "human gaze." Marshall states, "Acute concern as to how to react to the gaze of others as well as how to control one's own eyes—where and when to look and for how long—lies at the heart of social phobia."

If you have trouble making eye contact and think that there is something wrong with you, please realize that even creatures of the animal kingdom can feel intimidated by the power of eyes. Certain butterflies have false eyespots on their wings which, when flashed at the right moment, produce alarm in predators. Similarly, the scales on the flanks of certain sea fish are amazingly designed to look like huge eyes to help keep the bigger fish away. In a village in India, where Bengal tigers had successfully attacked folks from behind, someone came up with an ingenious idea that scared off a good number of these striped man-eaters: villagers began wearing masks with huge eyes on the back of their heads. Recently, a friend told me that construction workers, working in isolated forest areas in Canada, have taken to painting large eyes on the backs of their construction helmets to ward off cougars.

In many species, eye contact is used to threaten other members of the same species. By studying eye behaviors between animals, researchers have been able to accurately assess each animal's status in the social hierarchy of its group. For instance, a head honcho chimpanzee may gaze steadily at an underling chimp as it approaches him. The lower-status animal usually lowers its gaze and bares its teeth in a sheepish grin, to appease the alpha male, who finally looks away.

Common expressions such as "if looks could kill" and "don't give me that dirty look," reveal our recognition of the power of eyes in the human realm. In his book, the *Tyranny of Malice* (p. 37), author Dr. Joseph H. Berke writes that in the 1800s, Roman Catholics were convinced that Pope Leo XIII's evil eye was the cause of death of numerous cardinals. Eastern European immigrants after World War II made sure to include garlic cloves among their meager material possessions, to ward off the evil eye and any other harbingers of bad fortune. Nowadays, the golden tiger's tooth, often worn as an amulet on a necklace, serves as protection against the evil eye.

Read how Sarah describes how she has been intimidated by eyes much of her life:

> Three months ago I quit my job as a teacher. I was so self-conscious in front of my students. All I could see was thirty pairs of eyes watching me, judging me. It was the same at home, while

I was growing up. I felt like I was living in a fishbowl. My parents were always watching me. I couldn't make a single move without a critical comment from them. If I was playing in the back yard, I'd catch sight of their eyes watching me through the venetian blinds. It was important to be perfect. I won everything at school. I was a straight-A student. I was first in athletics. Yet I felt like I could never do enough. They were always watching me. Eventually, I lost my appetite for competition. I just wanted to be me. But still, I felt watched.

—SARAH, thirty-four years old

Improving eye contact

A number of years ago, when Betty, a woman in one of my groups, mentioned that she had difficulty looking people in the eye, and she wanted to do something about it, Michael, another group member, shared how he had learned to look at people directly. He said simply, "I welcome people in." Then he explained.

If I'm walking down the street, for instance, and I see someone, I silently say inside my head, "I welcome you." I find my face softens and my spirit lifts. I do this all in the space of a second or two. That's all it takes. If the other person looks back in a friendly way, I feel good.

Beautiful! I thought. Here I had been teaching people to steel themselves against the fear of looking into others' eyes by slowly getting used to looking, first at different parts of the face, then closer and closer to the eyes. But in doing this, the power still lay outside of oneself, in those other people's eyes. By using those three little words, "I welcome you," the power shifts to the inside, to one's very heart. People in my subsequent groups, inspired by the story of Michael, practiced silently welcoming people as they met their eyes. They reported feeling comfortable doing so and remarked on how friendly people seemed in return. I must make an important point here. It is not necessary to welcome into your heart every single body that passes you. Sometimes we're in a rush, have our mind on something else, or just plain don't want to get close to certain people.

One day, John, a gentle, grey-haired man in a recent group, reported that he was eager to share what had happened to him the previous week. This is the story he told:

> I've been going to this particular dry cleaner twice a week for the past ten years. I go in on Mondays to drop off my clothes and I come back on Thursdays to pick them up. About three years ago, the store changed hands. I've been dealing with the new husband-and-wife team ever since. This Monday, as I opened the door and stood on the top step, I deliberately took my time and looked over to the husband and wife, caught the husband's eye and silently said to him, "I welcome you." As I signed my bill, I stopped for a moment to say, "You know, I've been signing my name here for three years. You know that my name is John, but I don't know your names." Right away, the husband said, "My name is Parmjit." And I pointed to his wife and said, "I don't know your name, either." She smiled and softly said, "Prab." I thanked them, took my clothes, started heading out, up the stairs. Just as I reached for the door knob, I could hear Parmjit and Prab sing out in unison, "Good-bye, John." I found myself smiling back and saying, "Good-bye," in return.

John continued his story as we listened intently:

> I realized, as I walked out the door, that I had just had a spiritual experience, a connecting of the hearts. It felt good. But I also started thinking that if one started using some of these things, like saying, "I welcome you," as just another technique, then the spiritual element would be lost. That could be dangerous.

Thank you, John, articulate, insightful John. Indeed, it is critical that none of the suggestions offered here or in any book becomes just another "technique," another trick in a bag of tricks. Unless you can find a place in your heart where, for instance, the words,

"I welcome you," feel genuine, these practices will lead only to surface changes, which don't last long. They are not good for the spirit. On the other hand, if you can remember that people are just human beings who all want to belong and be appreciated, it might not be too far a leap to send them a gentle welcome signal.

More on eye contact practices

So far we've explored eye contact mostly as it relates to the beginning stages of a social interaction. What about eye contact during a social interaction? Psychiatrist John Marshall cites a study of two-party conversations that suggests partners typically give each other eye contact between thirty and sixty percent of the time while they talk. The length of these glances is anywhere from one to seven seconds.

Apart from the length of each glance, there is also a rhythmic, my-turn—your-turn flow between the glances. As a person begins to speak, he usually makes eye contact, then looks away to signal that he will keep on speaking. As he finishes his part, he looks back to the listener and signals that he is done by pausing and perhaps smiling. Now the listener, who has been doing most of the looking, either directly at the speaker or in his general direction, picks up the conversational ball by looking away. If what she is talking about is long, she checks in with her partner, gives him eye contact to make sure he's still listening, to get clues as to her partner's reactions, and to see if it's still okay to carry on talking. Once she's done, she looks back at her partner, pauses, and in so doing, signals that it's her partner's turn to talk. These back-and-forth signals are usually unconscious. If you try to replicate them deliberately, it will feel awkward. What is important to remember is that eye contact does not consist of prolonged gazes. Prolonged eye contact is usually reserved for displays of intimidation or of love and concern. In normal social interactions, eye contact consists of repetitive glances only one or two seconds in length, interspersed with periods of looking away.

The above descriptions of social interactions relate to North American practices. If you are traveling to other countries, it would be wise to find out what the rules for eye contact are in those countries. For example, in North America, direct eye contact with a person of greater status often makes a good impression. It shows that you are confident and are to be taken seriously. In certain Eastern cultures, however, it would be a sign of disrespect for a young person to make a lot of eye contact with an older person or a person of authority.

If making eye contact has been difficult for you, now is the time to add eye contact to your goal list. You may wish to begin by practicing looking at yourself in the mirror. Notice the different messages your eyes can give, depending on how you change the muscles around your eyes. Notice how the message changes when you add a smile that increases the crinkles around your eyes. See how long you can maintain eye contact with yourself. Start with a moment. Then add another moment. Take the silent "I welcome you" approach with yourself. You may wish to practice the silent "I welcome you" approach with strangers and acquaintances that you pass in the hallway or on the street. And don't forget. As you continue to work on the other aspects of social anxiety and social confidence, you will find that your eye contact will improve spontaneously.

Smells

Although smell is not ordinarily included in body language literature, I would like to include it; first, because it is an aspect of how we present ourselves to the world, and second, it is an aspect that can speak very loudly to others. Ordinarily people don't go out of their way to sniff each other like dogs do. But without even trying, they pick up smells, which range from appealing to repugnant. It may be true that when Napoleon Bonaparte wrote to his Josephine that he would soon be home, he also told her not to wash so that he might be aroused by the aphrodisiac of her natural smells. However, in our day and in our culture, a culture privileged with the luxury of soap, it is usually agreed that "fresh and clean" is preferable, and everything else is second choice. Basic grooming and hygiene is all that is required.

In the tango community I dance with, several women have confided that they avoid dancing with a certain male because it is obvious he has not bothered to shower before coming to the dance. He smells stale and unpleasant. Also beware of the extra splashes of perfume or cologne. Today, with all the health information about allergies to perfumes, a lot of people either choose to forgo perfume and colognes altogether or apply them lightly, so as to leave only a subtle fragrance.

Clothing

What you wear is a form of self-expression. Your clothing communicates to the world who you are. Even Buddhists, devoted to simplicity and the good of all, express themselves through their simple, earth-red clothing. Your outward appearance makes a statement to others about how you feel about yourself. Socially anxious people who fret about not being attractive enough tend to either have a hopeless, "who cares anyway" attitude or tend to fuss and be excessively concerned about appearances. Naturally, your budget will influence how you dress. Also, your spiritual values will influence your wardrobe. Less concern about clothing may be considered virtuous.

My advice is aimed at those who have hidden behind their clothes and now wish to make themselves more visible and even more attractive. It is important that you feel good in whatever you wear, whether it be professional or casual, simple or elaborate, dark or light, tailored or flowing, flowery or plain, wild or conservative. If you've spent much of your life hiding in nondescript clothes that make you invisible, or in expensive designer clothing to compensate for any feelings of inadequacy, see if you can do something different. Experiment. The idea is to come out and be the real you. If you've been unnoticeable, try a little color, a little flair and dare, a new style. Consult a fashion specialist. Take a friend whose taste you admire and go shopping. Buy clothes that accentuate your best features. If you've been hiding in fashion, go more natural, with less makeup. Come out, come out, whoever you are.

Body posture

More important than what you wear is how you carry your body underneath what you wear. Next to facial expression, body posture makes the loudest statement about who you are, about your approachability and confidence. When socially anxious, we often draw into ourselves, in a self-protective position. We tuck in our heads, raise or hunch our shoulders, cross our arms or legs. When your body shrinks, what message do other people receive? "Stay clear, I'm too vulnerable to handle. I'm frightened. Go away, I'm small and insignificant, not worth bothering about." Not exactly inviting, is it? Perhaps even more importantly, what message does this body posture give to your own body? Try this experiment. Coil into as small a ball as you can. Bow your head; hold onto yourself; lift your knees toward your head. Notice what this feels like. Take your time.

Now try the opposite. Stretch out, in every direction possible. Stand tall. Hold your head high. Expand your chest. Extend your arms. Reach up and out with your hands. Spread your feet apart a little. Take your time and notice what this feels like.

In which position do you feel more ready to take on the world? For most people, of course, the second posture feels a lot stronger. Isn't it interesting how your body posture not only talks to others but also talks to you? This may be a good time to add body posture to your goal list. From now on, pay attention to how you hold your body.

Social space

Social space is that space occupied by each individual in any social interaction. Sometimes this space is shared equally, sometimes not. I remember working with a couple whose use of space was dramatically different from each other. The husband sat squarely in his chair, with his legs apart, his chest thrust forward, and his arms gesturing in large movements. His voice boomed as he bombarded me with his concerns about the relationship. The wife sat quietly on the edge of her chair, in a submissive pose with her head bowed and her eyes lowered. She whispered that she often felt insignificant because of the way her husband treated her. My first comment to the husband was, "You seem to take up a lot of space." I told the wife, "You seem to take up very little space."

Ideally, our use of social space is flexible. Typically, the socially anxious person takes only a little. In the first couple of groups I ran, one of the things that struck me was how group members typically made their entries and exits at the beginning and end of the evening. They drifted in quietly, like vapor, and drifted out quietly, like vapor. There was little or no eye contact and barely a sound. Linda, a co-member of one group, who happened to be an American in Canada, also noted this quiet ritual of entry and exit and remarked that when she went to American conferences, people often introduced themselves to each other and usually tagged themselves with some comment about where they came from and so on. From then on, I have encouraged people to take up space when they enter our meeting room and when they leave, by making eye contact and saying hello and good-bye. My acknowledging the tendency to enter and exit like vapor has brought smiles and relief to many group members, who immediately take on the challenge of becoming more visible. At the end of their first session they will say, "Good-bye, all," and "See you next week," and they continue to do so for the duration of the group. Many of these people decide to make it a daily practice to take up space at work by being more vocal with hellos and good-byes.

Another aspect of social space is the physical distance between people during social interactions. Anthropologist Edward T. Hall found four typical distances used in face-to-face contact. In North America, they are

INTIMATE DISTANCE:
from no distance at all because of touching, to about eighteen inches away. Lovers, people dating, very close friends, and family members usually feel comfortable within this distance from each other.

PERSONAL DISTANCE:
from eighteen inches to four feet. This is the zone in which people who feel comfortable with each other interact.

SOCIAL DISTANCE:
from four feet to twelve feet. This distance is usually reserved for people who work together and for people involved in business transactions.

PUBLIC DISTANCE:
twelve feet and more. This is the distance that strangers usually keep from each other. It is understood that the space in between can serve as a barrier to involvement.

Cultural differences will influence the degree of distance in social interactions. For instance, Latin Americans, Mexicans, and Southern Europeans usually prefer closer distances than do North Americans. People will move in and out of these distance zones depending on their ethnic backgrounds, their sense of personal safety, their sense of confidence, and their interest in closing or widening the gap between themselves and certain people. If you have tended to keep more space between yourself and other people out of a sense of insecurity, you may wish to experiment with the use of social space. Move in a little closer, a little farther, and notice what difference it makes to your relationship with others, what difference it makes to your sense of comfort with others. Claiming your rightful space in this world is a powerful communication to others. It signals that you're ready to make connection with others.

The handshake

Your handshake also communicates a lot about you, about your approachability, about your confidence. In our culture, when people meet for the first time or meet after not having seen each other for a long time, greetings usually take the form of a handshake, or if the people involved are very close, hugs. Men almost always shake hands and women may or may not shake hands, depending on the local custom. It is thought that the handshake originated in Roman times. It was used to reassure the other party that intentions were friendly, a man would show his open hand to prove that he held no weapon, then would extend it to grasp the other party's hand, reinforcing friendly intentions and pledging an absence of hostility.

In one of the warm-up exercises that I give my groups, my first instruction is to introduce themselves to each other while shaking hands very gently or passively. I ask people to notice what they feel inside themselves during this type of handshake. Once this first round is accomplished, I ask people to introduce themselves again, this time with a lot of energy, aggressively, like a bull in a china shop. Again, they are to notice how they feel inside. Finally, I ask the group members to introduce themselves one last time, this time shaking hands firmly, in a matter-of-fact way, and with welcoming energy, or put another way, assertively. Again they notice how they feel about themselves and about the other person, during this type of handshake. In the discussion that follows, without fail, people report that they felt most connected to each other during the final, assertive handshake. If they shook hands too limply, they felt like they didn't matter. If they shook hands too forcefully, they felt like the other person didn't matter. But in the firm and friendly handshake, both people mattered. It was easier to make eye contact. It was easier to feel connected.

Again, I hasten to add that these descriptions of handshakes are set in mainstream North American culture. I was informed by a First Nations' person that generally speaking, aboriginals in this country often consider firm handshakes barbaric, just as most other people might consider aggressive handshakes coarse and inconsiderate. Certain Asian cultures may also be negatively impressed by firm handshakes. If you live in a culture that welcomes handshakes, I heartily recommend that you include handshakes in your repertoire of body language.

Gestures

Physical gestures are another aspect of body language. Certain cultures encourage generous use of hand and arm gestures to add visual flourishes and dramatic effect to conversations. Other cultures prefer minimal use of gestures. There are also nervous gestures that flow out of anxious feelings. Fidgeting with your hair, face, clothing, or with articles close at hand tells others that you are not at ease. Nervous gestures during presentations are particularly distracting.

Voice

The quality of your voice often communicates more to your audience than what you're actually saying. The smooth and steady voice that has varying intonations is easy to listen to and often signals friendliness. A loud, gruff voice can be jarring. A too-soft, whispering voice can be annoying, because people may have difficulty hearing you. If you mumble your words, people may have difficulty understanding you. When I was a teenager, my mother used to complain about my mumbling. So I used to practice saying the alphabet out loud, in front of the mirror, pronouncing each letter clearly, exaggerating the movements of my lips to get the distinct sounds I wanted. It worked. My mother stopped complaining and I enjoyed the fact that people weren't always asking me to repeat myself. How you use your voice can tell people "Come here" or "Go away"; "I'm interested" or "I'm not interested." Notice how you use your voice and decide whether voice work might be something that you want to add to your goal list.

This chapter has focused on making our presence known in the world. It has been about shedding the cloak of invisibility and telling the world through body language, "Here I am," ready and willing to engage. Let us move on to engaging through verbal communication.

KEY REFLECTION POINTS

➤ To avoid the anxiety of engaging socially, people often hide through a variety of ingenious methods. They may hide behind nondescript clothing, long hair, a shrunken posture, or a too-quiet voice.

➤ Practicing an "open face" helps others feel at ease and increases your own sense of comfort.

➤ Across human cultures and animal species, eye contact can either threaten or welcome.

➤ Silently saying, "I welcome you," when you meet the eyes of others can help improve eye contact.

➤ How you smell, use your voice, dress, hold your posture, and keep your distance from others are all important aspects of body language that tell others whether you are approachable.

➤ Reaching out to others through body language sets the ground for making contact through verbal language.

The one thing I want to remember from this chapter is:

_____

_____

I will translate this one thing into action in the following way:

_____

_____

_____

_____

FOURTEEN

HI!

Reaching Out through Verbal Communication

No amount of philosophizing, no amount of encouragement from someone else could substitute for that existen-
tial moment of taking the initiative....
—M. BLAINE SMITH

IN JACK CANFIELD and Mark Victor Hansen's first
Chicken Soup for the Soul book, Alan Cohen, motivational
speaker and author, (Web site: www.alancohen.com) tells
the story of his crush on an attractive girl who worked in a
pet store. He learned that her birthday was approaching
and decided to ask her out. After staring at the phone for
half an hour, he finally dialed her number. Caught in the
middle of excitement and dread, he hung up the phone just
before it started to ring. When he did finally drum up the
courage to ask her out, she thanked him but said she had
other plans. Crushed, he was ready to give up but something inside him urged him to try again. He found a lovely
birthday card in which he wrote a poetic note. As he walked
toward the pet store, his fear that she might reject him again
took over. He made himself a deal. He decided that if she
showed him some sign of interest, he would give her the

card, but if she didn't, he'd keep it under his shirt. No sign came. With disappointment, he headed for the door. Again, an inner voice encouraged him to seize the opportunity. "What's the worst that could happen?" he asked himself. At that fateful moment of decision, he felt a surge of courage shoot through him. As he handed the girl his card, he felt an "incredible aliveness and excitement—plus fear." But alas, the girl simply thanked him and put the card aside without even opening it. Feeling totally rejected and dejected, he left the store. Then something unexpected happened. A huge swell of exhilaration and satisfaction washed over his entire being. This feeling deepened to a warm bliss. Cohen realized something important: by daring to follow through with his need to express his inner self to this girl, he was, first and foremost, deepening his relationship with himself. It mattered less whether the girl was interested in his gift of self-expression. This life-changing experience taught Cohen, "It is not about what comes back; it is about what goes out!"

I love this story. I tell this story to my group members to illustrate the value of taking initiative and expressing one's self.

INITIATIVE, INITIATIVE, INITIATIVE

Iꜰ ʏᴏᴜ ᴡᴇʀᴇ attending my group, you'd hear me repeat, like a broken record, "Initiative, initiative, initiative." When socially anxious, we tend to hang back, be passive, adopt a wait-and-see attitude. Opportunities come and go before we've had a chance to get ourselves in gear and take advantage of them. Intrigued by the idea of exercising their initiative muscles, many group members include initiative practice in their weekly goals. For example, Mary will practice being the first to say hi to her coworkers when she arrives at work rather than wait to respond to their greetings. Dirk will initiate a short conversation with at least three people this week. Bob will plan a family function at home rather than wait for his wife to do so. I cannot stress enough the importance of taking initiative as you launch into making connections with others through verbal communication. Make sure it's on your goal list.

DEAD-END VERSUS FLOWING CONVERSATIONS

ALL OF US have experienced conversations that never really take off, let alone keep on going. Sometimes that's just the way it is. People who are shy or who experience social anxiety often feel it's their fault. For some reason they believe that the responsibility of keeping the conversation going rests solely on them. Consequently, the prospect of entering into a conversation brings on anxiety. It's important to realize that the other person is just as responsible as you for carrying on the conversation. What do you notice in the following two conversations?

MARY: Do you live near here?
DRAKE: No.
MARY: What did you think of the concert?
DRAKE: Not much.
MARY: See ya!

MARY: Do you live near here?
GERRY: Actually I live pretty close, near Kitsilano Beach, by Elsie's Bakery.
MARY: Kitsilano Beach! I haven't been there for ages. I used to go there all the time with my friends when I was a teen. Do they still have that train engine sitting out in front of the tennis courts?
GERRY: Oh, that train's long gone, but they still have the tennis courts. Do you play tennis?

The first conversation is like a car without fuel. No gas, no go! By contrast, the second conversation is fueled with two major ingredients. Manuel Smith, in his book, *When I Say No, I Feel Guilty*, calls these ingredients "free information" and "follow-up."

Free information

Free information is information given freely, without being specifically requested. In the above conversations, you can see that

Drake gave nothing extra, whereas Gerry volunteered three bits of information: that he lived close by, near Kitsilano Beach, by Elsie's Bakery. In the first conversation Mary had nothing to go on and had to think of a new question, which also went nowhere. In the second conversation, she was given several options. It so happened that Mary knew about Kitsilano Beach and the conversation was up and running. Even if Mary didn't know anything about Kitsilano Beach, she now had a launching pad from which she could ask questions related to Kitsilano, to beaches, to beach activities, to bakeries, and so on.

Follow-up

Mary did a great job of following up on Gerry's volunteered information. She was *actively listening* by asking questions to get further details about the topic at hand. She also volunteered her own bits of free information, which gave Gerry the opportunity to follow up with questions of his own. You can imagine how the conversation could have sailed on.

Other follow-up, or active listening, skills include *paraphrasing* or summarizing what the other person has said. For example, "So you think that Kitsilano is developing too fast." *Open-ended questions,* which typically begin with the words "how," "why," and "what," help extend conversations. For example, "What kinds of activities are you interested in when you're not at the beach?" Closed-ended questions, which usually begin with the words *"do," "are," "who," "when," "where,"* and *"which,"* usually elicit responses of only one or two words. Luckily for Mary, even though she began by asking a closed-ended question in the conversation, Gerry's free information made it easy for Mary to continue with more questions. Asking questions for clarification and for information also helps the conversation along.

Some socially anxious people have difficulty listening well because they are distracted by their own inner dialogues, rehearsing what to say next, or wondering what people are thinking of them. Other socially anxious people tend to be good listeners. In fact, some confess that they make sure they listen well so that the other person remains the focus of attention. In either case, giving free information and following up on such information will go a long way toward improving the back and forth of a conversation. You might like to add either or both of these skills to your goal list.

Body language further communicates to your partner that you are actively listening. Eye contact, occasional nods, facial expressions, tilt of the head, and moving in closer all show interest and help keep the conversation going. Naturally, if you're not interested, your body will signal non-interest, for instance by looking away at other things and other people, keeping your head still, turning or moving away slightly, and so on.

LEVELS OF PROGRESSION IN CONVERSATION

SOME PEOPLE WITH social anxiety report they have difficulty with small talk and prefer talking about the meaningful things in life. Others say they have difficulty having intimate conversations; consequently, friendships remain superficial. Let's look at the different levels of conversation. Remember, this is not a prescription for how a conversation should progress; it is merely a description of the typical progression of a conversation. Sometimes conversations don't progress beyond level one or two, and they can still be delightful social interchanges that nourish the heart. Sometimes conversations start at a deeply intimate level because of the context of the situation. Often conversations skip back and forth between different levels. Each of the six levels of conversation has its own rewards.

Level one: The start of a conversation

If you are among strangers at the grocery store, in a lineup, or at a show, a typical conversation starter is to comment on the immediate surroundings. "Aren't these tomatoes gorgeous and cheap!" "Wow, it's crowded here tonight! Is it crowded like this every night?" "Do you know it's started snowing already?"

Giving a compliment can also be a good opener. "I really like that tie you're wearing. I'd love to get one like that for my husband." "Mmmm, that's a lovely fragrance you're wearing. Do you mind telling me what it is?" Women usually find it easier to give compliments than men do. Men and women would do well to practice the art of acknowledging positively whatever it is that catches their fancy. It helps conversations along. It helps relationships along. I have one caution about compliments: Don't give compliments just because it's a nice to thing to do. Giving genuine compliments keeps you honest. The connection with the other person feels more honest.

How you receive a compliment can also influence the flow of a conversation. People whose self-esteem is low often feel awkward when they receive a compliment. They don't like being the focus of attention; they don't trust that the person genuinely means the compliment; they fear that the person would never give them such a compliment if they knew the "real me"; or they worry that they won't come across as modest enough if they go along with the compliment. They end up downplaying the compliment by saying things like, "Oh, this old thing; I bought it at a garage sale." It is far better to say a simple "Thank you." Confident people might even say, "Thank you, I like it, too."

Level two: Safe personal starters

If you're at an event where you face the possibility of a longer conversation, self-introduction, ritual questions, and requests for information are good starters. As you extend your hand for a handshake, you might say, "Hi, my name is Fran. What's yours?" "How are you enjoying the show?" "How are you connected to the host of this party?" "What did you think about the class?" "What do you do when you're not attending conferences?" These are considered common questions people ask of each other when they first meet. If, in the process of asking these questions, you find out your conversational partner is interested in something that you know little or nothing about, you have an excellent opportunity to ask questions that are requests for more information. People often feel complimented when someone shows interest in what they have to say.

Level three: Common interests

In the course of conversation, you may discover that you have common interests. Make sure to give free information about yourself in respect to the common interest. Follow up on the other person's stories. When you share your thoughts, feelings, and opinions about these interests and stories, you reveal more of who you are to the other person, and the conversation deepens.

Level four: Personal history

Moving along the continuum of intimacy, asking people questions about their family ties, their background, and their personal aspirations, and sharing details about your own life opens up possibilities of a more personal nature. "Do you have family nearby?" "What's it like to have family so far away?" "I wish mine were closer" (or "farther" as the case may be). Sharing not only facts, but also feelings and thoughts, about these facts reveals more and more about who you are. For the socially anxious person, the prospect of revealing oneself can be a frightening one. We'll discuss this further under the topic of self-disclosure. For now, let's just say that sharing who you really are, warts and all, can be a freeing experience, and a necessary experience if you are interested in really making connection with others.

Level five: Sharing feelings about the other

Philosopher Martin Buber said that the one thing that distinguishes humans from animals is the ability to have an "I—thou" relationship with another person. Animals have an "I—it" relationship with others. Let me explain. Suppose a cat were to watch you, listen to you, and even be petted by you. It has its experience of you and keeps its experience to itself. It doesn't have the capacity to describe to you its experience of you. It walks away. You remain an "it" to the cat. Now suppose I were to look at you, talk and listen to you, even be moved by something you have said; I will have an experience of you. I then have the option of keeping this experience to myself or sharing it with you. If I share it with you, I may say things like, "Gerry, you strike me as a very adventurous fellow. Your enthusiasm is contagious. I'm so glad we talked. You've inspired me to phone the YMCA tomorrow and ask about kayaking trips. I'd love to talk with you again." I've just told you how I feel being with you, the effect you have on me, my sense of you. You have become a "thou," not just an "it." As you listen to me describe my sense of you, more likely than not, something will stir in you—something warm and touching. This is connection. Unfortunately, many people, even married couples, continually pass each other, like proverbial ships sailing in the night, not telling each other their experience of the other. If you're interested in cultivating more intimate relationships, practicing "I—thou" statements is a definite must. By the way, "I—thou" statements are not necessarily always positive and cheery. I may tell a friend, "Erin, when you give me the silent treatment, I feel helpless, hurt, and angry all at the same time. I miss you when you distance yourself from me." Sharing my innermost feelings about Erin with Erin, rather than keeping them to myself, is being intimate. It opens possibility for further discussion, for sorting things out, for learning from each other, and for growing even closer to one another.

Level six: Ending conversations

It's not unusual to feel a little awkward about conversational endings. Sooner or later, a topic of conversation will have run its course and a gap or lull occurs. Either people try to bring up a new topic. "Have you any plans for vacation this year?" or "Wasn't last night's football game outstanding?" or people simply tell the other person they must be moving along. "Thanks for the interesting information. I see a friend over there who I need to catch up with. See you later." Or, "It's been nice chatting with you. I'm feeling really thirsty. I think I'll go see what's happening in the kitchen." Or, "I hate to run, but I've got a train to catch." Don't forget. If you're at all interested in seeing this person again, take the initiative. If you discovered that you have a common interest, you might suggest getting together to pursue that interest. If you've really enjoyed the conversation, say something like, "I've enjoyed talking with you. Perhaps we can talk again some time." You might offer the person your business card or your phone number and invite her to give you a call to get together over coffee or tea some time. This tells the person you're interested but also gives her the option not to follow through if she's busy, or not quite as interested. Again, if you haven't enjoyed talking with the person, don't fake it.

FEAR OF SELF-DISCLOSURE

SOME PEOPLE HAVE no difficulty whatsoever telling others all about themselves. Others find the prospect of such self-disclosure intimidating and even dreadful. This is perfectly understandable. If your parents delighted in you and showed interest in you, naturally you'd find it easy telling people who you are, confident that someone will be happy to know you. If, on the other hand, your parents, caretakers, or other important people in your life did not accept and welcome you wholeheartedly, you may prefer to lay low and hide your real self in order to not run the risk of feeling rejected again. Not only would you not share your real thoughts, feelings, and opinions, you may have even lost touch with what they are. If this is your situation, it is critical that you take action to get back in touch with yourself. Keeping a daily journal of whatever thoughts, feelings, and opinions you happen to notice will heighten your awareness of these inner parts of you. Remember, whatever your thoughts, feelings, and opinions are, and however you judge them, they are no different from what others have had, at some time in their lives. It's part of being human. What we think is very personal often turns out to be universal.

Frank, an older chap in one of my groups, reported to us a

discovery that he said had helped liberate him from his fear of self-disclosure. He had been going to seniors' dances for the last few years. He had no trouble asking women to dance but had an awful time having conversations that lasted longer than a few minutes. His goal for the week was to take a risk and disclose more about his real self. This is what happened.

> I sat down with two women and we started chatting about the music. Then we talked about other group functions that we attended. Suddenly I went for it. I told them that I was coming to this group because I was shy. I told them I wanted to learn how to be more confident in my conversations with people. Well, they both started telling me how they, too, felt shy in certain situations. The conversation went on for quite a while. We laughed. I felt so relieved. I felt like I belonged.

How much to disclose

People vary in their sense of privacy. Generally, the more you let people get to know you, including your strengths and your vulnerabilities, the more likely you'll develop a relationship with that person, be it as a colleague, friend, or lover. Having said that, there is wisdom in figuring out how much to tell and to whom. Allow me to share a personal experience to illustrate my point. In my twenties, I was talking to two male mental health colleagues of mine about the use of dream work in therapy. I even related a personal dream of mine, to provide an example. As I concluded my enthusiastic sharing, I waited for a response. Nothing! No response from either of them. I had laid bare my naked little heart and there it sat pulsing, out in the open, vulnerable and without a suitable reception. That night, I had a dream of two flies sitting on my head, slurping from a wound out of which a bit of my brain was seeping. I learned my lesson. Do not expose your inner self to just anyone.

I usually suggest to my group members that they test the waters. Go ahead, be the first to share a private thought, feeling, or opinion. Think of it as dipping your toes into the water. If your sharing is met with interest and respect, and better yet, an equal amount of tit for tat, think of the water as warm and inviting. Consider wading in further. The other person may follow and even step in a little deeper. Then it's up to you to meet the person or not. Eventually, you will both settle at a level of conversation that is mutually comfortable. If, on the other hand, your toes receive a chilly reception, it may be prudent to stay in the shallow end and be content with superficial small talk.

You can slowly wade into meaningful conversations as described above, or you can plunge in. Context has a lot to do with how slowly or quickly people begin sharing intimate details with each other. A client once told me a story about a woman friend of his who was on a singles' cruise. She was alone, contemplating the sunset as she stood over the ship's railing. Another single woman came along, a perfect stranger, and my client's friend turned to her and asked, "What do you do about loneliness?" The two became immediately immersed in a long heart-to-heart conversation. The context was there. This was a cruise for singles, people seeking connection. The common interest offered a natural entry into the discussion of loneliness. If, on the other hand, you were in an elevator with a single stranger, imagine the response you'd get if you asked, "What do you do about loneliness?" You'd probably witness a baffled individual make a panicked exit through the escape hatch.

Disclosing your shyness or social anxiety

In the first section of this book, we met a few socially anxious people who reported that they would never tell anyone, including a husband, about their shameful secret—that they were socially anxious or shy. Such is the power of unhealthy shame. It separates you from others. It keeps you in an emotional straitjacket, unable to feel relaxed about exposing the real you, lest others disapprove.

Recently, I went to a tango lesson on Salt Spring Island, one of the Gulf Islands off the west coast of British Columbia. I'd been staying at a friend's unoccupied summer home nestled on the side of a woodsy hill, far from the distractions of home and family in Vancouver city, so that I might complete this book. The host of the tango practice introduced me and I was warmly welcomed by Salt Spring's tiny tango community. After the lesson, three people asked me, separately, what I was doing in Salt Spring. When I told each of them that I was writing a book about shyness and social anxiety, each had an immediate reply. The first woman told me how, in her younger years, she coped with shyness by playing the social butterfly role so that no one would ever guess that she was shy. It worked, except for the fact that she never felt like her real self. The second person told me he felt that, as he was growing older, he was becoming shyer and shyer. The third person told me that he could write a book about shyness and certainly could stand to read about it. I get this response most frequently of all. Anytime I mention that I am writing a book on shyness and social anxiety, someone will invariably tell me that she could benefit from reading such a book. What is the moral of my story? Again, what seems most personal is often most general. Shyness and social anxiety are common human experiences.

I encourage you to share your shy nature or your social anxiety with others. As I said earlier, it's a good idea to figure out how much to tell and to whom. But tell you must; otherwise shame wins out and continued inhibition rules. Next time you admire someone for speaking up, you can tell him so. "Wow, I really liked what you said to that person. I wish I could do that. I tend to be a little shy when it comes to that sort of thing." If you're asked to go out somewhere, you might say, "You know, part of me would really like to; another part of me is kind of shy about going." If you're giving a presentation, you might say, "You know, folks, giving talks isn't exactly my strong suit. Frankly, I'd rather jump through a hoop of fire than give a talk, but I've got some things to tell you that I think you'll find really interesting." And don't forget your body language. If you tell your story timidly, with eyes lowered and body shrunken and turned away from others, you may hypnotize the other person into giving you a chilly reception. If you tell your story confidently, people will tend to take your information in stride.

Nothing to say?

A common problem for people who tend to shy away from conversations is that they have difficulty finding anything to talk about. Again, remember, it's not all up to you to come up with topics. The other person will have something to say and you can follow up. All the same, it is reasonable to expect that you will do your share of contributing to the conversation by bringing up your own topics. Here are a few ideas that should help.

Speak your awareness

I was once referred a client whose wife complained that he never talked to her. When I met James, he told me, "There's nothing much to talk about." I told James about an awareness exercise and asked him if he was willing to give it a try. He was game. The instructions are simply to notice what is going on inside and outside of you. You might notice any number of sensations, thoughts, feelings, or impulses. As each bit of information that enters your awareness, you tell the other person what you're noticing. For instance, you might say, "I notice the sun shining on those leaves. I notice your earrings sparkling in the sunlight. I notice your smile. I notice that I am now smiling." You can literally carry on this exercise for hours. There are millions of bits of information available to you at any moment, only a fraction of which registers in your conscious awareness. You can end up talking nonstop. James tried the exercise and had no trouble finding things to talk about. Some people do find it difficult at first, often expressing their awareness that they feel silly. I tell them, "Bravo, you just shared a lovely awareness; now, just keep on going." It does get easier. Anyway, I suggested to James that he continue to practice this awareness exercise and that he ask his wife to be his audience. The next time I saw James, this is what he reported.

> I was having dinner with my wife and I started to tell her that I noticed her spaghetti sauce tasted a little different from usual and I liked it. I told her that there seemed to be a hint of cinnamon in it. She nodded and looked really pleased. Things have been going

pretty well between my wife and me. But I want to tell you what happened at work. I'm the manager in a garage shop. The other day, one of the employees was looking kind of down in the mouth. Remembering my awareness exercise, I said to him, 'Hey, Joe, you don't look that great; are you okay?" Joe came over and told me that he and his girlfriend had broken up the night before. We sat down and talked a while. I told him that I thought he should take the rest of the day off and come back in the morning. The following morning, he came over and thanked me for the support I had given him. He said that it meant a lot to him. You know, before this awareness exercise, I would have barely noticed that look on his face, let alone said anything about it!

James was on the road to having meaningful conversations and connections not only with his wife but also with others.

Only two steps: Be aware. Speak your awareness. You might like to add these to your goal list.

Do interesting things

If shyness and social anxiety have ruled your life, chances are your life has been restricted and dull. It's difficult to tell interesting personal stories if you haven't been experiencing what life has to offer. Take a class, join a study group, sign up for a hiking club, buy a ticket for a travel tour, pick up a hobby, do volunteer work, attend local talks. If you're so inclined, keep a journal of your experiences. As you continue to fill your life with these kinds of experiences, you'll find it easier to tell personal stories.

Prepare topics

Another way of increasing the contents of your story bag is to stay tuned to what's going on in the world. Keep up with weekly news magazines; listen to the news; read good books, both current and classic; watch the latest movies or videos. If you're going to a social gathering, you might like to prepare two or three topics of conversation based on the news stories or fictional stories you've just heard or read about.

Form opinions

Expressing opinions can feel like risky business for the shy and socially anxious. If you express an opinion, won't someone shoot it down? Isn't it safer to keep a low profile and just go with the majority? Besides, some of us don't even know what our opinions are. We learned a long time ago to tuck away our opinions for fear of a slap in the face or some other form of rejection. Well, that's a long time ago, and now is now. Hiding no longer serves us well. It keeps us distant from others and from ourselves.

To help get into the habit of forming opinions, I suggest to group members that they watch the news. As each news story concludes, they are to figure out what they just thought about that story. Did it inspire them, disgust them, sadden them? Did they like it or not like it and why? If they find themselves sitting on the fence about any particular story, I encourage them to move over to one side or the other and see what it feels like. Pretty soon, people find that they're back in the business of forming opinions.

As for anyone shooting you down, there are a few things to remember. First, remember realistic thinking. The probability of someone going out of her way to put you down for having an opinion is extremely unlikely. Most people are courteous to others even if their opinions differ. Second, you are entitled to your thoughts, feelings, and opinions. Don't let anyone try to convince you otherwise. Third, if you do run across the odd character who gives you a rough time and criticizes you, there are a number of skills you can use to deal with the situation. They are listed below. Don't forget your calming techniques, in such a situation: Breathe. Ground yourself. Fourth, remember the exhilarating satisfaction that comes from expressing your real self. There's nothing like it!

DIFFICULT CONVERSATIONS

As WE REACH OUT and connect with people, the inevitable will happen once in a while. We feel hurt by others or others feel hurt by us. Tense and difficult moments follow. How to deal with these difficult moments is challenging even for the best of conversationalists, let alone for people who feel shy or socially anxious. Because social anxiety has to do with the fear of being judged, let's begin by looking at what we can do in the event of an actual judgment or criticism.

Criticisms

Details of how to deal with criticisms can be found in any number of books on assertiveness. The book I usually recommend is Manuel Smith's *When I Say No, I Feel Guilty*. Here are a few general tips that should help.

DON'T GET DEFENSIVE.

Arguing or trying to prove the other person wrong tends to increase criticisms.

GO ALONG.

When you have little or no emotional investment in the person who is criticizing or in the situation, as in lighthearted teasing at work, going along with the criticism is an effective strategy. A general agreement might sound like, "You could be right." An example of a specific agreement would be, "You're right. I can be so clumsy. You should see me at home. I'm forever bumping into things." Either way, the wind is usually taken out of the critic's sails and the criticisms come to a halt.

INVITE DETAILS AND FURTHER CRITICISMS.

You don't necessarily want to shut down conversations, when it comes to persons or situations that are important to you. In fact, when it comes to your friends, your colleague, or your lover, it is important to keep the conversation going. One way to do this is to ask the person questions that invite further details about the criticism. These questions often start with words like, "How exactly . . . ?" "What exactly . . . ?" "Where specifically . . . ?" For example, you might say, "How exactly have I been inconsiderate? Can you give me an example?" The confident person will even ask for further criticisms. For example, "Is there something else you didn't like about my presentation? I'd appreciate your feedback." In the process of inviting details and further criticisms, you accomplish one of two things. If the criticism is constructive, you will get useful information that will help you decide whether and how to improve something. If the criticism is meant to manipulate or hurt you, you will help the critic take responsibility for her criticisms. Either she will retreat from her critical stance, or she will be more honest about what is underlying her need to criticize.

Asking for what you want

Expressing yourself includes asking for what you want and need—not an easy task for many shy or socially anxious people. Some of us learned that it's not okay to impose on others. Some of us don't feel entitled to ask for what we want. It's time to challenge these beliefs and realize that human beings are social animals that are biologically designed to depend on each other. We need one another to fulfill all sorts of needs: food, shelter, material goods, emotional connection, security, assistance, adventure, love, personal development, and growth. In this interdependent exchange, we may not always get what we need or want, but it is still important to ask. Add "asking" to your goal list. Ask for help with a project. Ask for a date. Ask for a refund. Ask for information. Ask for an earlier/later appointment. Ask for a favor. Ask for quiet. Ask for directions. Ask for a hug. Ask to be treated with respect. Because asking used to be difficult for me, I tried an experiment when I first started dating my husband to be. I asked him if I could practice "asking" with him. The rules were that I would ask, but I would not expect him to necessarily deliver. Not expecting anything in return was freeing. I asked to my heart's content. Any impulse, any whim, I asked. I asked if we could hold hands. At the corner of Broadway and Main, I asked if I could have a kiss. I asked to go across the street to see a shop. Whether the requests were fulfilled or not, and mostly they were, the asking was exhilarating. Dare to ask.

Telephone panic

Kim says that she screens all her calls on her caller ID display. George reports that his heart starts racing at the mere thought of having to make a call. The inability to see people's reactions makes Harry uneasy. Phil hates feeling on the spot with unexpected phone calls. If any of this applies to you, put telephone calls on your goals list. To start with, stop screening your calls and treat each call as an opportunity for practice and mastery. Eventually, the telephone can be a wonderful aid in furthering human connection. You can make phone calls to let people know you enjoyed a certain event to which you were invited, to thank people after an interview, to ask people for a favor, or to suggest an evening out.

Before making a call, you can jot down a few points you wish to remember. As with any other social challenge, prepare yourself by using your calming techniques, by imagining a relaxing conversation, by telling yourself that you can do it. If you're making a call, the first thing you do is identify yourself. Don't assume people will recognize your voice. "Hi, this is Terry." If you're calling someone that you've just met, be sure to include some information that will remind the person who you are. "Hi, this is Terry, the tall lanky fellow with the German shepherd. We met last week on the marathon run in Stanley Park."

Next, it is a good idea to ask if you've called at a convenient time. The person you're calling may be preparing to eat dinner or go out the door. If so, make arrangements to call again or quickly mention why you are calling.

If you're in the middle of a conversation, it's awkward to leave a person waiting while you check your call-waiting feature to see who else is on the line. My advice is, don't do it. When you focus only on the person with whom you are talking, you let her know that your communication with her is important and you won't let an interruption get in the way. Even though the other person can't see you, it doesn't hurt to keep your body moving, to smile, to make gestures to make a point. This keeps your energy flowing, which will be reflected in your voice. Remember to focus on the other, not on how you are coming across.

Ending telephone conversations is like ending face-to-face conversations. If it's a business call, you can thank the person for her time. If it's a personal call, you can tell the person you enjoyed talking with her.

FINAL CONVERSATIONAL TIPS

THE FOLLOWING ARE a few additional tips that will enhance your conversational skills and increase your chances for connection with others.

Avoid distancing words

At least two or three people in each of my groups have had the habit of saying "you," "one," or the royal "we" when they are actually referring to their personal experience and should be saying "I." Using the "you" word is a way of hiding. Dare to take ownership of your statements. When you use the "I" word, people get a better sense of who you are and tend to feel closer to you. So rather than saying "You get nervous when the phone rings," say "I get nervous when the phone rings."

Don't monopolize

Although most socially anxious people tend to talk less, not more, nervousness for some can leak out in the form of overtalkativeness that leaves no room for pauses, no room for the other person to join in. Take your time and practice active listening.

Don't jump in too soon

Sometimes another person's story will remind you of a story of your own. In the excitement of remembering, you can jump in too quickly and start telling your tale. The other person retreats and you may not even notice that you have cut him off. Hear the person out, continue asking questions, and leave your story on the back burner until a more appropriate moment.

Ask for time to think about things

You can feel on the spot when you are asked to do something or to go out somewhere. Asking, "Can I have a couple of days to think about it?" is a great way to take care of yourself while letting the person know that you'll consider his request or invitation.

Be yourself

Being yourself, expressing who you really are, is an exhilarating experience.

KEY REFLECTION POINTS

➤ Taking a risk and expressing yourself can be exhilarating.
➤ Initiate, initiate, initiate. Be the first to make contact.
➤ Giving free information and following up on the other person's free information helps a conversation move forward.
➤ Fear of revealing things about yourself usually is accompanied by the fear that people will reject you if they find out about you. Remember that what we think of as very personal often turns out to be universal.
➤ If you feel that you have nothing to say, try the following: speak your awareness, do interesting things, prepare topics in advance, and get into the habit of forming and expressing your opinions.
➤ Instead of becoming defensive when criticized, try going with it. Agree with the possible grain of truth and ask for more information. You'll soon find yourself capable of dealing with criticism without getting overwhelmed.
➤ Practice asking for what you want.

➤ Reduce telephone panic by using a few prepared scripts to get you started.

➤ Using words such as "you" or "we" when you actually mean "I" creates distance between you and your conversational partner. Own your thoughts and your feelings by using the first person, "I."

➤ Dare to be yourself.

The one thing I want to remember from this chapter is:

_____

_____

I will translate this one thing into action in the following way:

_____

_____

_____

_____

FIFTEEN

FIRST IMPRESSIONS

Job Interviews and Presentations

Speak the speech, I pray you, as I pronounced it to you,
trippingly on the tongue; but if you mouth it, as many
of your players do, I had as lief the town-crier
spoke my lines.
—SHAKESPEARE, *Hamlet* (3.2.1–2)

YOU'RE THE CENTER of attention. Here's one scenario: Anywhere from one to a half-dozen people, possibly with paper and pen in hand, have their eyes fixed on you while they fire off questions and evaluate your answers. Will you pass the interview and get the job? Here's another scenario: You must introduce a speaker to three hundred people at a conference—or worse yet, you *are* the speaker. Will the audience applaud and smile or will they boo and laugh at you?

If job interviews and public speaking aren't a recipe for social anxiety, nothing is. For the socially anxious person, the job interview is a formal ritual that blatantly contains everything the socially anxious person fears most: a social setting where scrutiny and evaluation are the name of the game. With public speaking, scrutiny and evaluation multiplied by the number of people in the audience push the fear of fumbling and public humiliation to catastrophic proportions.

Have you ever noticed that the more you want something, the more anxious you become about whether you will get it? How nervous would you be, for instance, if you applied for a one-in-a-million dream job or if you were to talk to an audience of educated professionals? As the stakes go up, so does the motivation to make a good impression. As this motivation increases, so might self-doubt. The more a person doubts that she will succeed in creating a favorable impression, the greater the social anxiety. Taking what I call the four-pronged "P" approach (prepare, practice, present, and post-evaluate) can help reduce that social anxiety to manageable levels. Notice how aspects of body, mind, and action move in and out of the picture, in varying degrees.

PREPARATION

Preliminary groundwork is a must for both job interviews and presentations. A certain amount of pre-event investigation will help you figure out the direction you need to follow when you prepare your material. The following chart outlines what to think about and do when preparing for an interview or presentation.

Job Interview

Find out about

The organization: Its structure, history, mandate, goals, customer base

The field: The current trends, conflicting philosophies and ideas

The job: The job description; the job setting (formal or informal; fast-paced or laid back); the nature of the job (is there training? mostly individual work or team work?)

The interview format: Is it a group interview with several interviewees at the same time? One or several interviewers? Formal or informal?

Presentation

Find out about

The purpose of presentation: to inform, instruct, entertain, persuade, or a combination of any of these?

The audience: How large? Who? How old? Male and female audience members, all-male, or all-female? A majority or minority group? Is audience members' presence required by their job, or do they want to come? Do they want basics or sophisticated details?

Job Interview

Prepare

Answers for common interview questions, such as: Tell us about yourself. Why do you want to work here? Why did you leave your last job? Can you explain this gap in your resume? Don't give the impression that you've been doing nothing. Perhaps you've been taking care of the family or pursuing interests in reading, travel, or research. What are your strengths and weaknesses? Highlight those skills and personality traits that fit the job. Have one weakness ready and make sure it's not extreme. Perhaps you work too hard, or you need to round out your computer skills, in which case you've signed up for a course to take care of that. (Peter Desberg has a good section on job interview preparation in his book *No More Butterflies*.)

Readiness checklist: Directions to destination; name of interviewer; list of questions to ask; reminder to bring pen and paper, updated resume. Organize appropriate clothing. Reminder to practice grounding, breathing, imagery work. List of positive affirmations ("I can do this"; "I am calm"; "I am the person for the job.").

Presentation

Prepare

The presentation material: Choose topic. Research, brainstorm key ideas, and organize. Write out the presentation with introduction, body, and conclusion. Prepare supportive materials such as handouts, overheads, props, slides, videos. (Check out Peter Desberg's *No More Butterflies,* for more details on presentations.)

Readiness checklist: Directions to destination; name of person who will meet you; list for organizer, given ahead of time, of what you need (felt pens, flip chart, overhead projector, microphone, water, PowerPoint equipment); list of what you will bring (paged presentation with highlighted key points, handouts, evaluation sheets, bottled water); appropriate clothing chosen; reminder to practice grounding, breathing, imagery work; list of positive affirmations ("I can do this"; "I am calm"; "I am giving something of value to these people. They are interested in what I have to say.")

PRACTICE

REHEARSING BOTH IN imagination and in real life will help you to believe that you can actually do what you set out to do. Don't forget to include mind and body preparation as you proceed in the action of practice. You can use the affirmations mentioned above, as well as any calming techniques that you learned in Chapter 3. You might like to review rehearsals in Chapter 8, "Just Imagine" and Chapter 12, "Let's Do It!"

PRESENTATION

THE CURTAIN IS up and you're on. All your preparation work is about to pay off. If you get last-minute bursts of anxiety, remind yourself that this is normal. Tell yourself that this is excitement. Practice grounding. Breathe. Put things in perspective. Remember that all interviewers were once interviewees and in the same spot you are in now. Remind yourself that many great speakers were once poor speakers. Think about Demosthenes of ancient Greece. As a student, he was ridiculed because he stammered. Determined to become a great speaker, he practiced reciting verses at the beach with pebbles in his mouth, adding to the challenge by reciting loudly as he ran alongside the roaring waves of the seashore. Eventually, he succeeded in delivering an exquisitely elegant speech to the open skies with a pebble-filled mouth. What a day of triumph that must have been. He became one of the greatest orators of his time.

Job Interview

First impression

Arrive on time, in spotless, possibly new, clothing, smelling clean and fresh. Avoid distracting smells such as from smoking, too much cologne, or garlic.

Stretch yourself from the inside so that your posture reveals strength and confidence.

Smile.

Do your grounding and breathing.

Give a welcoming look to the person who meets you and initiate a warm handshake.

Make a friendly comment about the immediate surroundings.

Stay positive.

Follow through

Ground and breathe.

Presentation

First impression

Arrive early. Do as suggested for job interview. In addition, take charge and feel free to ask for what you need as you set up for your presentation.

Follow through

Take a moment to welcome various

Job Interview

Follow through

Welcome your interviewer(s) with your eyes and open face. Be prepared to talk about yourself, stating why you think you are the ideal person for this job.
Pause when you need time to reflect.
Make occasional eye contact.
Be yourself.
Ask a few prepared questions.
Thank your interviewer.
Follow up with a thank-you note.

Presentation

Follow through

members in the audience with your eyes and open face. If feeling a little jittery, remember that most speakers experience a thirty-second window of nervousness as they begin to speak. Ground and breathe. As you focus on the topic, the anxiety will pass.
Be yourself.
If anything goes wrong, don't ignore it. Comment on it casually, humorously.
Stay involved with the audience: make eye contact, smile, ask questions, ask for a show of hands to some of your questions, ask if anyone has questions.
Thank your audience for their interest and participation.

POST-EVENT EVALUATION

Once the interview or presentation is over, make sure to take the time to evaluate your performance so that you can learn from it. Start by celebrating the fact that you've done it! You've actually faced the number one fear of most people, that of public speaking, whether before an audience of one or several hundred. Bravo! As you review what happened, be kind to yourself. People who are socially anxious tend to be ruthless in evaluating their performance, often minimizing the good points and maximizing the not-so-good points. Why not do the opposite? Maximize the good points and minimize the others. The point of reviewing your performance is to learn what you can continue to do well and what you can strive to do better the next time.

JOB INTERVIEW/PRESENTATION
Sentence completions
Strong points:

Read the following sentence stem and complete it with the first thing that comes to mind. *What I liked about my presentation* *(interview) was:*_____

_____

_____

You might complete it by writing "that I told a good joke. The audience laughed." Repeat the sentence stem: *What I liked about my presentation was:* _____

_____

_____

Add something else. Keep doing this until you've run out of ideas. If you think of something later, add it to your list of things that you are proud of.

Things to improve:

Complete the following sentence stem: *One of the things that I would have done differently in my presentation (interview) is:* _____

_____

_____

You might complete it by writing, "I would not have rushed through it, especially at the end." Add one or two things more and then stop. No use going overboard. Savor what you are proud of and make plans for improving your presentation or interview the next time.

Objective feedback

Evaluation sheets:

If you or your sponsor gave out evaluation sheets, make sure to go over them. Note what worked and didn't work. Keep this feedback in perspective. Like everywhere else, people in audiences are positive and negative. There's usually someone who will be very negative in his comments. Don't take this personally. Again, enjoy the positive comments and consider whether to pursue the suggestions for improvement.

Conversational inquiry:

If you have a chance, ask audience members what they liked and didn't like about your presentation. This may be easier if you know someone in the audience.

Plan and follow through:

The next steps:

Once you have identified your strengths and weaknesses, decide what you want to do next. In terms of job interviews, there are often employment resources that offer courses that teach skills for successful job searching. Look these up in the Yellow Pages or ask your local librarian for help.

With public speaking clubs in over sixty countries, Toastmasters International is the best-known organization devoted to helping people overcome their fear of public speaking. Check its website at www.toastmasters.org. Public speaking courses are often included in adult continuing education curricula listed with local school boards.

You can also improve your public speaking skills by learning from others. Whether you watch speakers on television or in real life, notice which speakers you like and which ones leave you cold. What makes the difference? See if you can incorporate some of your discoveries into your own style of public speaking.

Like learning anything else, learning to speak confidently before others can take time. Stick with it. Eventually, like the Greek orator Demosthenes, you will find your voice and use it for all kinds of wonderful purposes.

KEY REFLECTION POINTS

➤ Being the center of attention during a job interview or while doing a presentation is nerve-racking for most people and can be excruciating for those with social anxiety.

➤ If you want to reduce your anxiety, use the four-pronged "P" approach: prepare, practice, present, and post-evaluate.

➤ Preparing involves searching for information and organizing relevant material for future use.

➤ Practicing refers to rehearsing in imagination and in real life, using all the skills described in earlier chapters.

➤ Presenting is the opportunity to share something of value with others, whether this something is you or your thoughts, opinions, knowledge, or talents. It is an opportunity to allow all your preparation and practice to come to fruition for the benefit of others as well as yourself.

➤ Post-event evaluation enables you to identify your strengths and your weaknesses. Celebrate your strengths and make plans to adjust what needs adjusting.

➤ As you continue to take risks and put yourself out there in the world, you will find a stronger voice, which you can use for all kinds of wonderful purposes.

The one thing I want to remember from this chapter is:

_____

_____

I will translate this one thing into action in the following way:

_____

_____

_____

_____

SIXTEEN

LET'S GET TOGETHER!

Friendships

The only way to have a friend is to be one. . . .
A friend may well be reckoned the masterpiece of Nature.
—RALPH WALDO EMERSON

W E ARE SOCIAL ANIMALS. Apart from needing each other for our basic survival, we also need each other for our emotional survival. Except for hermits and holy men, friends are considered essential to a balanced life. Although many people with social anxiety do have satisfying friendships, others have no friends at all or no close ones. If you are not satisfied with the number or quality of friendships in your life, it's time to explore your options and take action.

GROUNDWORK: BE YOUR OWN BEST BUDDY

As CHRISTOPHER McCULLOUGH says in his book *Always at Ease*, "The only way to be truly comfortable with others is to be truly comfortable with ourselves." I totally agree. If you're troubled by a negative self-image or poor self-esteem, it will be difficult to forget about yourself and truly enjoy the company of others. Consequently, the first step toward developing friendships with others is cultivating a solid friendship with yourself. You need to become your own best buddy. What does this mean? You like yourself. You enjoy spending time with yourself, pursuing interests and hobbies. You do nice things for yourself. You give yourself compliments. You stay clear of negative judgments of yourself. You tell yourself, "Bravo," when you've done something well, and you say, "It's okay, live and learn," when you've done not so well. You support your dreams and goals by following through with action. You respect your own thoughts, feelings, and opinions and share them with others. If you can be this kind of friend to yourself, your chances of developing satisfying friendships with others will increase dramatically.

THE NATURE OF FRIENDSHIPS

FRIENDSHIPS COME IN an assortment of shapes and sizes. We can have long-time friends whom we've known for years and are likely to continue knowing for years. We can have short-time friends whom we're not likely to see again but whose company has enriched our lives in some way. Some friendships develop quickly, because we feel an instant kinship or because of the intensity of shared experiences. Other friendships develop slowly, over time. Friends may drift apart because interests, values, or life circumstances change. With other people, we stay in touch on a regular and frequent basis. Some friends only meet now and again and pick up easily from when they last saw each other. Close friends share their real selves with each other, in good times and in bad. In contrast, you may only share doing special projects or leisure activities with casual friends.

There are also differences in the numbers of friendships a person cares to have or is fortunate enough to have. According to Henry Adams (1838–1918), "One friend in a lifetime is much; two are many; three are hardly possible. Friendship needs a certain parallelism of life, a community of thought, a rivalry of aim."

Adams, of course, is speaking of close friendships. For some people, having one or two close friends is plenty. Others enjoy the stimulation of several or many friendships. How many and what kinds of friendships people choose to cultivate is an individual matter that depends on individual needs and circumstances.

THE RIGHT INGREDIENTS

THE LIKELIHOOD OF a friendship developing increases when the following factors come together: regularity and frequency, proximity, openness, need, similarity, self-disclosure, and positive regard. Let's look at each, one at a time.

Regularity and frequency

The more often you see a person on a regular basis, the more familiar he or she becomes. Short-term regularity applies to attending a ten-week course or a three-day seminar. Long-term regularity may mean you both frequent the same gym, swimming daily, or wait at the same bus stop at the same time each day. It's just a matter of time before a simple "hi" becomes a short conversation and from there, a long conversation. If the other ingredients exist and a friendship develops, regularity of visits helps to strengthen this friendship.

Proximity

People who occupy the same space are naturally more likely to become friends than people who are physically distant from each other. A nearby neighbor or fellow student who repeatedly sits next to you in class is easier to talk with or visit than a person who lives in the next state.

Openness

Whom would you prefer to approach? The fellow sitting at the end of the bench with his head down, looking glum, or the one standing against the railing, smiling with interest as he watches the boat dock? Most people would be drawn to the fellow with the friendly face and the open stance. Various factors influence just how open you feel on any given day. Being in a good mood certainly helps. Freedom from stress and pressures promotes openness. Your expectation of how the other person will respond to you has a tremendous impact on how open you feel. If, for instance, you assume that the other person is going to like you, you're going to be open. If, on the other hand, you doubt that person will be interested in you, you're likely going to shut down.

Need

A person who already has many friends, perhaps more than she can keep up with, will obviously not need to make more friends. This person may not be eager to approach you. Nor will she be as open to your approaches as someone who is looking for new friends. Need for camaraderie is likely what makes travelers such friendly people. They are temporarily without their friends and are often open to approaching strangers and being approached by them.

Similarity

Friends become close when they are similar to each other. They have similar interests, values, beliefs, and attitudes. They don't have to agree on everything, but generally they do view the world through similar lenses. Other things that they may have in common include family backgrounds, religious affiliations, economic status, education, ages, and jobs. They often even have similar personalities. So much commonality creates a familiarity that makes people feel at home with each other. Of course, unique differences between these friends add the spice that keeps things interesting.

Self-disclosure

As mutual trust develops, the ability to reveal one's true self to another and feel accepted by that person is the substance of true friendship. To be able to share both strengths and weaknesses with each other, without judgment, contributes to a sense of profound connection.

Positive regard

Letting friends know that you like, enjoy, and even admire them goes a long way in deepening a friendship. There's showing and there's telling. You can show friends that you have positive regard for them in a variety of ways. Your eyes twinkle and your smile widens when you see them. You are affectionate. You hug and kiss (depending on your culture). You respect your friends' thoughts, feelings, and opinions by actively listening. You do favors. You go out of your way to delight your friends in some small way. You share your true feelings with them. You can also tell your friends directly that you like them, perhaps even love them. Most people find it easier to tell friends what it is they like about them. They might comment on their honesty, daring, loyalty, and so on. They might share how these qualities inspire them.

FRIENDSHIP BUSTERS

JUST AS THERE are factors that help create friendships, there are factors that help destroy friendships. The following are a few of the most common friendship busters.

Self-absorption

As we have already learned, people with social anxiety tend to become preoccupied with worries about how they are coming across to others. This kind of self-absorption diverts attention from what's going on in the immediate surroundings. If a new friend happens to be sharing a story about herself, and you're busy figuring out how and what you are going to say next, she'll soon figure out that you're not really listening. She may wonder whether you really care about what she's relating. If this becomes a pattern, she'll lose interest in the friendship, because there is no real connection. Another way self-absorption is expressed is through monopolizing the conversation, leaving little room for the other person to have his share of the stage. Although most people with social anxiety tend not to monopolize, there are those who do exactly this, out of a sense of nervousness.

Overdependency or possessiveness

Little else spoils a good friendship as swiftly as desperate neediness or possessiveness. There's nothing wrong with friends spending a lot of time with each other, as long as this a mutually agreed-upon arrangement. However, as soon as one friend begins to regularly demand more time than the other wishes to give, the friendship is at risk. Demanding behavior does not have to be active. It can also be passive, as when one friend withdraws or acts hurt whenever the other friend wants time to be alone or to pursue other interests or friendships. No one likes to feel suffocated by the neediness of another. Sooner or later, the person who is suffocating will want to break free of the relationship. That is why it is important to have as full and satisfying a life as possible, before entering into an important friendship; that is why it's important not to have all your eggs in one basket. Having a range of interests and friendships helps to shrink the desperation that often accompanies a life with only a few sources of satisfaction. Think of it this way: the life you build for yourself is your cake. The richer the life, the better the cake. A healthy friendship is icing on that cake. It cannot be the cake. That is too much to ask of anyone.

Lack of self-disclosure

It is critical to learn how to talk about yourself, about your thoughts, feelings, fears, hopes, and dreams. Otherwise, how can a friend get to know and love you? If you still hide your real self, for fear of being rejected, then it may be time to seek counseling. Find a therapist with a good reputation. As you learn to trust that your therapist will listen to you without judgment, you'll begin to experience the joy of being received as a wonderful human being, regardless of your shortcomings. As your therapist listens, asks questions, and makes observations, you'll learn the vocabulary of self-disclosure.

Negativity

It's no fun being around someone who constantly finds fault with the world and everyone in it. Nor is it uplifting to be with someone who is frequently down in the dumps. If you're prone to negativity, it's time to clean out the mental cobwebs that darken your view of yourself or the world. If you're depressed, seek help.

THE RISKS AND REWARDS OF FRIENDSHIPS

DEVELOPING FRIENDSHIPS, LIKE anything of value in life, has its risks and its rewards. The main risks are loss and hurt. Friends can move away or drift away, carried off by changing life circumstances. Friends can even die. They can leave a vacuum in your life that is difficult to get over. The pain of loss and grief is never easy.

Friends can also hurt you in other ways. They may get angry with you. They may say or do stupid and hurtful things. They may be insensitive, selfish, or inconsiderate. They might even break a trust. They are not always perfect and you might get hurt as a result. In fact, since you're not perfect either, you might do the same to them. You may feel the pain of shame and regret. Friendships are tested through these difficult times. Through honest communication with each other, friends share their feelings, make amends, and learn how to be better friends to each other. Many friendships survive and even grow stronger in the process. Other friendships do not survive. The necessary communication doesn't happen. The hurt and bitterness remain a wedge between the two people. Or, friends mutually decide that they weren't really cut out for each other, after all, and go their separate ways.

By now, you may be thinking, "Hmm, maybe life would be much simpler without friendships." You would be absolutely right. Life would be much simpler. Life would also be simpler without a flower garden that you have to weed and water; without a pet that you have to feed and worry about during vacations; without a passion that you have to pour time, money, and effort into. Life would be simpler, but would it be as thrilling, amusing, satisfying, or enriching? On to the rewards of friendships!

> A joy shared is twice the joy,
> A sorrow shared is half the sorrow.
> —Anonymous

Research shows that friendships contribute to overall emotional and physical health. In good times, friends get together for pleasurable activities like plotting surprise parties, sharing secrets, exploring new interests, or playing games or sports. Physical exertion, laughter, and excitement all release feel-good hormones such as endorphins, which, in turn, help to combat stress hormones. Your friend's positive regard and genuine interest in your well-being bring joy and comfort, not to mention, a boost to your self-esteem.

During times of crisis, friendships can make the difference between whether you cope or not. A friend's emotional support, practical assistance, guidance, and problem-solving skills console you and help you meet most of life's challenges. Interestingly, even mere thoughts and memories of ties with people you care about can sustain you through difficult times. If friendships do complicate lives, they also make life easier.

THREE STAGES OF FORMING FRIENDSHIPS

BEARING IN MIND some of the earlier information about making and breaking friendships, let's look at the three main stages of friendships: meeting, cultivating, and keeping.

Meeting people

You may be surprised at how many places and situations offer a chance to meet people who later develop into friends. Consider the following seven places for meeting people.

1. *People from your past:* To start with, consider calling up old friends or acquaintances from the past, even the distant past. Miriam told our support group that she had let slide a couple of relationships with high school pals over the last few years. She decided that her goal for the week was to call these women and invite them out for lunch. The following week she reported that she couldn't track down one of the women, but the other one had been absolutely thrilled to hear from her. They had had lunch, caught up on each other's news, and planned to meet again in a couple weeks' time.

2. *Family:* Family members can be friends. If you've lost touch with family members, perhaps even had a rift with them, maybe it's time to give them a call and see whether you can set things right. Not always, but often, family members are touched that you've taken the first step in making peace. Hope for the best and give it a shot. You may be in for a pleasant surprise.

3. *Work/School:* Work and school are common places for friendships to start. You meet with each other regularly and frequently. Through chats during breaks and through working together, you discover that you have things in common. Why not ask someone at work or school out for lunch or dinner? Or ask him if he'd like to join you to see a movie, play a game of tennis, or attend a local event. Some people find it easier to organize a group outing, so that more people can share the responsibility of keeping the conversations and activities going.

4. *Neighbors:* Another common starting point for friendships is in your own neighborhood. Whether it's with the fellow

in the next apartment or with the parents down the block whose children go to the same school as yours, why not take the time to say hello and chat a while?

5. *Service providers:* Not to be overlooked are the people who provide you with a service and who are likely to see you repeatedly. Through informal chats, you might discover that you have some things in common. For instance, my hair stylist, whom I've known for twenty years, works with her husband in their own shop; he's crazy about Latin dancing. She, he, my husband, and I are of a similar age, with grown children. On occasion, we all go out dancing and enjoy each other's company. Other service providers include, for example, teachers, accountants, carpenters, bankers, lawyers, pet groomers, and so on.

6. *Settings related to interests:* Because similarity is a key component in the formation of friendships, it makes sense that you'll increase your chances of meeting like-minded people in settings where people pursue the same thing, whether it's engaging in physical activities, learning a skill, listening to someone speak, or working for a cause. If you're not already pursuing interests and hobbies and don't know where to begin, comb through local papers, library bulletin boards, the Internet, the Yellow Pages, the adult continuing education flyers, and see what tickles your fancy.

Look for one-time events such as lectures, readings, travel slide shows, home and garden shows, sports events, concerts, dances, tournaments. Also look for repeated events, such as religious services, civic community meetings, parent committee meetings at schools, professional or trade conferences and meetings, club meetings, political activist meetings, and so forth.

A great way to meet people is to volunteer. This will give you and others a chance to get to know each other better. Why not take the initiative and ask one or more of the other volunteers whom you are drawn to if they would join you for a cup of coffee, lunch, or dinner?

7. *Interests and hobbies:* Alicia, an attractive, socially anxious person in one of my groups, recounted to us the following:

> I never felt like I fit in. In high school, there were the popular people who were in cliques, there were the sports people who played together and stayed together, and there were the geeks who talked about their computers. I felt lost. Then something happened. I'll never forget the first day I went to one of my music classes in university. There were people interested in the same thing I was interested in. We were speaking the same music lingo. I couldn't believe it. I made friends and we're still friends today.

Grange, a soft-spoken man who graduated from one of my social anxiety support groups, later told me that he had finally met a friend in circumstances that surprised even him. He explained that he enjoyed driving his remote-controlled mini car on the pavement of the local university parking lot in the evenings, when the lot was empty. During one particularly quiet evening, as he was directing his blue Ranger model toward the crest of a miniature slope, a twin Ranger model—only in brilliant red—made its way to the top of the same slope, from the other side. Its appearance startled Grange into a burst of surprised and delighted laughter. He looked around and discovered a young man his age, smiling and waving from across the lot. The two began to chat and plot about different maneuvers they'd attempt at future meetings.

I cannot stress enough the importance of having and pursuing healthy and satisfying interests. It doesn't matter what they are, as long as they interest you. People without interests or hobbies inevitably find their lives lacking in stimulation and luster. They complain of boredom. They even feel boring. Unfortunately, they might *be* boring, because they find little to talk about. Having an interest adds texture to your life. Because you are absorbed in something, you become more interesting. If others know little or nothing about what fascinates you, learning something new will be stimulating. If they share your interests, exchanging stories and experiences will be enjoyable. Developing and pursuing interests is wonderful for its own sake. Using interests as a springboard for conversation and possible future friendships is an added bonus.

CULTIVATING FRIENDSHIPS

Once you've met people and discovered some common ground, the next step is to arrange to meet again. If all goes well, you will continue to meet. The seeds of a lasting friendship are sown during these initial meetings. The art of cultivating friendships includes the following steps:

- ➤ Initiate
- ➤ Persevere
- ➤ Take turns
- ➤ Expect rejections
- ➤ Encourage others
- ➤ Meet regularly and frequently
- ➤ Plan ahead
- ➤ Be spontaneous
- ➤ Show interest and caring
- ➤ Be kind
- ➤ Be positive
- ➤ Be genuine
- ➤ Practice self-disclosure
- ➤ Be trustworthy
- ➤ Allow trust to develop
- ➤ Be generous, expansive, and inclusive
- ➤ Enjoy yourself

Initiate

In Chapter 14, we learned about the importance of initiating conversations. It is just as important to take the initiative in cultivating friendships. Making the first move and opening yourself up to the risk of rejection shows the other person that you care. At social gatherings, be the first to suggest meeting again.

Persevere in your initiatives

I remember Barbara's perseverance. She was a colleague in a neighboring mental health team. She initiated several contacts with me without my reciprocation. I was so busy and didn't think I was really in need of new friends at the time. I was especially preoccupied about getting pregnant with the help of an infertility specialist. My heart leapt with joy at the news that I was finally pregnant and plummeted with sorrow, a week later, at the discovery that I was miscarrying. Barbara visited me at the hospital with her husband. She brought me a single red rose in a vase. I was moved by her compassion and struck by her bravery to dare to visit on such a personally sad occasion, since we didn't know each other that well. But that was the beginning of a long-lasting and satisfying friendship. Do initiate. Reach out. Persevere.

Take turns initiating

Ideally, people take turns initiating. But, as illustrated in the story above, this is not always the case. Because of a person's personality, need, or circumstance, certain people may initiate more often. Don't be too concerned if you initiate more than the other. On the other hand, if the balance starts to tip too much in one direction, and you feel like you're the only one who ever takes initiative, it may be time to back off. Perhaps the other person is hinting that he's not that interested in the relationship. By the same token, if you rarely initiate, your friend may think that you're not that interested and may stop approaching you. It's nice to have a balance, but don't get obsessed with keeping things absolutely even.

Expect rejections

Not everyone needs friends at the same time. And face it, not everyone is going to select you for friendship, just as you won't necessarily want friendship with everyone who comes your way.

Encourage the other person to talk about herself

Cultivate a genuine interest in the other person's stories, in her welfare. Practice active listening: ask questions, respond to comments, and pay attention and remember details. When you meet again, include some of these details in your conversations. "How did your daughter's exam turn out? Did you get the apartment you were hoping for?" People will appreciate that you cared enough to remember and even follow up on previous conversations.

Meet regularly and frequently, if possible

Create opportunities to enjoy each other's company whether talking, engaging in physical activities, or pursuing similar interests.

Plan ahead

It's a good idea to fill in your calendar with at least one social event a week. The social event doesn't have to be formal. For some people, going for a walk, sharing conversation over coffee or tea, or talking over the phone can be considered a social event. Of course, the frequency of social events will vary according to your personality and needs. Writing plans down in a calendar will help keep you motivated. Give people the chance to prepare for an event by giving them one or two weeks' notice. This helps to avoid last-minute disappointments by people who cannot accept your invitation because they have already made other plans.

Be spontaneous

Not everything has to be planned in advance. If you've just been shopping or running together, for instance, suggest a swim at the beach or a drink at the kiosk. Suggest another run tomorrow.

Show interest and caring

After you've enjoyed a particular experience with a friend, follow up with a phone call, note, or e-mail and let that person know how much you enjoyed sharing time. If your friend is facing a crisis of sorts, whether a loss, an interview, or a new home, send a thoughtful note or card to express sympathy or congratulations, or to simply let her know that you're thinking of her. Send a note even when there is no particular reason to send it.

Be kind

Offer to help when the occasion arises. Do favors.

Be positive

Nothing is as appealing as positive energy. Notice what you like about the other person and comment on it. Notice what you like about your environment and comment on it. Share your enthusiasm. Being positive doesn't mean pretending that everything is fine when it isn't. Sometimes it's important to acknowledge and talk about unpleasant things, even downright horrible things. Being positive does mean choosing to focus, for the most part, on whatever is good and delightful.

Be genuine

Be yourself. It's no use trying to please others by telling them what you think they want to hear. If you lose your true self in a relationship, there is no relationship. Remember to be your own best buddy, respecting your thoughts and your feelings and sharing them with others.

Practice self-disclosure

The most important thing in cultivating a friendship is letting your friends know who you really are. It is heartwarming to share one's humanness with another person and discover that the other person has similar interests, passions, fears, dreams, hopes, and disappointments.

Be trustworthy

Earn people's trust by being true to your word and by taking care not to hurt them needlessly. If you say you're going to do something or be somewhere at a certain time, follow through.

Allow trust to develop

Naturally, if people have let you down in the past, you might have difficulty trusting new friends to not let you down as well. Give them a chance. Understand that people are only human. They might, indeed, let you down, but hopefully, they won't make a pattern of it. When they do let you down, talk about it. See how they respond. If a friend shows regret and makes changes to accommodate your needs, you've got a friend who cares. You will learn to trust that this person has your best interests at heart. If, on the other hand, the person doesn't take your grievance seriously and repeatedly refuses to take you seriously, it is time to move on.

Be generous, expansive, and inclusive

Cultivate a spirit of generosity. This might mean sharing your friend with other friends, by hosting events such as dinners or parties. Avoid cliques. Welcome newcomers into your conversations. Introduce them to your friends.

Enjoy yourself

Whether you're a guest or you're hosting a social event, relax and enjoy yourself and the company of others. As a host, prepare your foods ahead of time so that you're not buried in the kitchen cooking elaborate dishes while your guests chat in the living room.

Leave the cleanup until everyone has left, unless of course, everyone insists on continuing the party by working together in the kitchen. As a guest, don't hide out alone in the kitchen doing dishes. Share yourself with others.

KEEPING FRIENDSHIPS

TENDING A FRIENDSHIP is just like tending a house or garden. It must be kept in good repair. Although one of the nice things about a solid friendship is that you can take a lot of it for granted, it is important not to take "too much" for granted. Just as a well-established garden almost takes care of itself, it still needs some tender loving care. Here are a few of the more important do's:

➤ Stay positive. Focus on what's going right in the relationship, and from time to time express appreciation for the other person's contribution to the friendship.

➤ Keep doing things together. Find time to enjoy each other.

➤ Offer emotional and practical support whenever your friend needs it.

➤ Talk about difficult things—not necessarily every little difficult thing—but the things that are big enough to make the carpet lumpy if you were to sweep them under. It's no good brooding and stewing over a real or imagined hurt that will drive a wedge between you. Get it out in the open, clear up any misunderstandings, and learn from the experience. Reaffirm the importance of your friendship with the other person.

➤ Make amends. Whenever you've hurt your friend through thoughtlessness or forgetfulness, make sure to do something to set things right. Send a card, take flowers, offer a favor. Resolve to take better care the next time. Reaffirm the importance of your friendship with the other person.

➤ Forgive and forget. Be understanding when your friend has hurt you through a flippant remark or misdeed. There will probably be a time when you need his forgiveness. Reaffirm the importance of your friendship with the other person.

➤ Finally, remember: the best way to make a good friend is to be a good friend!

KEY REFLECTION POINTS

➤ We are social animals who need friends. Friendships contribute to overall emotional and physical health.

➤ It is difficult to feel good with others unless you first feel good about yourself. You need to be your own best buddy.

➤ The likelihood of a friendship developing increases when the following factors come together: regularity and frequency, proximity, openness, need, similarity, self-disclosure, and positive regard.

➤ Self-absorption, possessiveness, a lack of self-disclosure, and negativity can destroy a friendship.

➤ The three main stages of friendships are: meeting, cultivating, and keeping. Each involves specific tasks.

➤ Ultimately, the best way to make a friend is to initiate and strive to be as good a friend as you can be.

The one thing I want to remember from this chapter is:

_____

_____

I will translate this one thing into action in the following way:

_____

_____

_____

_____

SEVENTEEN

SHALL WE DANCE?

Dating

This bud of love, by summer's ripening breath,
May prove a beauteous flower when next we meet.
—SHAKESPEARE, *Romeo and Juliet* (2.2.129–130)

"DATING IS TORTURE," says Julie, a thirty-year-old woman in one of my groups. "I don't even know where to start. Just thinking about the dating scene intimidates me. Everybody who's any good already seems taken. What if I see someone I like? What do I say? How do I know he likes me? How will I know that he's the one for me?"

Bob also has concerns: "How can I tell whether this woman is single or already has a boyfriend or husband? What if she senses my shyness? How do I make the first move? What will she think when she finds out that I've always been single?" The prospect of dating can be daunting for several reasons, many of which have to do with expectations.

EXPECTATIONS

MANY PEOPLE FORM expectations about dating based on the infinite number of messages about love and sex presented in movies, television shows, and commercials; books, magazines, and advertisements; research articles, courses, and conferences; songs, tabloid headlines, greeting cards, and of course, fairy tales. These messages are everywhere, and they affect our expectations about love and connection.

Falling in love is a must

Stories of love and partnership abound. People may expect to find happiness and fulfillment only if they are in love. In reality, many people in this world lead fulfilling, happiness-filled lives without mated love relationships. In some cases, they may be happier because they are not distracted by a love relationship. Once you free yourself from the notion that you *must* be in love, some of the pressure around dating will decrease.

Only one true love

Is there but one true love for each person, one love that will or should last forever? In the murder mystery movie called *A Stranger among Us*, Melanie Griffith plays the role of an undercover police detective who falls for a handsome orthodox Jewish rabbi. He is also attracted to her but keeps her at arm's length. At one point, he tells her about an ancient story that says there is only one true love destined for each person, and that this beloved is called one's *basherte*. Although this idea of only one love provides the romantic with a hopeful ideal, it also promotes a mentality of limited opportunity. The notion of scarcity increases anxiety. I prefer to think otherwise. I tend to agree with Bea, who describes her relationship in the book *Love and Limerence: The Experience of Being in Love*, by Dorothy Tennov. Bea explains,

I love Bruce. I love him more than I have ever loved anyone. I am quite helpless about it. Fully involved. But I also know that I would have fallen in love with any fairly decent-looking unmarried man who happened to move into the apartment next door. Anyone. I know that and yet, now, it could not be anyone else. That's just the way it is.

I think Bea makes a very good point. First, you're likely to be attracted to someone who meets certain rough criteria (more on this later), and then, over time, you will become increasingly attached to this person. As the trust and caring between you grow, so do the history and memories you build together. You'll know what your partner likes and doesn't like; you'll know about his hidden scar, his sensitive ear lobe, and his favorite getaway spot. It is this kind of attachment that makes all the difference in the world. Attachment to that one special person makes him like no other person. It is at this point that your beloved becomes your one and only true love.

The perfect partner

Another myth that adds to dating anxiety is the myth of the perfect partner. Thanks to the romantic portrayals of exceptionally good-looking people with heroic character traits, people often develop unrealistic expectations about finding the perfect partner. When you become too attached to an ideal image of a person, you risk overlooking some potentially wonderful love partners. Just because someone is a little shorter, taller, heavier, lighter, older, younger, balder, hairier, bustier, flatter, louder, or quieter than your ideal image doesn't preclude the person from being an excellent, loving partner. Don't make the pool of potential dating candidates smaller than it really is by adhering to unrealistic expectations. Being open to a broader range of possibilities will reduce dating anxiety and increase the chance of surprise discoveries. For example, Becky, a thirty-two-year-old lawyer, said that she would never have imagined falling for Rick. He wasn't as tall or as handsome as she had imagined her boyfriend would be, nor was he as accomplished in his career as she had hoped. However, over dinner she found herself laughing at his jokes; she discovered his intelligence and kindness; she found his mannerisms terribly sexy. She found herself melting. She started falling in love. And interestingly, Rick started looking attractive, after all.

Yet another anxiety inducer is the idea that we have to *be* the perfect partner. I must be drop-dead gorgeous, clever, intelligent, witty, rich, interesting, well-traveled; I must be able to juggle, prepare pheasant under glass, dance the salsa, and speak several languages; otherwise that special person won't find me appealing. These types of demands reflect the kind of pressure some people put on themselves as they weigh their merits on the dating scene. Drop these impossible standards. Real people are the most attractive people.

This date means forever

Another expectation that contributes to dating anxiety is the premature focus on the future. I've had a number of male clients, in particular, who have admitted that the moment they are attracted to someone, they instantly play out, in their minds, a lifelong scenario with this person. Without having said so much as a single word to her, or having heard her say a single word, they begin to imagine being in bed with the woman of their dreams, which is normal enough, but they also imagine being unable to perform or please sexually. They imagine being married and they worry whether they can pull it off as a husband, even as a father. Whew! Talk about creating unnecessary anxiety. Let's take it easy. Let's take it one day at a time, one hour at a time, even one minute at a time! Let's put dating in perspective and realize it's just one step in the process of finding love.

DATING CAN BE FUN

WHAT IF, INSTEAD of looking at dating as a test that determines your future, you look at it as an adventure that defines your present? Dating is a little like shopping at a clothing store. You try on an outfit that you think will look great on you, but it just doesn't fit or the color is wrong. You keep on looking. Finally, you find an outfit that fits like a glove. It's the same with dating. Imagine the pressure if you expect the first date to fit like a glove. Be prepared to accept the fact that you will be attracted to some people and not to others, just as some people will be attracted to you and some won't be. All you can do is put your best foot forward, be as real as you can be, and hope that even if your date doesn't turn out to be Mr. or Ms. Wonderful, you'll still have had a good time. At the very least, you'll have learned something worth learning. In other words, with an open and positive attitude, you can't lose.

THE FOUR STAGES OF DATING

TO MEET PEOPLE you have to make yourself available. No one is going to notice you, and you are not going to be able to meet anyone, if you're stuck at home watching television. Once you're in the company of other people, you must tune in and be able to recognize the potential for romance. If both of you are attracted, you need to connect with each other. Next, continue connecting so that you get to know each other. If, over time, you continue to be attracted to each other, emotional and physical intimacy usually begins to develop. Often these stages overlap, melting into each other so that it's difficult to say where one stops and the other begins. Let's look at each of these stages.

Stage I: Making yourself available

Attitude

Being available is not just a matter of getting out of the house. It is also a matter of attitude. This is the time to say to the world, "Ready or not, here I come. Surprise me, delight me, teach me; disappoint me on occasion, if you must, for I am open to all sorts of possibilities." If you are available for life, you are available for love.

Places to meet other singles

➤ *Anywhere and everywhere, including places that support special interests*

As with friendships, you can find a potential date just about anywhere. Review the sections called the Right Ingredients and Meeting People in the previous chapter for detailed lists of places to find other people. These places also apply to finding potential dates. Don't forget to tell family and friends that you are interested in meeting people. When people know that you are available, they may think of you when they invite other available people to social gatherings.

➤ *Singles clubs and associations*

Many places cater to singles. Kathy Tait, in her book, *Love Smarts: A Singles Guide to Finding That Special Someone,* has a thirty-page appendix called "Connections throughout North America," which lists a myriad of singles organizations, clubs, associations, and services that serve as sources for finding dates. She suggests that you can use your Yellow Pages to find similar organizations in your own community, under the listings, "Clubs, Associations, or Dating Services." She cautions the reader to phone first.

To find out about singles groups in your community, also talk to your local librarian and look for ads in local papers. Look for singles courses in continuing education flyers. For instance, a successful course at one of our local colleges is called "Suddenly Single." It helped one of my social anxiety group members get over the devastation of a divorce and supported her as she learned how to open a new and exciting chapter in her life that she had never thought possible.

➤ *Dating services*

You've probably heard of or seen personal ads in the newspaper, advertisements for telepersonals on the telephone, video dating services that promise to match personality profiles and introduce people to each other, and online Internet services that allow you to describe yourself and list your preferences in terms of your potential date. It used to be that many people shied away from these public matchmaking services. They thought that relying on these services would be admitting that they couldn't find or attract a partner in the usual, conventional way. Attitudes are changing. The fact that these services have only continued to expand is testimony that they are meeting the needs of singles looking for other singles. Life in the city, in particular, has become increasingly busy and complex. People either feel they don't have the time to figure out who's single and who's not, or they are tired of or uncomfortable with the bar scene, where people often collect, hoping to find romance. Dating services have been around for quite a while now, and stories of successful unions are plentiful. When you start to hear that even couples you know have met through the Internet, you might realize that this kind of date finding is increasingly common. I myself know at least three married couples who met through such services, and I have heard of many others.

Dating services have advantages and disadvantages. A much-appreciated advantage is that dating services take the guesswork out of determining who's single and available. Everyone is participating in the service for the same reason—to meet people. Another advantage is the extent of the pool of candidates from which to choose your potential love partner.

There are also disadvantages to dating services. Predators who want some action with no real consideration for the person involved do not lurk only in bars. I've heard of an actor who treated dates like auditions. He'd woo and dazzle his date and as soon as he knew he had captured her heart, he would disappear, preparing to win over the next hapless victim. Internet dating has its share of dishonest people. Some people exaggerate their attractiveness, post pictures that are years old, lie about their age, or lie about their jobs and interests. Be prepared that whatever is advertised on the Internet may not be what you actually get when you meet the person. If you're prepared, at least you won't be caught off guard. Keep your meeting short. If you feel you need to explain your hasty retreat, simply state, "You're not what I had in mind."

Another disadvantage that can occur with Internet dating is emotional investment that goes nowhere. Bill, a fellow in my social anxiety group, reported that he had cultivated a rather delightful relationship, sending several e-mails back and forth, happily discovering shared values and interests. Bill and his new friend felt so close to each other that when they finally met, they were taken aback by how much they felt like total strangers. As Bill put it, "We were strangers but we were not strangers. It was totally awkward. I had thought we knew each other so well and yet, when we met, here stood this completely new person." Bill and others who have tried dating through Internet services recommend that people not invest too much time in getting to know each other on the Internet before actually meeting. It's better to meet after a couple of e-mail exchanges. If there's no chemistry, all the e-mail exchanges in the world are not going to fuel a romantic union.

Stage II: Tuning in, recognizing attraction and connecting

What makes a person generally attractive? What makes one person attractive to another? Why are some people attracted only to certain types of people and not to others? There are several layers of answers to these questions.

➤ *Genetic layer*
Evolutionary psychologist David Buss and his team conducted a monumental study, asking over 10,000 people in thirty-seven cultures about what they found

attractive in their mates. Typically, men valued physical attractiveness and youth in a mate more than women did; and women, just as consistently, valued ambition, status, and resources in their mates. We knew that, right? Women have complained for years about being treated as sex objects; men have complained about being status symbols. Jokes epitomize this gender difference. For instance, the older, rich man says, "Darling, if I lost all my money, would you still love me?" to which Lolita replies, "Of course, I would, honey, and I would miss you, too!"

In case you're concerned about being good-looking enough or rich enough to attract a mate, perhaps you will find it comforting to know that Buss's study also finds that the two most highly valued qualities for both men and for women, above attractiveness and access to resources, were intelligence and kindness-understanding.

➤ *Psychological layer*

Most people would be able to describe their image of an ideal mate. The closer a potential mate matches this image, the more you are attracted to this special person. Let's take a brief look at some sources that help to shape a personal image of an ideal mate.

Some people are drawn, for better or worse, to the same kind of person over and over. Something about the person reminds them of someone familiar, usually a parent or sibling. It is this sense of familiarity that is alluring. This can work for both the good and the bad. If you've had good childhood experiences with nurturing parents, you may be drawn to people who have the same nurturing qualities, who may even have some vague or not-so-vague physical resemblance to one of your parents. On the other hand, if your childhood experiences have been traumatic, due to abuse or neglect, you may, unfortunately, have a tendency to reenact the abuse or neglect, by being drawn to abusive or distant mates. The relationship is familiar and in this sense comforting, even if also disturbing.

All kinds of early impressions can also help feed our image of an ideal mate. Our first love, whether consummated or not, can set the physical and emotional standard for the mates we seek out in the future. If we grew up surrounded by books, art, or sports equipment, we may feel drawn to people who are intellectuals, artists, or athletes. Again, familiarity makes us feel "at home" with the person who reminds us of our original surroundings.

Understanding the makings of ideal images should take away some of the sting of rejection we may feel when a person is not as attracted to us as we are to them. Do not take this rejection personally. You may be a wonderful human being; however, you may not fit the ideal image that the other person has cultivated from a unique blend of personal experiences. You may not be familiar enough—their loss.

➤ *Being attracted is attractive*

Not to be overlooked is the fact that your attraction to another person can be very attractive to that person. I've given numerous talks on shyness and dating to mixed audiences, both large and small. I find it interesting that many men have stated that the single thing that attracts them most is a woman's smile. A simple smile is all it takes to attract a lot of people! In *Interpersonal Attraction*, Ellen Berscheid and Elaine Walster write that attraction theorists have generally agreed that the beginning of personal attraction is some promise of reward. We are attracted to persons who reward us. The more they reward us, the more attractive we find them. Shows of interest through body language, verbal communication, and later, physical communication, can be viewed as rewards of recognition. The other person recognizes that we are worthwhile. If you want to appear attractive to another person, then it is important to show your attraction to him. Smile away. Even blush away. A blush can be very appealing to a person who interprets it as a show of interest.

➤ *Connecting*

When people are attracted to each other, at least one of the pair starts to send "come hither" signals to the other. Helen Fisher, a research associate in the department of anthropology at the American Museum of Natural History in New York City, describes some of these natural signals in her fascinating book *Anatomy of Love: The Natural History of Monogamy, Adultery, and Divorce.* She reports, for instance, that women around the world share common flirting gestures. They smile, lift their eyebrows, give prolonged eye contact, drop their eyelids and look away, giggle, and retreat.

Men and women swell and shrink, similar to males and females in the animal kingdom, to signal importance, defenselessness, and approachability. Perhaps we can relax a little, finding comfort and amusement in the fact that we're simply being creatures of nature when we tilt our heads and thrust our chests forward.

Although we can count on nature for some of these courting ploys, which emerge unconsciously, it is not a bad idea to take active responsibility for the art of connection. This is no time to be a shrinking violet. Body language that is confident and welcoming is essential. Standing or sitting up tall, making eye contact, and having an open face and a ready smile are messages that tell people, "I'm here."

Remember your conversational skills and be the first to talk. Remember that what you say is not as important as how you say it. A gentle, melodious "hello" will signal friendly interest, whereas a clipped, matter-of-fact "hi" shows no particular interest. The human voice reflects caring and interest as much as, and sometimes more than, facial expressions. The human voice also reveals other qualities about a person; it reveals a person's background, education, and even, to some extent, temperament. Any of these will match or not match our image of an ideal mate. If there's enough of a match, conversation will continue. If not, the connection may come to an abrupt halt.

Stage III: Getting to know each other

➤ *Arranging the first date*

Once a connection is made, it's time to arrange ways of getting to know each other better. This is where dating comes in. Whether you've been chatting in real life or on the Internet, one person takes the lead in suggesting that it would be nice to spend more time with each other. Why not let that person be you? You can try something simple like "I've enjoyed talking with you. I'd love to get together again, perhaps over a cup of coffee."

Usually, it's a good idea to keep the first date short, especially if you don't know the person well or are unsure how much you like her. Meeting for coffee or having lunch in a restaurant is a great way to have an extended conversation and determine whether you share enough interest and attraction to want to continue spending time with each other. If you don't know much about the background of the person you're dating, it's a good idea to plan the first date for during the day, and in a public area, for the sake of safety. If you keep the date short—coffee or lunch—and you don't want to see the person again, it will be easier to end the date quickly. Furthermore, the intensity of a longer date, for dinner or a movie, may feel unsettling.

Of course, longer first dates are not out of the question, if you've already decided that this person is safe, desirable, and potentially a good match for you. If you have established that you share a common interest, you can say, "I've enjoyed talking to you about skiing (kayaking, gourmet cooking, bowling). I'm going to the Ski and Snowboard Show at the Coliseum this weekend; would you be interested in joining me?" If you're not sure what kind of outing to suggest, invite the other person to make a suggestion. Most people appreciate the fact that you are interested in finding out their preferences.

Don't make the mistake of making all the decisions yourself, from where to go, to when to go, to how to go.

Although some people might find it a treat to not have to figure any of this out, others might feel excluded and that their thoughts and feelings were not considered. Not a great beginning for a relationship!

There are a number of other concerns people share about first dates; for instance, who pays, when do you call, and so on. These fall outside the scope of this book. I'd suggest you search on "dating etiquette" on the Internet or go to the library to get a few ideas. Again, don't feel bound to any of these ideas. Mull them over and see which ones suit your values and tastes. In the end, kindness and consideration form the basis of all good manners, and certainly, the foundation of all good relationships.

➤ *Ending dating*

At the end of your first or second date, each of you will decide whether you care to see each other again. If you mutually decide that it's a good idea to stop seeing each other, ending dating is a little easier. You state things simply and move on. For instance, "Well, I guess it's fairly obvious that we're not exactly cut out for each other. It's been good meeting you. Good luck in the future." If, however, one person wants to continue dating and the other doesn't, ending dating can feel awkward. The importance of kindness and consideration still holds true at this stage of dating. If you're the one who doesn't want to continue, you can start by saying something like, "I'm not sure how it's going for you, but I have to tell you that I'm starting to realize that this isn't going to work for me. Nothing personal. You seem like a great human being, but it's just not there for me. I've decided to continue meeting other people. It's been fun. Good luck in the future." Most people will understand. If the other person wants to convince you otherwise, or starts asking you questions to defend your decision, the simplest way to deal with this is to acknowledge his difficulty in accepting your decision, and then repeat your decision. Do not get pressured into arguments. You might say, "It looks like I may have said something you didn't want to hear. I'm sorry, but I have made my decision." If it's the other person who has decided to stop seeing you, read on.

➤ *Rejection*

Fear of rejection in the initial stages of dating is a common concern. To start with, using the word "rejection" is risky business. If you try on an outfit and it doesn't suit you, do you state, "I reject you"? Not likely! You simply note that you and the outfit were not made for each other, and you move on. It may be time to toss out the idea of "rejection," which only increases the chance of feeling like a "reject" should things not work out as you had hoped.

Remember that dating is a try-it-on-for-size kind of affair, for *both* parties. Either two people fit together, more or less, or they don't. People with social anxiety all too often put themselves in the role of the only person being sized up and *possibly* rejected. They forget that it's a two-way street. Both you and the other person are trying to figure out whether there's a good fit or not. Remember that you, too, will have good or not-so-good feelings about the other person. Although you might have hoped to continue dating a certain person, and it didn't work out this time, remember that as you continue dating, the shoe may be on the other foot the next time. Sometimes it will be you who doesn't want to continue dating.

As mentioned earlier, people can often tell within moments of meeting each other whether they feel attracted. Some people are quick to feel that chemistry; others feel that warmth and sizzle only after they've spent some time with their potential mate. Still others won't feel it at all, no matter how much they know and like the person. We've already looked at the various components that make one person attractive to another. It could be that, through no fault of your own, you simply don't meet the criteria that the other person has in mind for a potential mate. There is no chemistry. Don't take it personally!

Finally, remember the old folk adage, "There are

plenty of fish in the sea." The fantasy that there is no one
else out there for you and you're going to be alone for the
rest of your life is often only that—a fantasy. Heather, a
fellow therapist, found her "amazing man" after having
dated twenty other men through an Internet dating service. She said that her preconceived idea of scarcity went
right out the window as she became acquainted with all
these potential partners. Somewhere, there's someone!

➤ *Continuing to get to know each other*

　　Just as with friendships, frequency and proximity are
key ingredients in the development of a love relationship.
After a while, dates don't feel like dates. They are simply
times you spend with each other, talking, asking questions,
responding to the world in its many aspects, watching the
other person respond to the world, and taking in all kinds
of information about each other. Spending time together
is no longer about making good first impressions; it's
about being more and more our true selves. If the other
person can accept who we really are, the ground is fertile
for love. Nature has probably already turned on the physical yearnings for each other, and it becomes time to move
on to more intimacy.

Stage IV: Developing physical intimacy

　　For some people, becoming physically intimate feels as natural
as taking a promenade in the sunshine. For others, the process is
fraught with anxiety, questions, and doubt. "What if he turns
away?" "When is it the right time to kiss, to hug, to make love?"
"What if she finds out I'm inexperienced?" "Where do I start?"

　　First, realize that it is natural to feel physiologically aroused
when on the threshold of physical intimacy. Interpreting this as
excitement rather than anxiety will help keep things going. Other
things that can help you make the transition from a platonic relationship to a loving relationship include intimate conversations,
initiative in reaching out, awareness, and Mother Nature. Let's
look at each.

➤ *Converse intimately*

Intimacy has to do with revealing who you really are—not necessarily all at once, but a bit at a time, as trust builds between the two of you. One difference between intimate conversations with friends and with lovers is the tendency of lovers to share even more of their feelings about each other. Making heartfelt comments such as, "I absolutely love being with you," or "Your smile warms me right to the core," or "I feel soooo comfortable with you," help to increase the sense of closeness to each other. Also, communicating your anxieties can help develop closeness. For instance, you might say things like, "I feel like a six-teen-year-old right now, nervous on her first date." Chances are, the other person will either feel the same way or will reassure you and invite you to just be yourself.

➤ *Reach out*

Some studies show that women are often the first to touch, often subtly, and it's up to the man to realize he has just been given a signal. Touching is easy for people who have grown up in touchy families. But if you've grown up with very little touching, no touching, or bad touching, reaching out to touch and being touched can both be chal-lenging. Give yourself permission to surrender to the pleas-ure of being touched. If you've had a history of bad touching, you may wish to consider therapy, to help overcome the unpleasant associations connected with touching.

Once you feel ready to touch, dare to reach out to your partner. Initiate, initiate, initiate. Start with tiny touches, on the elbow, on the shoulder. Reach out to hold hands as you walk across the street, as you sit side by side. Give a lit-tle kiss on the cheek when you say goodnight. Some-times the signals are clear and you can go ahead and do these things without saying a word. Sometimes you might like to ask, "Is it okay if I give you a kiss?"

➤ *Speak your awareness*

If ever there was a time to speak your awareness, this is it. It's possible that you may have already touched, held hands, and kissed without so much as a word about these expressions of tenderness. However, if you are contemplating a sexual encounter, in the interest of physical safety, open communication is critical. Think of speaking your awareness prior, during, and after sexual relations.

At some point during dating, it becomes time to find out what both of you hope for in a relationship. Talking about what makes for a good relationship in general terms offers an opening to discuss sex in general terms. For instance, you might ask, "What do you think makes a good relationship work?" Or, you might ask, "What are you hoping for in a relationship?" Eventually, one or the other of you may mention that good sex or physical intimacy would be important. You might learn that your partner is not interested in having sex for religious reasons, or not until marriage, or not until he is absolutely sure about the person he's dating. Listen closely to the other person and to your own heart and mind. Is this relationship a match for your values and ideas? Do you wish to continue or not continue being with this person? Think of sexuality as being a continuum. You don't have to have intercourse to feel sexual pleasure with each other. Just being in each other's close presence, smelling each other's scent, and holding hands can feel sexual. Or, you may learn that the person feels that sexual relations would be a natural step in continuing to express interest in and caring for each other. Then you can ask, "With all these concerns about HIV and sexually transmitted diseases, do you ever worry? How do you handle it?" People can agree that it may be awkward to talk about sex, but it's getting talked about!

If you've established that you both value sexual expression, in general terms, it's time to get specific. Share your awareness of your sexual longings. One way might be to express how desirable the other person is to you. For instance, "You're looking mighty good to me"; "Just looking at you makes me excited." You get the idea.

Speaking your awareness is, of course, also important *during* your sexual encounter. Stereotypically, men feel they should know everything about how to make love, and women feel they shouldn't say much for fear of insulting a man. Forget all that. Talk, ask, tell. I'm not about to go into the art and practice of love and sex. You can do your own research; there are excellent books on the subject. But I can give a general tip to men and women. Men: Realize that women can be different from each other in terms of how and where they like to be touched. Jill might like soft touching, whereas Jayne prefers strong caresses. Jill might like her nipples nibbled, whereas Jayne would sooner have gentle massaging along her inner thighs. Even the same woman might like things done one way one day and another way on another day. So it's more than okay to ask. A woman will appreciate that you are taking care to please her, according to her actual needs, not according to what you think she needs. Women: Do not be afraid to guide your lover. You can take his hand and silently put it wherever you want. You can tell him, "A little slower, faster, lighter, harder," and so on. And, of course, vice versa. Women can ask and men can guide. Checking in with each other, making sure that everything is going along okay, is another nice way of sharing your awareness in the consideration arena. "Is this okay?" "Would you prefer something else?" "Your turn, what would you like?"

Speaking your awareness is important whenever you notice you are not feeling comfortable with something. If you don't say anything and continue with whatever is going on that you don't like, something inside you will turn off. You'll be going through the motions on the outside, but inside, you'll be somewhere else. Inside, you may feel like a log or a stone statue, putting up with whatever it is you don't like, hoping it will be over soon. You may feel angry with your lover or yourself. Worse still, you may go numb and not feel anything at all. Simply state, "Sorry, honey,

I'm not comfortable with this. Let's do something else instead." Sometimes humor breaks the tension, helping you both to relax. Some aspects of sex are funny, like other experiences you've shared together. If you feel any pressure from your mate, take notice. Perhaps this person isn't as considerate as you thought. Perhaps it's time to cool things off for a while, discuss things, renegotiate, try again—or not.

And finally, speaking your awareness *after* a sexual encounter also helps to deepen intimacy. When you're relaxing together after an enjoyable romp between the sheets, it's always nice to say something that affirms the experience. A simple, "That was lovely!" is often enough to keep each other smiling. If, for some reason, the experience was not so "lovely," you may choose to gently explore what happened so that things work out better the next time. Or you may simply choose to acknowledge that lovemaking is often variable, depending on energy levels, your sense of closeness to each other, and a host of other factors.

Speaking your awareness the day after making love is considered good manners. In fact, I heard one woman refer to a man as a snake when he didn't call her back after they had made love. She felt used and vowed never to see him again. Besides, verbally acknowledging that you enjoyed the previous day's intimate connection helps to either build or maintain the story of you as lovers.

➤ *Trust Mother Nature*

Now that you've read everything you ever wanted to know about sex and dating, consider the following. Animals and human beings have been mating for millions of years without any instructions. So you certainly can, too. Sure, it's fun and interesting to read about the birds and the bees, if only to be reassured that your feelings are normal. Furthermore, a little inspiration about all the ins and outs (pun intended) of sexual possibilities can't hurt. In the end, however, what really counts is your ability to tune into your own impulses and to surrender to them, while considering the needs of your partner. Making love is ultimately an exercise of awareness and surrender; that is, surrender to the process of loving. As you sit, lie, or stand with your partner, notice how your body wants to move. Where does your hand wish to move? When it gets there, what does it want to do? Glide, explore? Touch? Caress? Squeeze? What else does your body want to do? Your body holds within it millions of years of stored bits of information about how to enjoy the pleasures of physical intimacy. Give yourself permission to relax and sense into the different parts of your body that are communicating to you and to your partner. Luckily for you, if you've experienced social anxiety or shyness, you're more likely of the sensitive ilk. Let your sensitivity work for you. Tune into all those sensual feelings, surrender to them, luxuriate in them. A world of shared sensations and intimate moments awaits you and your partner!

KEY REFLECTION POINTS

➤ The prospect of dating can be terrifying if you believe that you must have a mate in order to have a fulfilling life; that there is only one person who is right for you; that you must find and be the perfect partner; and that your whole future hinges on your first encounter.

➤ Dating can be fun if you see it in the proper perspective. Dating is the process of meeting with people, doing enjoyable things, and deciding whether you and the other person are a good match.

➤ You can be a wonderful human being and still not match the other person's ideal image, which is based on his or her personal past experiences. No need to take things personally if things don't work out. Besides, not everyone will meet your ideal image of a mate, either.

➤ Dating involves four stages: being available to meet people, recognizing the potential for romance and initiating connection, taking steps to continue this connection, and finally, engaging in physical intimacy.

The one thing I want to remember from this chapter is:

_____

_____

I will translate this one thing into action in the following way:

_____

_____

_____

_____

EIGHTEEN

YOU CAN DO IT!

Maintaining Motivation and Social
Confidence in Spite of Setbacks

Not fare well,
But fare forward, voyagers.
—T. S. Eliot (1888–1965), from "East Coker"

D URING THE TENTH and final session of the
social anxiety support group, members typically
express both elation and apprehension. They are elated that
they have made progress. Some are simply happy that
they're not so shy about being shy any more. They
accept that they have a shy nature and trust that they will
undertake social events and enjoy the company of others.
Many members state that they now look forward to events
they formerly avoided. Harry may state, for instance, "My
wife couldn't drag me to a party in the past; now, I'm actually looking forward to going! I can hardly believe it."

Group members also voice apprehension. "Is this going
to last?" "What if I slip back?" "What's going to happen if
I don't have the support of the group?" "This program was-
n't the magic bullet I hoped it would be. I've finally realized
that gaining social confidence is hard work. It requires

discipline and determination. I'm not sure I can keep up the momentum." These are valid concerns. In the normal course of living, focus turns to everyday demands. Bit by bit, efforts to increase social confidence may wane. Add to these daily demands the inevitable crisis that life will throw your way, and the path is paved for setbacks. Even when things are going great, increased anxiety and the tendency to avoid social situations may return. Temporary setbacks are normal—absolutely normal. Do not become alarmed or discouraged by setbacks. In fact, expect them. If you expect them, you can do things to prevent them from becoming too overwhelming. You can stop them from developing into full relapses. Let's begin the work of dealing with setbacks by looking, again, through the landscapes of body, mind, and action.

BODY

GENERAL STRESS, TRAUMATIC events, and discontinuation of medication can all influence the body's tolerance for social demands.

General stress

Financial hardship, health concerns, work-related stress, lack of employment, family tensions, relationship problems, poor diet, poor sleep, unbalanced lifestyle, experiences of failure, too many responsibilities and obligations, new relationships, losses, unexpected and even expected life changes, noise, and pollution all contribute to general stress. Any one of these or any combination of these stressors takes its toll on the body. Stress chemicals keep the body in a state of constant arousal. Furthermore, a steady dose of stress, with no relief, finally leads to exhaustion, and for some people, to depression. Is it any surprise that a depleted body will have a hard time mustering the energy it takes to feel socially confident? Wherever possible, minimize stress. Create opportunities for recreation and relaxation. Get plenty of sleep, nutrition, and exercise.

Traumatic events

Traumatic events overwhelm the nervous system in dramatic ways. If there has been little or no work done to resolve these traumatic experiences and to learn how to regulate your nervous system, you will continue to have extreme stress reactions in the face of threat. For example, if a person has been the victim of brutal ridicule and criticism in the past, and has experienced intense neurophysiological reactions as a result, she will tend to experience equally intense reactions in the face of a repeated incident of ridicule, even if the ridicule or criticism is slight. It doesn't take much to stimulate an alarm reaction in the brain, once it's already been triggered by a major event in the past.

If you can understand your body's stress reaction to trauma, it may be easier not to take future negative events so personally and not to take any return of social anxiety so personally. It is not your fault. It's just the way the body works. Your main tasks are to resolve the trauma and teach your body ways of coping with stress. Review the grounding, self-regulation, breathing, and relaxation techniques in Chapter 3. If necessary, seek professional help from someone who specializes in trauma counseling.

Medication

Increased social anxiety can also be due to stopping medication. Some people stop medication too early. Usually a good trial of medication lasts anywhere from six to twelve months. If you stop medication earlier than this, you may find that you end up at square one all over again. Naturally, if you haven't been solely dependent on medication and have also learned to think and behave differently, you'll be further ahead. You'll be able to draw on recent memories of social confidence. You'll remember coping skills and thinking strategies that you can continue to practice. Eventually you will regain and possibly exceed your most recent level of social confidence. Then you may simply need to return to taking medication and take it for a longer period. If this is the case, remember to continue working on the other body/mind/action strategies you have learned.

There is also the danger of stopping one's medication suddenly. Most medications need to be tapered off gradually, under the supervision of a doctor. Otherwise, withdrawal symptoms can result. Withdrawal symptoms often include symptoms of anxiety. People may mistake these withdrawal symptoms for a return of social anxiety and enter into a vicious cycle of worrying about being socially anxious again, which, in turn, will feed into increased social anxiety.

MIND

THREE MAJOR FACTORS that can contribute to a return of social anxiety: lack of motivation, negative thinking, and lack of mindfulness.

Motivation

Motivation is fuel for the engine. No fuel, no motion. Many people start out with the best of intentions, promising themselves to stick to their goals and follow through with their action plans. Then, the normal demands of everyday life take over and pretty soon these folks, once full of hope and enthusiasm, lose sight of why they wanted to work toward change in the first place. Motivation and energy peter out.

For fifteen years after my first son was born, I was too busy to engage in regular exercise. I admired anyone who had the interest and discipline to exercise regularly in whatever fashion they chose. I was plain too busy and couldn't find the time. Then something happened. My back went out horribly. The pain was agonizing. For a while, I couldn't move. Then I could only make baby steps. Sitting for any length of time was unbearable. I was incredibly afraid that the rest of my life would be like this. The back specialist explained why it was important to build up the muscles that supported my spine. If I could exercise faithfully, I would be able to live free of debilitating back pain.

I was desperate for results. Suddenly, I found the time to exercise. For the first year, I exercised religiously, every single day. I was afraid that if I skipped even one day, I'd start descending the slippery slope to exercise-slothville. I noticed an improvement not only in my back but in general limberness. Initially, my motivation was strictly to avoid the misery of pain. Then it included the desire to move toward continued limberness. I became confident that morning stretching and strengthening exercises had become a part of my life, like brushing my teeth. I felt sure that even if I missed a day, I'd resume the routine with no trouble. My hunch was correct. Years passed and I'd miss weekends or holidays and I'd always return to my routine.

About a year back, I became cocky and took my back for granted. I'd let a few days go by without exercising, week after week. And then it happened: the inevitable setback. My back went out and I was back in bed, off work for a week, and recovering for another few weeks. Ever since, I've been exercising faithfully, missing, at the most, one day every couple of weeks. It's been nine years since I started to exercise, and I still exercise regularly.

Sometimes we just need a little reminder to get us motivated again. Why did you pick up this book? Why did you start making goals? Was it the desire to be free of the pain of isolation? Or was it to be free of overwhelming anxiety symptoms? Were you tired of an unsatisfying personal or work life? Or was it the desire to be in control of your life, rather than have social anxiety rule the day? If you want to increase your chances of staying on track in your efforts to manage social anxiety and gain confidence in certain social situations, writing down your reasons for undertaking such efforts is an excellent way to maintain the motivation and energy necessary to sustain your efforts. Take a moment and write down any reason that comes to mind. Include them all, big and small.

Reasons I want to manage social anxiety:_____

_____

_____

_____

_____

_____

_____

_____

_____

_____

_____

_____

_____

_____

Negative thinking

Flawed thinking, irrational beliefs, negative assumptions and expectations, poor self-image, negative self-criticisms, excessive worrying, and self-absorption can all contribute to setbacks. Each of these mind traps can worm its way into the best of plans and efforts. Be vigilant about how you talk to yourself. Guard against defeating thoughts that sabotage your best efforts and slowly erode your confidence, your motivation, and your spirit. You may wish to review Part Three, "The Mind," and continue to identify and challenge those negative thoughts. Make a habit of replacing them with constructive, realistic, compassionate, and encouraging thoughts.

Mindfulness

Without mindfulness, setbacks are almost certain. Without mindfulness, we live our lives on automatic pilot, like robots, moving this way and that, depending on how we've been programmed. We take the road of least resistance, becoming slaves of habit. If shyness is our habit, we may continue to avoid.

Living life mindfully means paying attention. Notice how you behave and why you behave the way you do. Notice how you think and how your thoughts propel you or stop you. Be aware of the many points in life where you can choose to behave differently, even think differently. Mindfulness usually requires slowing down, taking the time to reflect. Keeping a journal of reflections is an excellent way to help cultivate mindfulness. Reflect on how you embrace or avoid the opportunity for social engagement. Recognize tendencies to hide, seek safety, and minimize visibility. It helps to be honest by looking at yourself without judgment. As you open yourself to what you discover, you may also be more open to the idea of experimenting, daring to do things differently. Life becomes more interesting, even exciting!

ACTION

IN THE LANDSCAPE of action, the three major contributors to setbacks are avoidance, lack of practice, and lack of action goals.

Avoidance

There are both blatant and subtle types of avoidance. Blatant avoidance is simply not doing something. For instance, you don't invite someone out for lunch, you avoid eye contact, and you don't state your opinion. Subtle avoidance includes all sorts of safety-seeking behaviors. You focus exclusively on the other person, to draw attention away from yourself. You take a friend to an outing so that you don't have to deal with new people. You joke or talk excessively so you don't have to engage in serious conversation where people might find out about you. You over-rehearse what you're about to say, to minimize the chances of saying the wrong thing, or you go along with the popular opinion even if you don't really agree. The task here is to recognize both types of avoidance and dare to participate more fully, even if only one small step at a time.

Lack of practice

Once socially anxious people achieve a certain level of confidence in certain areas, they easily begin to take that confidence for granted. When this happens, they tend to relax their efforts to reach out and to move beyond their comfort zone. There's nothing wrong with relaxing your efforts. In fact, you've worked hard and deserve to relax and savor your hard-won gains. Sometimes, however, periods of relaxation become extended and the practice of making an effort in certain areas starts to fade. To prevent social anxiety and fear from returning, it's a good idea to practice exposure to the situations that have caused you concern in the past.

Sometimes people stop practicing because there's simply no opportunity to practice. Public speaking is an excellent example. Unless your job requires you to make frequent presentations, in the normal course of living, most people are not required to make public presentations. Consequently, there's little occasion to practice. This happened to Alice. She was thrilled that she could finally give class presentations without experiencing them as torturous ordeals. After school was over, she had no occasion to give another presentation. A couple of years went by, and she was asked to do the eulogy at the memorial service of a favorite aunt who had died after a prolonged terminal illness. Alice wanted very much to pay tribute to her aunt by speaking about her publicly, but she hadn't spoken publicly for so long and she began to wonder whether she could do it. Social anxiety returned with a vengeance. Worrying kept her up at night. Her stomach started doing somersaults, like it used to in university classes.

When the service was six days away, the panic took shape like an ominous storm brewing though her body. She called me for an emergency appointment. Once I reassured her that this kind of setback was normal, she relaxed a little and started taking stock of the matter. Together we reviewed what had worked for her in the past. Using these strategies, she prepared for the following week. Alice was delighted that she could find her voice and gave a wonderful tribute to her aunt.

Whenever possible, arrange to have the opportunity to practice exposures in whatever areas you find challenging. If it's in public speaking, attend Toastmasters regularly. Accept invitations to speak. Speak up in group settings. Offer to do talks. If it's dancing in public, join dance classes or dance clubs. If you're afraid to spill your drink in public, have tea with a friend, have coffee in a swanky hotel lounge, drink pop at the crowded beach, or have a beer at the pub. Practicing in all sorts of situations and contexts helps to prepare you for a wider range of challenges.

Lack of action goals

Another critical factor that contributes to setbacks is a lack of action goals. Specific goals help to motivate and mobilize. If you're having trouble with goals, review Chapter 9. When setting goals becomes a routine practice, you'll discover that your life becomes enriched in all sorts of ways, for years to come.

MAINTAINING PROGRESS IN SPITE OF SETBACKS

IF YOU STILL feel stuck, it may be time to seek help. If you've had trauma in your life, if you are depressed, if you are suicidal, if you have drug or alcohol addictions, if you have relationship problems, if you have other anxiety disorders, or if your social anxiety is so severe that it seriously hampers your ability to function in life, professional help can be of enormous value. A professional therapist can help identify obstacles, suggest new approaches, and give moral support.

Seeking help

Many people with social anxiety have made an art of keeping their anxiety a secret. The prospect of telling their secret to a perfect stranger—even a psychotherapist—can be formidable. Often, someone who has never sought help has the usual fear of being judged, rejected, and even ridiculed. He may be afraid of appearing silly. He may be concerned that no one can do anything for him. Or he may share the common misconception that going for therapy means a person is crazy. This last concern is often shared by people with little or no information about what therapy really is. Contrast this perspective to the view, in certain groups of society, that having a therapist can be a status symbol!

Alternatively, some people see therapy as a search for knowledge. Harriett Lerner, an accomplished author and psychologist, once told her workshop audience that since she came from a Jewish family and Jews value education highly, her mother sent her to therapy at age two, believing it would be good for her education!

There has never been a better time to seek help from therapists for social anxiety. Increasing numbers of professionals are learning to recognize social anxiety in their practices and are better able to deal with it either directly or by referring to professionals or programs specializing in social anxiety.

Finding the right person

Several professional groups offer therapy. They are psychiatrists, clinical psychologists, clinical social workers, psychiatric clinical nurses, and general clinical counselors. Psychiatrists have medical training and are the only ones specifically trained to give prescriptions for medications. Psychologists usually have their PhDs and are consequently addressed as "Doctor," but they are not medically trained and do not prescribe medication. There is a movement afoot, however, to promote added training so that psychologists can prescribe medication, to help cope with the increasing shortage of psychiatrists. Some psychologists do not have a doctoral degree but do have a master's degree, as do clinical social workers, clinical nurses, and clinical counselors.

Psychologists and all the other clinical professionals are trained to do therapy. One book on the different approaches to therapy counts over three hundred different approaches. Although some therapists are purists, drawing mainly from one approach or another, most therapists will draw from several approaches depending on the needs of their clients. No matter what the approach, all good therapists will treat their clients, whether individually or in groups, with respect and confidentiality. They will aim to help their clients reduce suffering and increase life options in order to live more satisfying and fulfilling lives. The question is: how do you choose the right person for you?

Ask for recommendations. Ask your doctor, colleagues, friends, family. You might try your local university medical center; ask staff members whether they have or know of any stress and anxiety clinics, and more specifically, whether they can recommend any resources that deal with social anxiety. Listen to talk shows. Search the Internet.

Just as there are good plumbers and bad plumbers, there are good therapists and bad therapists. First, make sure they have credentials and are licensed or registered with a professional association. Other things to look for in a therapist include

> experience with helping clients who have social anxiety
> experience in cognitive-behavioral approaches (cognitive restructuring and exposures)
> ideally, experience with trauma and appropriate desensitization techniques (current techniques include E.M.D.R. (Eye Movement, Desensitization, and Reprocessing); Bodynamics; and Somatic Experiencing and Self-Regulation Therapy. All pay some degree of attention to stress responses in the body.)

Not to be overlooked are the personal qualities of the therapist. The best way of assessing personal qualities is by actually meeting with the person. During the first interview, you will discover whether the therapist is warm, respectful, calm, understanding, nonjudgmental, at ease, open, actively interested in your story, able to focus on your concerns, and able to clarify the issues at hand. Basically, you will get a sense of whether you will be able to like and trust this person. If there is something about the therapist that rubs you the wrong way, or if the therapist's manner does not inspire confidence, it may be a good idea to keep on looking.

As long as your therapist is willing to learn and eager to help, he or she can offer you support and guidance. For therapy to be collaborative, you must be willing to teach your therapist about your condition. Be ready to talk about the full extent of your symptoms. Describe the impact of these symptoms on your life. The best therapists are willing to listen and learn. By joining your expertise on your condition and their expertise on helping clients move through obstacles, you can create an excellent team in figuring out the best approaches to deal with your social anxiety.

Once you've found the right therapist, be prepared to be as honest as possible. A therapeutic relationship, like any relationship, is bound to have its ups and downs. Practice speaking your awareness (as covered in Chapter 14). During therapy, you will become more and more adept at speaking freely about good things and bad. Everything and anything is grist for the therapeutic mill, including any difficulties you may have with the therapist. You are paying for the session (or your insurance company is), so this is your time. You have the right to complain, question, and seek clarification. Don't sit on issues that can get in the way of honest communication with each other. When you enter into therapy, you embark on an adventure that can be intense, demanding, and nerve-racking, but also gentle, slow and easy, reassuring, fascinating, inspiring, and life-affirming.

Support groups

It's one thing to sit alone with a receptive therapist; it's another to sit in a room with eight to ten other people. When prospective clients call me to inquire about my groups, at least twenty to thirty percent of them quickly tell me that they're not sure they would be able to sit with so many people for any length of time. Fred, for instance, told me, "Even as I talk on the phone with you and think about attending such a group, I can feel my heart beat faster." My typical reply is, "Join the crowd. The fact that you're nervous at the idea of being with people is a sign that you're an excellent candidate for the group. A lot of people tell me exactly the same thing."

Research literature invariably recommends group work over individual work when it comes to social anxiety. It makes sense. If you want to overcome the fear of people, the best way to face the fear is to be with people. It's usually less intimidating to sit with a therapist whose approach is based on acceptance. Naturally, if the prospect of attending a group is too overwhelming, then individual therapy is an excellent alternative. With the right kind of support and guidance, you will gain enough courage to join a group. I've had clients who, after having learned about the existence of my groups, have waited four, six, and ten years before joining. If the prospect of joining was that awful, then certainly they deserve admiration and congratulations for finally taking the plunge. What incredible courage to, at last, face their greatest fear!

Then there's the reality that there may be no group for you to join. This would be especially true in smaller communities. Even in larger cities, it is sometimes difficult to find a support group for social anxiety. Again, individual therapy is an option. The other is to ask your therapist whether she'd consider starting a group, as one of my clients asked me, so many years ago. Failing that, you might consider starting a group of your own.

Put an ad in the paper or make a notice for your library bulletin board: "Are you shy? Socially anxious? Join a support group and discover ways you can learn to be at ease with people. Please call: 555 1212." Even if you start with only one or two other people, you've got a group. Be the group leader, or decide to take turns as leader. Use the ideas in this and other books to help you organize topics for discussion, activities, and homework. Why would you go to all this trouble? Read on and consider the benefits of working in a group.

Benefits of a support group

➤ *Structure.* A group gives you a structure in which you can focus your efforts toward a common purpose. Meeting regularly, with the same people at the same place, helps people stay committed, to each other and to the goal of building social confidence.

➤ *Relief.* There is enormous relief to actually be in the presence of people who describe experiences similar to your own. People finally don't feel so isolated or "weird." A sense of community and belonging begins to form almost immediately.

During the second session I ask people, "How many of you think that your problem is the worst?" Usually forty to fifty percent of the people raise their hands. Again, another layer of relief. Another source of relief comes from finally talking openly about what for many has been a deep, dark secret. At long last, the secret's out and it turns out to be not so dark and not so unique, after all!

➤ *A new perspective.* Apart from the educational material that helps people gain a new, more compassionate perspective about shyness and social anxiety, people can see for themselves that people who experience shyness or social anxiety are actually really likable people. As George once put it, "I look around me and I have to admit I'm surprised. You guys are all nice, normal folks." People laugh and chuckle but the realization has a profound effect on the group. It's true: just because a person is shy or socially anxious doesn't make him "dorky," "geeky," or "weird." In fact, it could be that the sensitivity often associated with shyness and social anxiety almost ensures that people in the group are going to be of the nice and lovely variety. People start realizing, "Say, if all these people are so nice and normal, maybe I am, too."

➤ *Support, understanding, and encouragement.* One of the sweetest experiences one can have in life is to be received by another, without judgment. Because people know exactly what you're going through, they're quick to offer support. The effect is tremendously healing and uplifting.

➤ *Practice.* A group provides an instant forum in which to practice taking turns being the center of attention and speaking out. There is plenty of opportunity to ask and answer questions, to share experiences, and to give support. Within a few short weeks, trust builds among members, as does the level of conversations and laughter. Group members can also arrange phone calls or informal activities in order to practice the various social and conversational skills learned during the group sessions.

➤ *Inspiration.* Group members inspire each other. As Betty begins to speak more freely and as Michael reports, with great pride, that he has signed up for a class in soccer coaching, it is difficult not to feel the swell of energy in the room, in one's own chest. Watching people overcome all sorts of obstacles and slowly begin to blossom is incredibly moving. Hearing tales of courage is en-*courage*-ing. As people share how exactly they prepared for and finally accomplished their goals, they spark the imagination of others, who think, "Hmm, if she can do it, maybe I can, too." Mary, for instance, told the group that she had Betty to thank for her ability to finally speak up at her morning meeting at work. Turning to Betty, she said,

> I think back to the first few sessions and how quiet you were and then, last week, you told us that you walked up to your boss and calmly told her that you did not appreciate her running down a coworker in front of everyone. I was amazed and . . . proud. Something happened at work this week and I think you're partially responsible! There I was, sitting alongside ten other people at our daily morning meeting, listening to one of my coworkers make snide remarks to a junior worker. I could feel myself get angrier and angrier. I looked around and no one was coming to this poor girl's rescue. Then all I could see was an image of you confronting your boss. Without really thinking about it, I cleared my throat and told my coworker, right in front of everybody, that I was having a lot of difficulty with her negative remarks toward the junior worker. It was discouraging to see a senior worker treat anyone like that and it was not helping us move through the agenda. Everything went quiet. Then someone else agreed and we continued through the agenda. Afterwards, people came up to me and told me how glad they were that finally someone said something to this obnoxious person. The junior worker thanked me for my support and told me it had taken everything she had not to appear shaken by the mean remarks. So, Betty, thanks, your sharing really meant a lot to me.

Whew! Moments like these are what make a support group a support group.

➤ *Friendships.* Spending extra time with each other on the phone, during shared car rides to meetings, and through outside activities initiated and organized by the group, gives people added opportunities to get to know each other. Sometimes the short-term friendships that form during the group develop into longer-lasting friendships.

FAMILIES, FRIENDS, AND PARTNERS
AS SOURCES OF SUPPORT

As already mentioned, many people keep their social anxiety a secret even from those closest to them. This only adds to their sense of isolation in the world. Unless your family is totally dysfunctional and negative and your friends are deadbeats, I would heartily encourage you to share your story of social anxiety with someone close to you. You might be pleasantly surprised by the response.

If you don't know where to start, here are a few suggestions. If you're talking with a family member, ask if he knows of anyone in the family, including the extended family, who is shy or who becomes anxious in social situations. Approach the subject from a researcher's stance. Be curious as to how these other members experience their anxiety and how they cope with it. Eventually, this can lead to your disclosing that you, too, experience social anxiety. You can then talk about the books you've been reading on the subject and possibly invite your relative to read one of your favorites.

You can do the same thing with friends or partners. Approach indirectly. Ask if they have ever felt anxious in social situations or if they know anyone else who has had to cope with shyness or social anxiety. Again, this can lead to self-disclosure. Or you can use the direct approach. You might say, "Honey, I have something to tell you. It's really hard for me to talk about, but I want you to know something about me and I would really appreciate your support." Share your symptoms and how these symptoms have influenced the way you live your life. You can explain how you've learned that millions of people share this condition. You can describe the efforts you've been making to better manage your social anxiety. Often, people who love and care about you respond with relief. Finally they can make sense of situations in the past.

For instance, Harry reported that his wife thanked him for telling her. For twenty years of their marriage she had tried cajoling, pressuring, and threatening him into going to parties with her. She often took his refusal to join her as a personal rejection. Now she could appreciate the reason for his reluctance. She was relieved and thankful. She felt a renewed commitment to the marriage and offered support in any way she could give it. She started by learning more about social anxiety herself. Harry, in turn, was tremendously relieved. He didn't have to feel so alone anymore. He was encouraged and continued to work on managing his social anxiety with renewed energy.

It is true that not all family and friends will be as supportive as Harry's wife. If you are unfortunate enough to have someone tell you to simply get over it or to misguidedly reassure you that you have nothing to get nervous about, don't despair, and above all, do not take it personally. Chalk it up to the person's lack of understanding and education and move on. Or, if you think it might be worth the effort, let that person know that you are disappointed by her lack of understanding and support and offer information about this condition, in case she is interested. If the family member or friend still isn't interested, you've done your best. Move on and make sure to find support elsewhere.

NOURISH AND FLOURISH

As I said at the outset of this book, the growth impulse resides in the core of every living creature. If this energy has been dampened in your life by social anxiety, realize that it can be reawakened with proper care. Nourishing this energy by attending to your body, your mind, and your actions will release that special something in you that strives to flourish. Make those tiny goals, follow through, and learn from your mistakes and successes. As final words of encouragement, I offer these letters from participants in my previous groups. They wrote these letters in response to my request for a description of their experience and for a few tips to future group members.

Dear Newcomer,

I felt very self-conscious, inadequate, not a part of things, when I first came here. This support group does wondrous things to help you get through it, but you have to work at it. I have noticed great changes in myself; I'm more the real me. It can happen. I used to think that it couldn't, but it really can. You can feel better about yourself, have more confidence, but you just have to work at it. Good luck!

Dear Newcomer,

I know it seems tough going right now. But taking it one step at a time and practicing what you learn in the group make it easier as time goes by. Taking risks is a very freeing experience!

And here's a letter written to me, from a graduate of one of my groups.

Dear Erika,

Since the group ended, my dread of social situations has dwindled to the point where I almost never dread them! Even if the events don't go as well as I would have wished, I am not tempted to "hide" anymore. I was so elated, after years of struggling with social anxiety, to be able to see such a dramatic improvement in my courage and outlook. My determination to "get out there and live" quadrupled! I still have some trouble with eye contact, and I still need to make myself practice in all kinds of situations, but I look on these practices mostly as fun challenges. Early this July, I went all on my own to an old friend's wedding in Boston. As an unofficial "matron of honor," I was on call to meet, talk to, and be helpful to a whole range of people, including some intimidating ones, none of whom I'd ever met. Using skills that I learned in your group, I didn't let myself get excessively nervous, I didn't berate myself for my shyness. I plunged in and—I had an absolutely marvelous time! In fact, I made some new connections I hope I can hang on to.

I hate to think how often I used to feel, "I'll never get over my shyness." The anxieties didn't vanish; I would hate for people to think that they're failures because they can't solve overcoming social phobia in a couple of months. From my vantage point, I'd say that overcoming social phobia takes a lot of work and a never-say-die attitude. Every tiny bit of progress should be celebrated. I am celebrating and this is how I plan to live the rest of my life.

You can do it!

KEY REFLECTION POINTS

➤ In the normal course of living, focus turns to everyday demands. Gradually, efforts to increase social confidence may wane. Setbacks are inevitable. They are absolutely normal.

➤ One can take measures to prevent setbacks from becoming full relapses. Examining factors that contribute to setbacks through the lens of body, mind, and action can help.

➤ If you still feel stuck, consider seeking support from a therapist, a support group, or your own family and friends.

➤ If your life impulse has been dampened by social anxiety in the past, realize that it can be reawakened with proper care. Attend to your body, mind, and action. You can do it.

The one thing I want to remember from this chapter is:

_____

_____

I will translate this one thing into action in the following way:

_____

_____

_____

_____

Farewell, fellow voyagers!

Abdominal or Belly Breathing

WHEN TENSE, WE usually breathe from our upper chest. When relaxed, we breathe from our lower chest or belly. How is it that belly breathing helps us to relax? First, it increases the supply of oxygen to the brain and to the muscle tissues. If the body is regularly nourished with oxygen, it is under no strain. Second, belly breathing stimulates the parasympathetic nervous system, which, as you remember, slows the body down and restores it to a state of relaxation. And finally, while concentrating on belly breathing, our focus moves to the body and away from the worrying mind. The following are a few breathing exercises.

Four, Four, and Eight Breathing

Breathe in to the count of four

First, breathe in slowly through your nose to the count of four. If you put your hand on your belly (the part between your belly button and the bottom of the sternum), you'll feel your belly rising as you breathe in. Imagine that freshly oxygenated blood is traveling to the tips of your fingers and toes.

Hold to the count of four.

Exhale to the count of eight

On every exhalation, notice yourself moving into deeper and deeper relaxation.

Repeat this sequence of four, four, and eight about four or five times. Most clients report an immediate sense of relaxation after doing this exercise. Adjust the pace of breathing to suit your breathing needs. If at any time, you feel lightheaded, return to normal breathing.

Two Normal, One Deep

A less complicated breathing exercise is to take two normal breaths followed by one deep breath. Again, make sure you're breathing right to the bottom of your lungs, so that your belly rises with every inhalation. If you notice thoughts distracting you from your concentration on breathing, just acknowledge the thoughts and let them go. With every breath in, imagine oxygen-rich air swirling inside every nook and cranny of your body, energizing, enlivening, strengthening, and relaxing every single cell. With every breath out, imagine the carbon dioxide–laden air leaving, drifting into space, leaving your body cleaner and more relaxed.

Normal Breathing

Finally, we have the easiest but also the most difficult breathing exercise. It's the easiest because there's not much to it. It's the most difficult because there's not much to it. As you breathe in, count "one" to yourself. As you breathe out, say the word, "relax," to yourself. Then count "two" on the next inhalation and think "relax," on the next exhalation. Keep this going until you reach "ten." Sounds simple, doesn't it? For some people, this exercise is very difficult. It is perfectly natural for thoughts to come into your mind and start distracting you. Your job is simply to notice the thoughts and refrain from pulling up a chair and inviting them to stay and visit. If distracting thoughts intrude, just notice them briefly, then return to counting, from the beginning, at "one." To be able to focus on your breathing for extended periods of time is a real gift. You will be able to induce relaxation and maintain relaxation. Remember to keep your breaths smooth and regular.

As with the previous breathing exercises, don't forget to breathe low into your lungs, letting your stomach rise and fall with every breath like a baby riding on the waves of a blissful sleep.

As you become more skilled at controlled, belly breathing (also called abdominal breathing), practice in places that are a little more stimulating. It only takes a few minutes each time. Practice two, three, four times a day; more if you like. Proper breathing is to an anxious body as water is to a parched lily. Discover which breathing exercise works best for you. Then, as you would nourish your garden, nourish your body. Breathe and relax.

PROGRESSIVE MUSCLE RELAXATION

PROGRESSIVE MUSCLE RELAXATION was developed over sixty years ago by Dr. Edmund Jacobson, a U.S. psychologist who felt that muscle tension and emotional tension were related. Because it is so effective in bringing about a deep sense of relaxation, it remains a popular method of relaxation even today. Muscle relaxation involves systematically tensing and relaxing particular muscles in the body. You can start with your hands or your feet. I prefer starting with my feet and working my way up to my head, then my hands and arms. It's usually a good idea to sit or lie down in a quiet spot, making sure you have as much support for different parts of your body as possible. The object of this exercise is to tense each particular muscle for four or five seconds, without causing pain or discomfort, and then to let go and relax for about ten seconds. Some people like to slowly say, "Relax," or "Let go," to themselves each time they release a set of muscles.

As with other exercises, the effectiveness of the exercise is increased when you are mindful about what exactly is going on. Sense into the sensations of tension and relaxation and notice the difference. The first version of this exercise focuses on individual small muscle groups. Once you have mastered tensing and relaxing the small muscle groups, usually after a few days or so, you might like to try the second, shorter version, which focuses on larger muscle groups.

Small Muscle Groups

1. Sense into your breathing. Take three full breaths and relax.
2. Stretch out your legs and point your toes downwards. Then let them go and relax.
3. Tighten your calf muscles by pointing your toes up and toward you. Let go and relax.
4. Tighten the muscles in your thighs and buttocks by squeezing your legs and buttocks together. Relax.
5. Tighten your lower back by arching it up. (Don't do this if you have lower back problems.) Relax.
6. Tighten your stomach muscles by sucking your tummy in. Relax.
7. Fill your lungs with air and expand your chest as much as you can, hold, then exhale and relax.
8. Tighten the muscles around your shoulder blades by pulling back your shoulders as if the shoulder blades were going to touch each other. Relax.
9. Bring your shoulders up, close to your ears. Relax.
10. Tuck your chin in, close to your chest. Relax.
11. Purse your lips as tightly as you can. Relax.
12. Clench your jaw and teeth. Relax.
13. Close your eyes tightly (unless you are wearing contacts). Relax.
14. Tighten your forehead by raising your eyebrows as high as you can. Relax.
15. Tighten your upper arms by bending your elbows and holding your fists towards your shoulders. Relax.
16. Bend both hands back at the wrists and lift hands toward you to tighten the forearms. Relax.
17. Clench your fists. Relax.

Large Muscle Groups

1. Tighten legs and feet. Relax.
2. Tighten lower back and buttocks. Relax.

3. Tighten your stomach. Relax.
4. Tighten your chest and upper back. Relax.
5. Tighten your head, neck, and shoulders. Relax.
6. Tighten your hands and arms. Relax.

Do the progressive muscle relaxation exercise twice a day, for about twenty minutes each time. As you become expert at identifying which muscles are tense and which are relaxed, you'll be better able to recognize the first whispers of tension and apply your "tense and relax" method before the tension becomes overwhelming.

Imagery Work

GUIDELINES

GUIDELINES ARE ONLY suggestions. You don't have to stick to all of these suggestions at all times. Experiment. Most of these ideas have helped people use their imagination effectively.

Prepare for imagery work

1. Choose a quiet place.
2. Get comfortable.
3. Close your eyes.
4. Relax. Focusing on your breath as you exhale once or twice will often do the trick.
5. Have an open mind. Images are a product of activity in the right side of your brain, which is not concerned with logic or facts. It is creative and can come up with all kinds of "fantastic" material. Anything is possible. Suspend your judgment and enjoy yourself.
6. Form an intention. Decide what it is that you would like to accomplish. Would you like to say "hi" to someone at work? Invite someone to a movie? Be sure to set a realistic goal. Impossible goals only lead to frustration or even hopelessness.

During imagery work

7. Imagine in the first person. There are two ways of imagining a scene. You can imagine it in the third person, as if you are watching yourself on a movie screen. Or you can imagine the scene in the first person, as if you are actually in the scene, aware not so much of how you look but very aware of internal and external sensations. It is often easier to start out by imagining yourself in the third person, but eventually, it is more effective to imagine yourself in the first person, inside your own body, smack in the middle of the scene.

8. Imagine in the present tense. Imagine that this scene is taking place in the immediate present, not in the future.

9. Bring the scene to life through the senses. Use all of your senses. See, hear, smell, taste, touch, and feel the details of the imaginary scene. The more you remember to involve all your senses, the more realistic your imagined scene will be.

10. Forget the words. The whole idea of using imagery is to engage the right side of the brain. If you choose an imagery exercise from memory, remember to focus on pictures and senses. Don't engage the left side of your brain, by using words to describe the scenes to yourself. For instance, don't say to yourself, "Now I am crossing the road. I can feel the pressure of the pavement against the soles of my feet."

11. Stay positive. Create positive thoughts and images that will nourish positive energy. Indulging in images of disasters and catastrophes is definitely out. If, on the other hand, an image comes up that portrays a minor disaster, such as seeing yourself trip as you walk onto the stage, don't worry. Use this as an opportunity to correct it.

12. Imagine with gusto. You're safe. No one is watching. Have some fun! Be dramatic. Exaggerate your parts in your imaginary scene. The word "gusto" originates from the Latin *gustare*, which means "to taste; to enjoy the taste of." So enjoy. In your imagination, move with gusto, talk with gusto, be gusto.

13. Keep it short. Some experts suggest that imagery work should last about ten to fifteen minutes; others say that two to three minutes is plenty. Meanwhile, many audiotapes of visualizations can last up to thirty minutes. In my experience, people have often found it difficult to make time in their busy schedules to sit down and do imagery work. When I've suggested that two to three minutes is plenty, their immediate response has been, "Oh, I can do that!" In other words, several short stints of imagery work are far more useful than longer stints that never happen.

14. Repeat, repeat, repeat. More important than the duration of the imagination exercise is the number of times you practice. I recommend doing imagery work two to four times a day: in the morning, at noon, around supper time, and before you go to bed. Positive images before breakfast will set a positive tone for the rest of the day. Just before bed is also a wonderful time, because your unconscious can continue working with these positive images while you're asleep.

15. Take it easy. Images cannot be forced. If you find yourself trying too hard, stop and relax. Ask yourself if you are focusing too much on the desired outcome and not enough on what's happening in the image. One way you can stay in touch with the process of imagery work is to focus on the immediate sensations of your images.

After imagery work

16. Add an affirmation. Although it is not a good idea to describe scenes in your head with words, as mentioned earlier, it is a good idea to reinforce the positive images with positive affirmations, before or after your imagery work. Saying things like, "I am making a wonderful presentation to my class," "I am relaxed and confident," and "I enjoy finding out about others," is an effective way of supporting your imagery work.

17. Be patient. Results can be immediate or delayed. The stronger your belief in imagery work and in yourself, the sooner you will witness your desired changes. The stronger your doubt about your ability to change, the longer it will take to chip away at the doubt with positive images. But don't worry. The positive images will eventually triumph, as long as you persevere.

CAUTIONS

IMAGERY WORK IS not for everybody. People who already daydream too much, people who have a psychotic disorder and have difficulty telling the difference between reality and fantasy, and people who are haunted by violent imagery are better off focusing on concrete, practical tasks. People with very low self-esteem, who don't believe they deserve the good things in life, will sabotage their imagery work with negativity, and when unsuccessful, they'll become even more convinced that they are not deserving. Energy would be better spent on first building positive self-esteem.

Goal Recording Charts

SAMPLE WEEK-IN-PROGRESS

GOALS Date:	Frequency	Mon	Tues	Wed	Thurs	Fri	Sat	Sun
BODY Grounding or 4, 4, 8 belly breathing	3 X daily	✓	✓	✓	✓			
MIND **A) IMAGERY** Imagine greeting coworkers with an open face and "I welcome you" eye contact	2 X daily	✓	✓	✓	✓			
B) WORDS Record flawed thinking and replace with realistic, compassionate thoughts	1 X daily							
ACTION Say hello at work Say good-bye at work	1 X daily 1 X daily	✓	✓	✓				

GOAL RECORDING CHART

Goals Date: _____	Frequency	Mon	Tues	Wed	Thurs	Fri	Sat	Sun
BODY								
MIND A) IMAGERY								
B) WORDS								
ACTION								

Suggestions for Goals

LOOK OVER THESE suggestions and choose one or two per week. Don't forget to make them specific to your situation. Example: "I will say 'hi' and 'bye' at work at least twice a day, all week."

Body

> practice grounding: sense into feet, seat, hands, back, breath
> do self-regulation work, back and forth between anxiety sensations and grounding
> practice breathing exercise: 4, 4 & 8; 2, 1; or normal
> practice progressive muscle relaxation
> pick up and listen to an audio tape on relaxation
> exercise
> get regular, adequate sleep
> reduce or eliminate:
>> junk food
>> caffeine
>> alcohol
>> sugar
>> smoking
> take vitamin supplements
> increase whole grains
> increase calcium-rich foods

➤ pursue leisure activities, have fun
➤ learn to dance, play tennis, etc.

Mind

IMAGES:
➤ identify images in mind as positive or negative
➤ review imagery guidelines (see Appendix II)
➤ practice positive images
➤ rehearse in imagination (visualize a specific incident)
➤ check Chapter 8 for specific imagery exercises
➤ imagine goals, overall and mini-goals
➤ review goal guidelines in Chapter 9
➤ use goal chart (see Appendix III)

WORDS:
➤ challenge negative inner voice: voice therapy
➤ record flawed thinking and substitute realistic, compassionate thinking
➤ create and repeat affirmations (Appendix V)
➤ focus on other
➤ focus on purpose
➤ identify major mind trap and challenge it

Action

➤ identify goal/specific action using hierarchy lists
➤ exposure: do the specific action (review exposure guidelines)
➤ keep record with goal chart
➤ celebrate successes, record what you've learned
➤ body language, become more visible:
    open face
    eye contact with silent "I welcome you"
    good hygiene
    clothing: experiment
    body posture

handshake
social distance
gestures
voice
➤ verbal communication, express and reach out:
    practice initiative, be the first to talk, to suggest an
        outing
    say "hi" and "bye"
    give free information in conversations
    follow-up in conversations
    review six levels of progression in conversations
    practice starters, commenting on surroundings, giving
        compliments
    practice self-disclosure
    speak your awareness
    find hobbies, pursue interests
    prepare topics
    form opinions, share opinions
    practice dealing with criticisms
    practice asking for what you want
    make telephone calls
    use the "I" word instead of "you, we," or "one."
    use four-pronged approach with job interviews or
        presentation (prepare, practice, presentation, post-
        event evaluation)
    call up old friends or family members with whom
        you've lost touch
    pursue interests and reach out to people while pursu-
        ing these interests
    do favors, ask for favors
    clear the air with friends, by speaking your awareness
    make yourself available to meet potential partners:
        take classes, attend singles activities
    if stuck or need support, seek help from a therapist,
        from family or friends, attend a support group,
        Toastmasters

Guidelines for Creating
Effective Affirmations

1. *Short.* Keep your affirmations short and simple. This way your unconscious gets the point quickly and is not distracted by too much information.
2. *Positive.* Keep your statements positive. Avoid negative words such as "don't," "no," and "not." For example, if you say, "I am not nervous," the unconscious mind doesn't seem to notice the "not" word. It usually latches onto the word that suggests an image, in this case "nervous," and the body obeys, becoming all the more nervous. It is far more effective to say, "I am calm," for the image of calmness will be communicated to the rest of the body and the body will obey.
3. *Present.* Keep your affirmations in the present tense. "I am calm," not "I will be calm when I give my presentation next week."
4. *Effortless.* As with imagery work, it is important to say your affirmations easily and effortlessly, without strain.
5. *Frequent.* Remember Suzuki, the violin and piano teacher, who played the "fa" note on key thousands of times before the so-called tone deaf student could hear the "fa" correctly. So it is with positive affirmations. Make a daily practice of saying your affirmations. Say them a few times a day on a regular basis.

6. *Gusto.* Don't forget to say your affirmations with feeling. This may seem strange at first, but once you see evidence of your affirmations making a difference, gusto will come naturally.

References

Shyness, Social Anxiety, Sensitivity

Aaron, Elaine N. *The Highly Sensitive Person*. New York: Broadway Books, 1996.

Antony, Martin. *10 Simple Solutions to Shyness: How to Ovecome Shyness, Social Anxiety, and Fear of Public Speaking*. Oakland, CA: New Harbinger Publications, Inc., 2004.

Antony, Martin M., and Swinson, Richard P. *The Shyness and Social Anxiety Workbook: Proven Techniques for Overcoming Your Fears*. Oakland, CA: New Harbinger Publications, 2000.

Berent, Jonathan. *Beyond Shyness: How to Conquer Social Anxieties*. New York: A Fireside Book, Simon and Schuster, 1993.

Bruno, Frank J. *Conquer Shyness: Understand Your Shyness and Banish It Forever.* New York: Arco Publishing, 1997.

Butler, Gillian. *Overcoming Social Anxiety and Shyness: A Self-Help Guide Using Cognitive Behavioral Techniques*. New York: NYU Press, 2001.

Carducci, Bernardo J. *Shyness: A Bold New Approach*. New York: Quill, HarperCollins, 2002.

Cheek, Jonathan, Cheek, Bronwen, and Rothstein, Larry. *Conquering Shyness: The Battle Anyone Can Win*. New York: Dell Publishing, 1986.

Dayhoff, Signe A. *Diagonally Parked in a Parallel Universe: Working Through Social Anxiety*. Placitas, NM: Effectiveness-Plus Publications, 2000.

Desberg, Peter. *No More Butterflies: Overcoming Stagefright, Shyness, Interview Anxiety and Fear of Public Speaking*, Oakland, CA: New Harbinger Publications, 1996.

The Diagnostic and Statistical Manual of Mental Disorders, 4th edition, DSM-IV. Washington, DC: American Psychiatric Association, 1994.

Leary, Mark R., and Kowalski, Robin Mark. *Social Anxiety*. New York: The Guilford Press, 1995.

Markway, Barbara G., Carmin, Cheryl N., Pollard, C. Alec, and Flynn, Teresa. *Dying of Embarrassment: Help for Social Anxiety and Phobia.* Oakland, CA: New Harbinger Publications, Inc., 1992.

Markway, Barbara G., and Markway, Gregory P. *Painfully Shy: How to Overcome Social Anxiety and Reclaim Your Life.* New York: Thomas Dunne Books, St. Martins Press, 2001.

Marshall, John R. *Social Phobia: From Shyness to Stage Fright.* New York: BasicBooks, HarperCollins Publishers, 1994.

McCullough, Christopher J. *Always at Ease: Overcoming Shyness and Anxiety in Every Situation.* Los Angeles: Jeremy P. Tarcher, Inc., 1991.

Miller, Rowland E. *Embarrassment: Poise and Peril in Everyday Life.* New York: The Guilford Press, 1996.

Rapee, Ronald M. *Overcoming Shyness and Social Phobia: A Step-by-Step Guide.* Northvale, NJ: Jason Aronson Inc., 1998.

Schneier, Franklin, and Welkowitz, Lawrence. *The Hidden Face of Shyness.* New York: Avon Books, 1996.

Shaw, Phyllis M. *Overcoming Shyness: Meeting People Is Fun.* New York: Arco Publishing, Inc., 1983.

Smith, M. Blaine. *Overcoming Shyness.* Downers Grove, IL: InterVarsity Press, 1993.

Soifer, Steven, Zgourides, George D., Himle, Joseph, and Pickering, Nancy L. *Shy Bladder Syndrome: Your Step-by-Step Guide to Overcoming Paruresis.* Oakland, CA: New Harbinger Publications, 2001.

Stein, Murray B., and Walker, John R. *Triumph over Shyness.* New York: McGraw-Hill, copublished with The Anxiety Disorders Association of America, 2001.

Zimbardo, Philip G. *Shyness: What It Is, What to Do about It.* Cambridge: Malor Books, ISHK, 1981, 1999.

Zimbardo, Philip G., and Radl, Shirley. *The Shy Child: Overcoming and Preventing Shyness from Infancy to Adulthood.* New York: Addison-Wesley, 1997.

Fear, Anxiety

Barlow, David H. *Mastery of Your Anxiety and Panic.* New York: Graywind Publishing Company, 1989.

Bourne, Edmund J. *The Anxiety & Phobia Workbook.* Oakland, CA: New Harbinger Publications, 1990.

———. *Healing Fear: New Approaches to Overcoming Anxiety.* Oakland, CA: New Harbinger Publications, 1998.

Foxman, Paul. *Dancing with Fear: Overcoming Anxiety in a World of Stress and Uncertainty.* Lanham, MD: A Jason Aronson Book, Rowman and Littlefield Publishers, Inc., 1996.

Hunt, Douglas. *No More Fears.* New York: Warner Books, 1988.

Jeffers, Susan. *Feel the Fear and Do It Anyway.* New York: Fawcett Columbine, 1987.

Kopp, Sheldon. *Raise Your Right Hand Against Fear: Extend the Other in Compassion.* Minneapolis, MN: CompCare Publishers, 1988.

Wolpe, Joseph. *Life without Fear.* Oakland, CA: New Harbinger Publications, 1988.

Trauma, Physiology of Emotion

Levine, Peter A., and Frederick, Ann. *Waking the Tiger: Healing Trauma.* Berkeley, CA: North Atlantic Books, 1997.

Pert, Candace B. *Molecules of Emotion: The Science Behind Mind-Body Medicine.* New York: Scribner, 1999.

Rothschild, Babette. *The Body Remembers: The Psychophysiology of Trauma and Trauma Treatment.* New York: W.W. Norton, 2000.

Scaer, Robert C. *The Body Bears the Burden: Trauma, Dissociation, and Disease.* New York: The Haworth Medical Press, 2001.

van der Kolk, Bessel A., McFarlane, Alexander C., and Weisaeth, Lars, eds. *Traumatic Stress: The Effects of Overwhelming Experience on the Mind, Body, and Society.* New York: The Guilford Press, 1996.

Mind, Body, Imagination

Borysenko, Joan. *Minding the Body, Mending the Mind.* Reading, MA: Addison-Wesley, 1987.

Coué, Emile. *La Maitrise de Soi-Même.* Paris: Club du Livre de L'Homme D'Action, Editions J. Oliven, 1970.

Epstein, Gerald. *Healing Visualizations: Creating Health through Imagery.* Bantam Books, 1989.

Fanning, Patrick. *Visualization for Change.* Oakland, CA: New Harbinger Publications, 1994.

Fezler, William. *Creative Imagery: How to Visualize in All Five Senses.* New York: A Fireside Book, Simon & Schuster, 1989.

Kehoe, John. *Mind Power into the 21st Century: Techniques to Harness the Astounding Powers of Thought.* Vancouver, BC: Zoetic Books, 1997.

Liggett, Donald R. *Sport Hypnosis.* Champaign, IL: Human Kinetics, 2000.

Communication, Connecting, Assertiveness

Avila, Alexander. *The Gift of Shyness: Embrace Your Shy Side and Find Your Soul Mate.* New York: A Fireside Book, Simon and Schuster, 2002.

Branden, Nathaniel. *"If You Could Hear What I Cannot Say": Learning to Communicate with the Ones You Love.* New York: Bantam Books, 1983.

Burns, David D. *Intimate Connections: The Clinically Proven Program for Making Close Friends and Finding a Loving Partner.* New York: Signet Books, 1986.

Gabor, Don. *Talking with Confidence for the Painfully Shy.* New York: Crown Trade Paperbacks, 1997.

McKay, Matthew, Davis, Martha, and Fanning, Patrick. *Messages: The Communications Skills Book.* Oakland, CA: New Harbinger Publications, 1983.

Smith, Manuel J. *When I Say No, I Feel Guilty.* New York: The Dial Press, 1975.

Stone, Douglas, Patton, Bruce, and Heen, Sheila. *Difficult Conversations: How to Discuss What Matters Most.* New York: Penguin Books, 1999.

Tait, Kathy. *Love Smarts: A Singles Guide to Finding That Special Someone.* Vancouver, BC: Self-Counsel Press, 1994.

Inner Work

Branden, Nathaniel. *How to Raise Your Self-Esteem: The Proven Action-Oriented Approach to Greater Self-Respect and Self-Confidence.* New York: Bantam Books, 1987.

Brazier, David. *The Feeling Buddha: A Buddhist Psychology of Character, Adversity and Passion.* New York: Fromm International, 1998.

Burns, David D. *Feeling Good: The New Mood Therapy.* New York: Signet Books, 1980.

Firestone, Robert W. *The Fantasy Bond: Structure of Psychological Defenses.* New York: Human Sciences Press, 1987.

Woodman, Marion. *Addiction to Perfection: The Still Unravished Bride.* Toronto: Inner City Books, 1982.

Inspirational

Canfield, Jack, and Hansen, Mark Victor. *Chicken Soup for the Soul: 101 Stories to Open the Heart and Rekindle the Spirit.* Deerfield, FL: Health Communications Inc., 1993.

Frankl, Viktor E. *Man's Search for Meaning.* New York: Pocket Books, Simon and Schuster, 1939/1963.

Osho. *Courage: The Joy of Living Dangerously.* New York: St. Martin's Griffin, 1999.

Steindl-Rast, David. *Gratefulness, the Heart of Prayer: An Approach to Life in Fullness.* Ramsey, NY: Paulist Press, 1984.

Tolle, Eckhart. *The Power of Now, A Guide to Spiritual Enlightenment.* New World Library, California and Namaste Publishing, Vancouver, B.C., 2004.

Other

Fisher, Helen E. *Anatomy of Love: The Natural History of Monogamy, Adultery, and Divorce.* New York: W.W. Norton, 1992.

Hegi, Ursula. *The Vision of Emma Blau: A Novel.* New York: Simon and Schuster, 2000.

Montessori, Maria. *The Absorbent Mind.* New York: Holt, Rinehart and Winston, 1967.

Pawlak, Laura, and Turner, Lisa. *Food Smart: A Nutritional Atlas.* Emeryville, CA: Biomed Books, 2000.

Suzuki, Shinichi. *Nurtured by Love: The Classic Approach to Talent Education.* Transl. Waltraud Suzuki. Smithtown, NY: Exposition Press, 1984.

Tennov, Dorothy. *Love and Limerence: The Experience of Being in Love.* New York: Stein and Day, 1979.

Acknowledgments

M Y HEART AND thanks go to my beloved husband, Don, who encouraged me to pursue my dreams and who was there for me in countless ways. Thanks go to my loving sons and mother who kept reminding me, "You can do it."

I owe much to Kirsten, a former client who urged me to start my social anxiety support groups. I am indebted to the hundreds of group members who shared their stories, experiences, and insights, many of which form the mainstay of this book. I am grateful to psychiatrist Dr. Ron Remick and neuropsychologist Dr. Ed Josephs, for their reviews of the sections on medication and the physiology of anxiety, respectively. This book would not have been possible without the expert knowledge and insights of the many authors, therapists, and spiritual and workshop leaders who have influenced me over the years.

It was my good fortune to have a top-notch literary team. I am particularly indebted to Elizabeth Lyon, my editor and mentor. She expertly unearthed my book from a too large tome. I continually marvel at her talent, wisdom, and compassion. I am very grateful to my agent, Cathy Fowler, who believed in this project from the start and helped me whenever the need arose. To my publisher, Matthew Lore, I owe many thanks. His life-affirming values, sense of integrity, and appreciativeness were welcome gifts, at just the right times. Thanks go to my publisher's assistant, Peter Jacoby, for his diligence and support.

I am grateful to friends Terry and Suzanne Boswell, and Jaime and Angie Martinez who graciously gave me their homes on Salt Spring Island when I needed a quiet haven. I owe special thanks to Sue Okuda, manager at Royal Columbian Hospital, who generously granted me leaves of absence as I needed them. Thanks go to so many other friends and colleagues whose support and interest in my book kept me going. To mention a few: Elsie Candlish, Judith Phanidis, Brian Muller, Mary Armitage, Connie Clark, Margo Weston, Irene Mahoney, Yvonne Savage, Lori Campbell-Ryan, Tammy Fiorillo, Mary Acheson, Janice Titleborn, and Jean-Louis Gendreau.

Permissions Acknowledgments

Index

About the Author

ERIKA BUKKFALVI HILLIARD, MSW, RSW, is a registered clinical social worker and seasoned therapist with thirty years of experience in mental health and psychiatry. She has been in private practice for over twenty years, nearly fifteen of which have included facilitating social anxiety support groups. In recent years she has devoted herself to the study of trauma, which has given her further insight into the phenomenon of social anxiety. She is a member of the Canadian Association of Social Workers and lives in Vancouver, British Columbia, with her husband and three sons, each in various stages of leaving the nest.